Microsoft®

Word 97

Illustrated Standard Edition,
A First Course

Microsoft®
Word 97
Illustrated Standard Edition, A First Course

Marie L. Swanson

COURSE
TECHNOLOGY

ONE MAIN STREET, CAMBRIDGE, MA 02142

an International Thomson Publishing company I(T)P®

Cambridge • Albany • Bonn • Boston • Cincinnati • London • Madrid • Melbourne • Mexico City
New York • Paris • San Francisco • Singapore • Tokyo • Toronto • Washington

Microsoft Word 97—Illustrated Standard Edition, A First Course

is published by Course Technology

Managing Editor:	Nicole Jones Pinard
Product Manager:	Jeanne Herring
Production Editor:	Nancy Ray
Developmental Editor:	Meta Chaya Hirschl
Composition House:	GEX, Inc.
QA Manuscript Reviewers:	John McCarthy, Gail Massey
Text Designer:	Joseph Lee
Cover Designer:	Joseph Lee

© 1997 by Course Technology — I(T)P®

For more information contact:

Course Technology
One Main Street
Cambridge, MA 02142

ITP Europe
Berkshire House 168-173
High Holborn
London WC1V 7AA
England

Nelson ITP, Australia
102 Dodds Street
South Melbourne, 3205
Victoria, Australia

ITP Nelson Canada
1120 Birchmount Road
Scarborough, Ontario
Canada M1K 5G4

International Thomson Editores
Seneca, 53
Colonia Polanco
11560 Mexico D.F. Mexico

ITP GmbH
Königswinterer Strasse 418
53277 Bonn
Germany

ITP Asia
60 Albert Street, #15-01
Albert Complex
Singapore 189969

ITP Japan
Hirakawacho Kyowa Building, 3F
2-2-1 Hirakawacho
Chiyoda-ku, Tokyo 102
Japan

ISBN 0-7600-5996-9

Printed in the United States of America

6 7 8 9 02 01 00 99

Illustrated Series™ Team

At Course Technology we believe that technology will transform the way that people teach and learn. We are very excited about bringing you, instructors and students, the most practical and affordable technology-related products available.

► The Development Process

Our development process is unparalleled in the educational publishing industry. Every product we create goes through an exacting process of design, development, review, and testing.

Reviewers give us direction and insight that shape our manuscripts and bring them up to the latest standards. Every manuscript is quality tested. Students whose backgrounds match the intended audience work through every keystroke, carefully checking for clarity and pointing out errors in logic and sequence. Together with our own technical reviewers, these testers help us ensure that everything that carries our name is as error-free and easy to use as possible.

► The Products

We show both how and why technology is critical to solving problems in the classroom and in whatever field you choose to teach or pursue. Our time-tested, step-by-step instructions provide unparalleled clarity. Examples and applications are chosen and crafted to motivate students.

► The Illustrated Series™ Team

The Illustrated Series™ Team is committed to providing you with the most visual introduction to microcomputer applications. No other series of books will get you up to speed faster in today's changing software environment. This book will suit your needs because it was delivered quickly, efficiently, and affordably. In every aspect of business, we rely on a commitment to quality and the use of technology. Each member of the Illustrated Series™ Team contributes to this process. The names of all our team members are listed below.

The Team

Cynthia Anderson	Mary-Terese Cozzola	Jeanne Herring	Elizabeth Eisner Reding
Chia-Ling Barker	Carol Cram	Meta Chaya Hirschl	Art Rotberg
Donald Barker	Kim T. M. Crowley	Jane Hosie-Bounar	Neil Salkind
Ann Barron	Catherine DiMassa	Steven Johnson	Gregory Schultz
David Beskeen	Stan Dobrawa	Bill Lisowski	Ann Shaffer
Ann Marie Buconjic	Shelley Dyer	Chet Lyskawa	Dan Swanson
Rachel Bunin	Linda Eriksen	Kristine O'Brien	Marie Swanson
Joan Carey	Jessica Evans	Tara O'Keefe	Jennifer Thompson
Patrick Carey	Lisa Friedrichsen	Harry Phillips	Sasha Vodnik
Sheralyn Carroll	Jeff Goding	Nicole Jones Pinard	Jan Weingarten
Brad Conlin	Michael Halvorson	Katherine T. Pinard	Christie Williams
Pam Conrad	Jamie Harper	Kevin Proot	Janet Wilson

Preface

Welcome to *Microsoft Word 97 – Illustrated Standard Edition, A First Course*! This book in our highly visual new design offers new users a hands-on introduction to Microsoft Word 97 and also serves as an excellent reference for future use.

▶ Organization and Coverage

This text contains eight units that cover basic Word skills. In these units students learn how to design, create, edit, and enhance Word documents. The units also cover creating tables, formatting pages, merging documents, working with multiple-page documents, and inserting graphics.

▶ Microsoft Office User Specialist Program Approved Courseware

This book, when used as part of a two-course sequence with the companion textbook *Microsoft Word 97 – Illustrated Standard Edition, A Second Course*, has been approved by Microsoft as courseware for the Microsoft Office User Specialist program. After completing the lessons and exercises in these two books, the student will be prepared to take the Proficient level Microsoft Office User Specialist examination for Word 97. By passing the certification exam for a Microsoft software program, students demonstrate their proficiency in that program to employers. Microsoft Office User Specialist exams are offered at participating test centers, participating corporations, and participating employment agencies. For more information about certification, please visit the Microsoft Office User Specialist program World Wide Web site at http://www.microsoft.com/office/train_cert/.

▶ About this Approach

What makes the Illustrated approach so effective at teaching software skills? It's quite simple. Each skill is presented on two facing pages, with the step-by-step instructions on the left page, and large screen illustrations on the right. Students can focus on a single skill without having to turn the page. This unique design makes information extremely accessible and easy to absorb, and provides a great reference for students after the course is over. This hands-on approach also makes it ideal for both self-paced or instructor-led classes. The modular structure of the book also allows for great flexibility; you can cover the units in any order you choose.

Each lesson, or "information display," contains the following elements:

This icon indicates a CourseHelp 97 slide show is available for this lesson. See the Instructor's Resource Kit page for more information.

Each 2-page spread focuses on a single skill.

Concise text that introduces the basic principles in the lesson and integrates the brief case study.

Excel 97

Changing Attributes and Alignment of Labels

Attributes are font styling features such as bold, italics, and underlining. You can apply bold, italics, and underlining from the Formatting toolbar or from the Font tab in the Format Cells dialog box. You can also change the alignment of text in cells. Left, right, or center alignment can be applied from the Formatting toolbar, or from the Alignment tab in the Format Cells dialog box. See Table C-2 for a description of the available attribute and alignment buttons on the Formatting toolbar. Excel also has predefined worksheet formats to make formatting easier. ▶ Now that he has applied the appropriate fonts and font sizes to his worksheet labels, Evan wants to further enhance his worksheet's appearance by adding bold and underline formatting and centering some of the labels.

Steps

CourseHelp
The camera icon indicates there is a CourseHelp available with this lesson. Click the Start button, point to programs, point to CourseHelp, then click Word 97 Illustrated. Choose the CourseHelp that corresponds to this lesson.

QuickTip
Highlighting information on a worksheet can be useful, but overuse of any attribute can be distracting and make a document less readable. Be consistent by adding emphasis the same way throughout a workbook.

Time To
✔ Save

1. Press **[Ctrl][Home]** to select cell A1, then click the **Bold button** B on the Formatting toolbar
   The title "Advertising Expenses" appears in bold.

2. Select the range **A3:J3**, then click the **Underline button** U on the Formatting toolbar
   Excel underlines the column headings in the selected range.

3. Click cell **A3**, click the **Italics button** I on the Formatting toolbar, then click B
   The word "Type" appears in boldface, italic type. Notice that the Bold, Italics, and Underline buttons on the Formatting toolbar are indented. You decide you don't like the italic formatting. You remove it by clicking I again.

4. Click I
   Excel removes italics from cell A3.

5. Add bold formatting to the rest of the labels in the range **B3:J3**
   You want to center the title over the data.

6. Select the range **A1:F1**, then click the **Merge and Center button** on the Formatting toolbar
   The title Advertising Expenses is centered across six columns. Now you center the column headings in their cells.

7. Select the range **A3:J3** then click the **Center button** on the Formatting toolbar
   You are satisfied with the formatting in the worksheet. Compare your screen to Figure C-8.

TABLE C-2: Attribute and Alignment buttons on the Formatting toolbar

icon	description	icon	description
B	Adds boldface		Aligns left
I	Italicizes		Aligns center
U	Underlines		Aligns right
	Adds lines or borders		Centers across columns, and combines two or more selected adjacent cells into one cell.

▶ EX C-6 **FORMATTING A WORKSHEET**

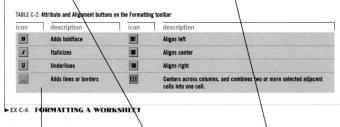

Quickly accessible summaries of key terms, toolbar buttons, or keyboard alternatives connected with the lesson material. Students can refer easily to this information when working on their own projects at a later time.

Hints as well as trouble-shooting advice right where you need it – next to the step itself.

Clear step-by-step directions, with what students are to type in red, explain how to complete the specific task.

Every lesson features large, full-color representations of what the screen should look like as students complete the numbered steps.

The innovative design draws the students' eyes to important areas of the screens.

Brightly colored tabs above the program name indicate which section of the book you are in. Useful for finding your place within the book and for referencing information from the index.

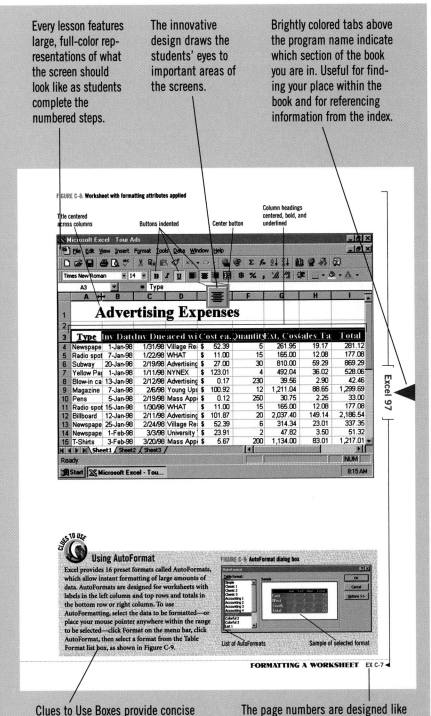

FIGURE C-8: Worksheet with formatting attributes applied

Title centered across columns

Buttons indented

Center button

Column headings centered, bold, and underlined

Excel 97

Advertising Expenses

Using AutoFormat

Excel provides 16 preset formats called AutoFormats, which allow instant formatting of large amounts of data. AutoFormats are designed for worksheets with labels in the left column and top rows and totals in the bottom row or right column. To use AutoFormatting, select the data to be formatted—or place your mouse pointer anywhere within the range to be selected—click Format on the menu bar, click AutoFormat, then select a format from the Table Format list box, as shown in Figure C-9.

FIGURE C-9: AutoFormat dialog box

List of AutoFormats

Sample of selected format

FORMATTING A WORKSHEET EX C-7

Clues to Use Boxes provide concise information that either expands on the major lesson skill or describes an independent task that in some way relates to the major lesson skill.

The page numbers are designed like a road map. EX indicates the Excel section, C indicates Excel Unit C, and 7 indicates the page within the unit. This map allows for the greatest flexibility in content – each unit stands completely on its own.

Other Features

The two-page lesson format featured in this book provides the new user with a powerful learning experience. Additionally, this book contains the following features:

▶ **Real-World Case**

The case study used throughout the textbook, a fictitious company called Nomad Ltd, is designed to be "real-world" in nature and introduces the kinds of activities that students will encounter when working with Microsoft Word 97. With a real-world case, the process of solving problems will be more meaningful to students.

▶ **End of Unit Material**

Each unit concludes with a Concepts Review that tests students' understanding of what they learned in the unit. A Skills Review follows the Concepts Review and provides students with additional hands-on practice of the skills they learned in the unit. The Skills Review is followed by Independent Challenges, which pose case problems for students to solve. At least one Independent Challenge in each unit asks students to use the World Wide Web to solve the problem as indicated by a Web Work icon. The Visual Workshops that follow the Independent Challenges help students to develop critical thinking skills. Students are shown completed documents and are asked to recreate them from scratch.

Instructor's Resource Kit

The Instructor's Resource Kit is Course Technology's way of putting the resources and information needed to teach and learn effectively into your hands. With an integrated array of teaching and learning tools that offer you and your students a broad range of instructional options, we believe this kit represents the highest quality and most cutting edge resources available to instructors today. Many of these resources are available online at www.course.com. The resources available with this book are:

CourseHelp 97 CourseHelp 97 is a student reinforcement tool offering online annotated tutorials that are accessible directly from the Start menu in Windows 95. These on-screen "slide shows" help students understand the most difficult concepts in a specific program. Students are encouraged to view a CourseHelp 97 slide show before completing that lesson. This text includes the following CourseHelp 97 slide shows:
• Moving and Copying Data
• Creating and Formatting Sections
• Understanding Mail Merge
Adopters of this text are granted the right to post the CourseHelp 97 files on any standalone computer or network.

Course Test Manager Designed by Course Technology, this cutting edge Windows-based testing software helps instructors design and administer tests and pre-tests. This full-featured program also has an online testing component that allows students to take tests at the computer and have their exams automatically graded.

Course Faculty Online Companion This new World Wide Web site offers Course Technology customers a password-protected Faculty Lounge where you can find everything you need to prepare for class. These periodically updated items include lesson plans, graphic files for the figures in the text, additional problems, updates and revisions to the text, links to other Web sites, and access to Student Disk files. This new site is an ongoing project and will continue to evolve throughout the semester. Contact your Customer Service Representative for the site address and password.

Course Student Online Companion This book features its own Online Companion where students can go to access Web sites that will help them complete the WebWork Independent Challenges. This page also contains links to other Course Technology student pages where students can find task references for each of the Microsoft Office 97 programs, a graphical glossary of terms found in the text, an archive of meaningful templates, software, hot tips, and Web links to other sites that contain pertinent information. These new sites are also ongoing projects and will continue to evolve throughout the semester.

Student Files To use this book students must have the Student Files. See the inside front or inside back cover for more information on the Student Files. Adopters of this text are granted the right to post the Student Files on any stand-alone computer or network.

Instructor's Manual This is quality assurance tested and includes:
• Solutions to all lessons and end-of-unit material
• Unit notes with teaching tips from the author
• Extra Independent Challenges
• Transparency Masters of key concepts
• Student Files
• CourseHelp 97

CLUES TO USE

The Illustrated Family of Products

This book that you are holding fits in the Illustrated Series – one series of three in the Illustrated family of products. The other two series are the Illustrated Projects Series and the Illustrated Interactive Series. The Illustrated Projects Series is a supplemental series designed to reinforce the sills learned in any skills-based book through the creation of meaningful and engaging projects. The Illustrated Interactive Series is a line of computer-based training multimedia products that offer the novice user a quick and interactive learning experience. All three series are committed to providing you with the most visual and enriching instructional materials.

Brief Contents

Contents

Word 97

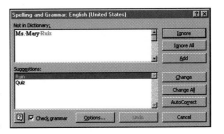

Contents

Formatting a Document

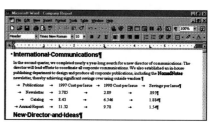

Working with Tables WD D-1

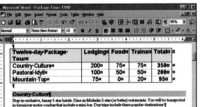

Contents

Formatting Pages — WD E-1

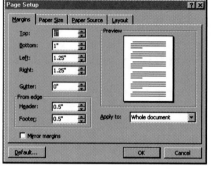

Formatting with AutoFormat and Styles — WD F-1

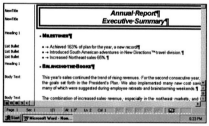

Merging Word Documents

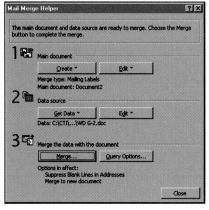

Working with Graphics

Contents

Getting
Started with Word 97

Objectives

- ▶ **Define word processing software**
- ▶ **Launch Word 97**
- ▶ **View the Word program window**
- ▶ **Enter and save text in a document**
- ▶ **Insert and delete text**
- ▶ **Select and replace text**
- ▶ **Get Help and with the Office Assistant**
- ▶ **Preview, print, close a document, and exit Word**

Welcome to Microsoft Word 97. Microsoft Word is a powerful computer program that helps you create documents that communicate your ideas clearly and effectively. More than an automated typewriter, it provides graphics, sophisticated formatting, proofing tools, and charts, to name just a few of its features. The lessons in this unit introduce you to the basic features of Word and familiarize you with the Word environment as you create a new document. ◀━━ Angela Pacheco is the marketing manager at Nomad Ltd, an outdoor sporting gear and adventure travel company. Angela's responsibilities include communicating with new and current customers about the company. To make her job easier, she'll be using Word to create attractive and professional-looking documents. She'll begin by exploring the Word environment while creating a letter to her shareholders.

Defining Word Processing Software

Microsoft Word is a full-featured **word processing** program that allows you to create attractive and professional-looking documents quickly and easily. You'll find that word processing offers many advantages over typing. Because the information you enter in a word processing document is stored electronically by your computer, it is easy to revise and reuse text in documents that you (or others) have already created. In addition, you can enhance your documents by giving text a special appearance, adding lines, shading, and creating tables. Figure A-1 illustrates the kinds of features you can use in your documents. Angela is eager to learn about some of the benefits she can expect by using Word. Table A-1 describes additional features she will use as she learns about working in Word.

Details

 Locate and correct spelling mistakes and grammatical errors

As you use Word to create documents use Word's proofreading tools to identify errors and correct them. The AutoCorrect feature even corrects many typing mistakes as you make them.

 Copy and move text without retyping

You can save time by copying text from other documents and using it again in the current document. Within the same document, you can easily reorganize and edit text.

 Enhance the appearance of documents by adding formatting

By applying different types of formatting (including shading and borders) to important parts of documents, you can create documents that convey your message effectively to your readers. Word features, such as the Formatting toolbar, styles, and AutoFormat, help you do this quickly.

Align text in rows and columns using tables

Although you can use another program such as Microsoft Excel, for complex financial analysis, you can also use tables in Word to present small amounts of financial information in an easy-to-read format. You can also format the tables to emphasize important points.

FIGURE A-1: Features in a Word document

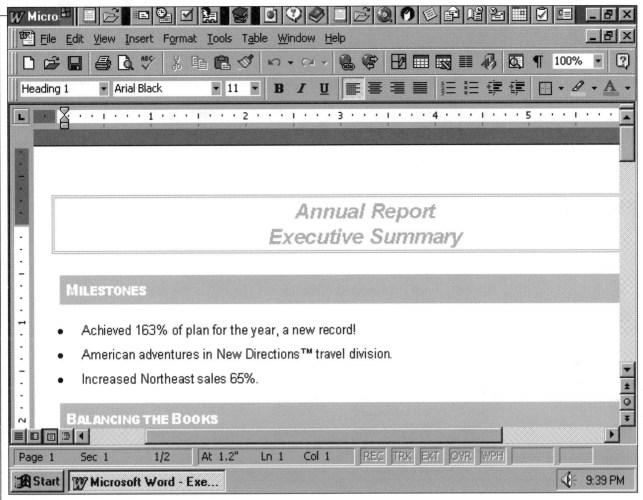

If you had a previous installation of Office on your computer, your screen may contain the Office 97 shortcut bar. Click the Close button on the shortcut bar.

TABLE A-1: Additional Word Features

feature	description	example
AutoSummarize	Allows you to see important ideas in a document	When you use the AutoSummarize command, Word highlights important words, phrases, sentences in the document. This feature helps you learn about the main ideas without requiring you to read the entire document.
Templates and Wizards	Provides the ability to create standard business documents using professionally designed formats	Word provides a number of preformatted business documents that help you quickly create the documents you need, including memos, letters, and faxes. You can even create your own templates for customized company documents.
AutoComplete	After you type a few characters of a word you use often, Word suggests the word it expects you to insert	This feature can save you a lot of time. As you work in Word, it keeps track of words and phrases you use often. Then when you type just a few characters, Word displays a word it expects you to type. When you press [Enter] Word inserts the remaining text.
AutoText	Allows you to store and insert frequently used words and phrases for fast document creation	By storing frequently used words and phrases as AutoText entries, such as a standard closing to letters, you can work faster and with fewer errors.
Document Map	Combines Outline view with Normal view	In a large document, use the Document Map to view the overall structure of the document and quickly locate headings and text you want to edit.

Word 97

Launching Word 97

To launch Word 97, you must first launch Windows by turning on your computer. You get to the Word program by clicking Start and then choosing Word from the Programs menu. The Programs menu displays the list of programs installed on your computer, including Microsoft Word. You can launch all programs this way. You can also create a shortcut on your desktop that launches Word without opening the Start and Programs menus. A **shortcut** is a faster way to open a program or a document. Because each computer system can have a different setup (depending on the hardware and software installed on it), your procedure for launching Word might be different from the one described below, especially if your computer is part of a network. See your instructor or technical support person for additional instructions. ◄── The marketing department at Nomad has installed Word 97 on all their computers, including Angela's. Angela's first step in learning to use Word 97 is to launch the program.

1. Make sure the Windows desktop is open, then click the Start button 🎯Start on the taskbar
The Start menu appears on the desktop.

2. On the Start menu, point to Programs
Each menu remains open as you point, as shown in Figure A-2. Depending on the programs installed on your computer, the programs you see on the Programs menu might be different from the ones shown in the figure.

3. On the Programs menu, click Microsoft Word
The Word program window appears, as shown in Figure A-3. The blinking vertical line, called the **insertion point,** | in the program window, indicates where text will appear when you begin typing. When you first launch Word, by default you can begin entering text and creating a new document right away. In the next lessons, you will continue to explore basic Word features.

If you have installed Microsoft Office on your computer, you might need to click Microsoft Office on the Programs menu, before you click Microsoft Word.

Creating Shortcuts

You can create a shortcut on the desktop to launch Word without going through all the menus. You just double-click a shortcut, and the program starts. To create a shortcut on the desktop, use either My Computer or Windows Explorer to locate the Program Files folder. In this folder, open the Winword folder, and locate the application file called Winword. Drag this file out of the window and onto the desktop. To eliminate the shortcut, just drag the shortcut to the Recycle Bin and confirm that you want to remove the shortcut from the desktop. Note: If you are working on a network or you share your computer with others, get permission from your instructor or technical support person before creating shortcuts on the desktop.

FIGURE A-2: Menus on the Windows desktop

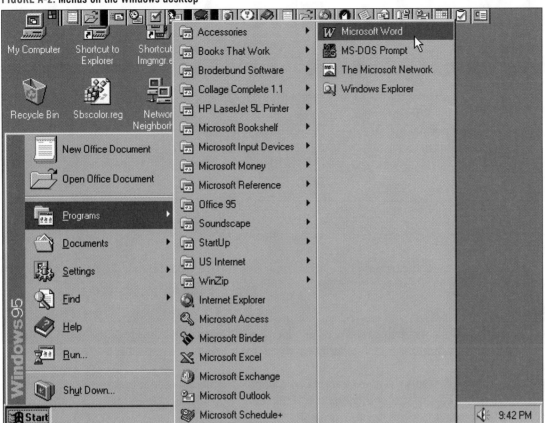

FIGURE A-3: Word program window

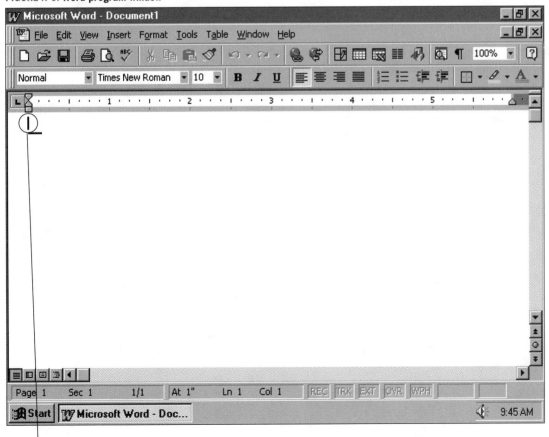

Insertion point

Viewing the Word Program Window

Now that you are in the Word **program window**, you can see some of the key features of Word. Word provides different views that allow you to see your document in different ways. In default view (called normal view), you see the features described below. On your computer, locate each of the elements described below using Figure A-4 for reference.

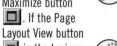

Trouble?

If your document window is not maximized, click the document window Maximize button ⬜. If the Page Layout View button ▤ in the horizontal scroll bar appears indented, indicating it is selected, the document window is in page layout view. To work in normal view, click the Normal View button ▤ in the horizontal scroll bar.

 The **title bar** displays the name of the program and the document. Until you save the document and give it a name, the temporary name is Document1.

The **menu bar** lists the names of the menus that contain Word commands. Clicking a menu name on the menu bar displays a list of commands from which you can choose.

The **Standard toolbar** contains buttons for the most frequently used commands, such as the commands for opening, saving, and printing documents. This toolbar is one of the two default toolbars. Clicking buttons on a toolbar is often faster than using the menu bar.

 The **Formatting toolbar** contains buttons for the most frequently used formatting commands, such as applying bold to text or aligning text. This toolbar is the other default toolbar. Other toolbars related to other features are also available.

 The **horizontal ruler** displays tab settings, left and right paragraph margins, and document margins.

 The **document window** displays the work area for typing text and working with your document. The blinking insertion point is the location where your text appears when you type. When the mouse pointer is in the text area of the document window, the pointer changes to an **I-beam**, I . You can have as many document windows open as your computer's memory will hold. You can minimize, maximize, and resize each window. When only one document is open, maximize the document window so that you see more of the document.

 The **vertical and horizontal scroll bars** display the relative position of the currently displayed text in the document. You use the scroll bars and **scroll boxes** to view different parts of your document.

 The **view buttons**, which appear in the horizontal scroll bar, allow you to display the document in one of four views: normal, online layout, page layout, and outline. Each view offers features that are useful in the different phases of working with a document.

 The **status bar** displays the current page and section numbers, the total number of pages, and the position of the insertion point (in inches and in lines from the upper-left corner of the document).

 When you position the pointer over a button, a **ScreenTip** appears showing the name of the button. You can customize the ScreenTips to display keyboard shortcuts. You also have the option to hide the ScreenTips.

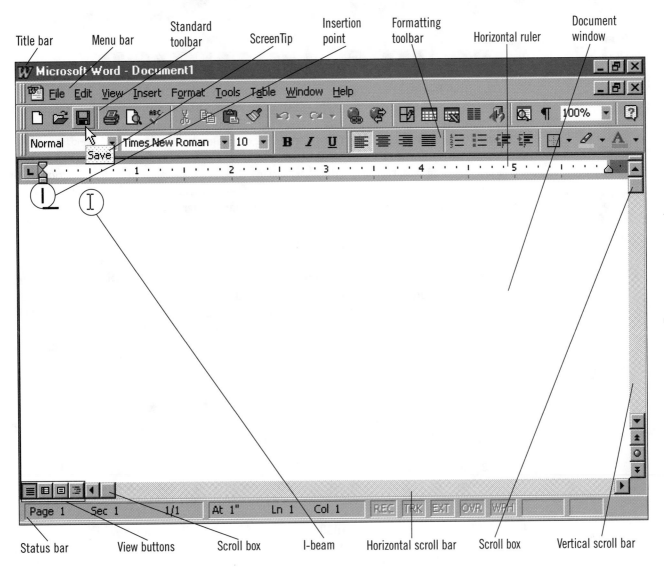

Title bar   Menu bar   Standard toolbar   ScreenTip   Insertion point   Formatting toolbar   Horizontal ruler   Document window

Word 97

Status bar   View buttons   Scroll box   I-beam   Horizontal scroll bar   Scroll box   Vertical scroll bar

Customizing ScreenTips

To display or hide ScreenTips, click Toolbars on the View menu, click Customize, click the Options tab, then select or clear the Show ScreenTips on toolbars check box. You can also hide or display keyboard shortcuts as part of the ScreenTip by deselecting the Show shortcut keys in ScreenTips check box.

Entering and Saving Text in a Document

When you launch Word, the program opens a document window in which you can create a new document. You can begin by simply typing text at the insertion point. When you reach the end of a line as you type, Word automatically moves the insertion point to the next line. This feature is called **word-wrap**. To insert a new line or start a new paragraph simply press [Enter]. It is also a good idea to save your work shortly after writing your first paragraph and every 10 or 15 minutes and before printing. You can save a document using the Save button on the Standard toolbar, or the Save or Save As commands on the File menu. ◢ Angela begins by typing the first two paragraphs in the body of her letter to Nomad Ltd's shareholders.

Steps 1 2 3 4

1. At the insertion point, type the following paragraph:

   The year has been an exciting and profitable year, at Nomad Ltd. As a shareholder, you will be interested to learn about our recent successes and the challenges we expect in the coming year and beyond. This letter includes the high points of the year and provides valuable details about our work in individual areas of the organization, including finance, communications, quality assurance, and travel. In the next few days you will receive a complete Annual Report for the entire organization and detailed profiles for each division.

   Do not press [Enter] when you reach the end of a line. Just keep typing.

2. Insert your Student Disk in drive A, then click the **Save button** 🖫 on the Standard toolbar

   The Save As dialog box opens, as shown in Figure A-5. In this dialog box, you need to assign a name to the document you are creating, replacing the default filename supplied by Word.

3. In the File name text box, type **First Draft Letter**

   Next, you need to instruct Word to save the file to your Student Disk. The name of the currently active drive or folder appears in the Save in list box.

4. Click the **Save in list arrow**, then click $3\frac{1}{2}$ **Floppy (A:)**, and then click **Save.**

   These lessons assume your Student Disk is in drive A. If you are using a different drive or storing your practice files on a network, click the appropriate drive.

5. Press **[Enter]** twice

   The first time you press [Enter], the insertion point moves to the start of the next line. The next time you press [Enter], you create a blank line before the text you type next.

6. Type the following paragraph:

   We are proud of our employees and encourage you to join us at the Annual Meeting to be held at the Ocean View Suites next month. Enclosed please find an Annual Meeting reply card, which you can return to let us know if you plan to attend.

7. At the end of the second paragraph, press **[Enter]** once

   Don't be concerned about making typing mistakes. Also, don't be concerned if your text wraps differently from the text shown in the figure. How text wraps depends on your monitor or printer. Next display the number of spaces between words and paragraphs, by displaying non-printing characters.

8. Click the Show/Hide button ¶ on the Standard toolbar

   The spaces between words appear as dots. New lines are represented by ¶ at the end of a paragraph. Compare your screen to Figure A-6 then click Save.

9. Click 🖫

   The document is saved with the name First Draft Letter on your Student Disk.

FIGURE A-5: Save As dialog box

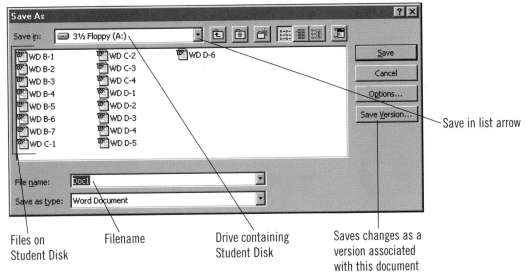

Files on Student Disk — Filename — Drive containing Student Disk — Saves changes as a version associated with this document

Save in list arrow

FIGURE A-6: Text in a Word document

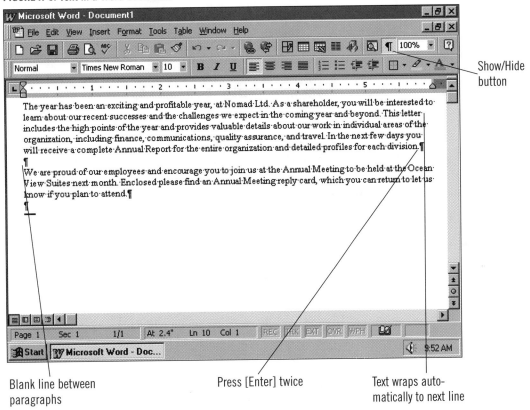

Show/Hide button

Blank line between paragraphs — Press [Enter] twice — Text wraps automatically to next line

Working with Automatic Corrections

If you make certain kinds of spelling or typographical errors, you might notice that Word automatically makes the necessary corrections as you type. This feature is called AutoCorrect. For example, some common spelling mistakes (such as typing 'adn' instead of 'and') are corrected as soon as you type the first space after the word. Similarly, if you type two capitalized letters in a row, Word automatically changes the sec- ond character to lower case as you continue typing (except in a state's abbreviation, such as 'WA'). If you misspell a word that is not corrected right away, Word underlines the word with a red, wavy underline. If you make a potential grammatical error, Word underlines the error with a green, wavy underline. After you finish typing, click the right mouse button on the word to display a pop-up menu of correction options.

Inserting and Deleting Text

After typing text, you often need to edit it by inserting new text or deleting text you want to remove. To insert text, place the insertion point where you want the new text to appear, then start typing. You can delete text to the left or the right of the insertion point. Word also offers commonly used AutoText entries that can be inserted in your documents for more information. Whenever you insert or delete text, Word adjusts the spacing of the existing text. ✎ First, Angela adds the inside address to her letter, then she'll make a few corrections by removing individual characters.

Steps 1234

Trouble?

If your typing overwrites existing text, check to see if the indicator "OVR" appears in black in the status bar. Press [Insert] or double-click OVR in the status bar to switch back to Insert mode, so that text you type does not overwrite existing text.

QuickTip

The Letter Wizard is a fast and easy way to create letters. Just click the Letter Wizard option in the Office Assistant balloon-shaped dialog box and complete the dialog boxes according to your preferences.

1. **Press [Ctrl][Home]** to place the insertion point at the beginning of the document and type the following address, pressing **[Enter]** after each line:
   Ms. Malena Jeskey [Enter]
   456 Greenview Lane [Enter]
   Shoreview, CA 90272 [Enter]
   Notice that a wavy, red underline appears under the word "Malena" and other proper names. This means that these words are not in Word's dictionary.

2. **Press [Enter]** again to insert a blank line and type **Dear Shareholder:** and press **[Enter]** twice

3. If the Office Assistant appears asking if you want to create a letter using a wizard, click **Cancel** in the Office Assistant balloon-shaped dialog box
   If you create a letter using the Letter Wizard, you simply respond to a series of dialog boxes. So that you can learn a lot more about using Word, for now type this letter without the aid of the wizard. Next, you want to change the word "The" in the first sentence to "This."

4. Place the insertion point after the word **The** (but before the space) in the first sentence, press **[Backspace]**, then type **is**
   This removes the "e" and inserts "i" and "s." Next, you will delete an unnecessary comma.

5. Place the insertion point after the second occurrence of the word **year** (but before the comma) in the first sentence, then press **[Delete]**
   This removes the comma. Next, you will add today's date to the beginning of the letter. First, move to the beginning of the document.

6. Press **[Ctrl][Home]**
   With the insertion point at the beginning of the document, you can insert the date.

7. Click **Insert** on the menu bar, then click **Date and Time**
   The Date and Time dialog box opens. Word displays the date based on your computer's system clock. Before you proceed, verify that the Update Automatically check box is cleared, so that the date is not updated each time you save or print the document. For formatting dates in letters and other business correspondence, choose the third option in the list.

8. In the dialog box, click the third option in the list, then click **OK**
   Today's date automatically appears in the document.

9. Press **[Enter]** twice
   Compare your document to Figure A-7. The date you see might be different.

FIGURE A-7: Letter after inserting and deleting text

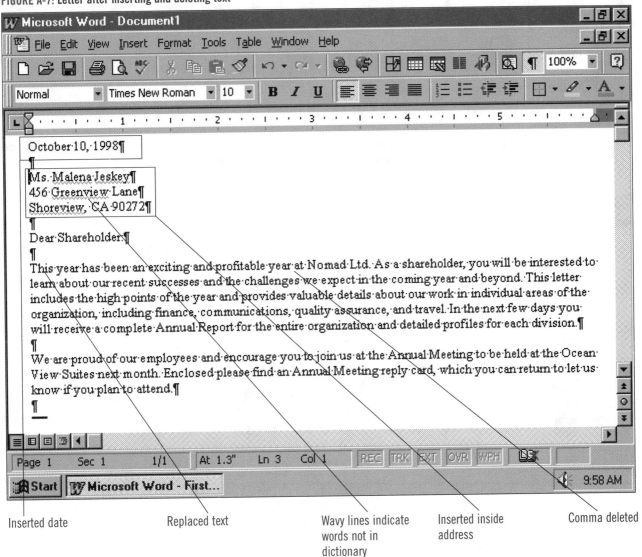

Inserted date

Replaced text

Wavy lines indicate
words not in
dictionary

Inserted inside
address

Comma deleted

Inserting built-in AutoText entries

AutoText entries are words or phrases that are
frequently used, such as company names or greetings
and closings in letters. Word includes various built-in
AutoText entries which are arranged by subject,
such as closings and salutations. To insert a built-in
AutoText entry, point to AutoText on the Insert
menu, click the desired subject, then click the desired
AutoText entry as shown in Figure A-8. The AutoText
entry is inserted at the place of the insertion point.

FIGURE A-8: Built-in AutoText entries on the Insert menu

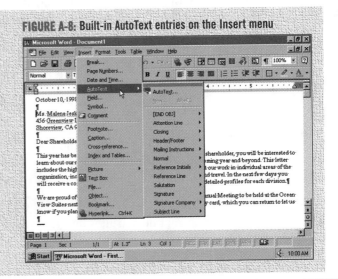

Selecting and Replacing Text

In addition to editing characters one at a time, you can also edit multiple characters, words, paragraphs, or the entire document. Most Word editing techniques require that you first select the text you want to edit. For example, to delete existing text and replace it with new text, you first select the text you want to remove, then type the new text. This feature is called **Typing Replaces Selection**. Table A-2 describes the different ways to select text with a mouse. You can also change your mind about the revisions you make with the Undo and Redo features. ✎ Next, Angela uses various techniques to select and replace text.

1. Place the insertion point in front of the second occurrence of the word year in the first sentence and drag across the word
The highlighting indicates that the word is selected. You want to replace the selection so that the word "year" is not used twice in the same sentence.

2. Type one
The word "one" replaces the selected word. Now you will replace several words with one word.

3. Place the insertion point in front of the word please in the last sentence and drag across it and the next word, find, then release the mouse button and type is
Both words and the spaces that follow the words are selected. If you drag across too many words, drag back over the text to deselect it. The word "is" replaces the selected text. Word inserts the correct spacing and reformats the text after the insertion point. You will replace the word "includes" in the third sentence.

4. Double-click the word includes in the third sentence, then type summarizes
The word "summarizes" replaces the selected text, along with the correct spacing. If you change your mind about a change, you can reverse it. You will reinsert the word "includes."

5. Click the Undo Typing button 🔄 on the Standard toolbar
The word "includes" replaces the word "summarizes." Clicking the Undo Typing button reverses the most recent action. The arrow next to the Undo Typing button displays a list of all the changes you've made since opening the document, so you can undo one or more changes. You can also reverse a change you have undone.

6. Click the Redo Typing button 🔄 on the Standard toolbar
The word "summarizes" reappears. As with the Undo Typing feature, the arrow next to the Redo Typing button displays a list of changes you can redo.

7. Position the pointer to the far left of the first line of the body of the letter until the pointer changes to ⬧, then click the mouse button
Clicking next to the line in the selection bar selects the text. The **selection bar** is the area to the left of the text in your document, as shown in Figure A-9.

8. Click anywhere in the document to deselect the text
The first line is no longer selected. Whenever you want to deselect text, simply click in the document window. Compare your screen to Figure A-10.

9. Click the Save button 💾 on the Standard toolbar.
Your document is now saved.

Trouble?
If text you type does not replace selected text, click Tools, click Options, click the Edit tab, then click to select the Typing Replaces Selection check box. Click OK to return to the document.

FIGURE A-9: Selected text and selection bar

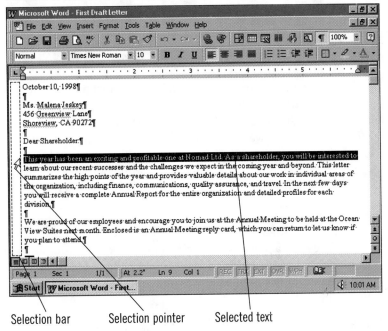

Selection bar   Selection pointer   Selected text

FIGURE A-10: Completed document

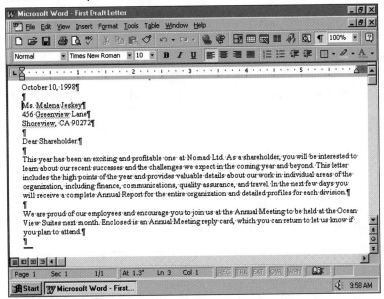

TABLE A-2: Mouse selection techniques

to select text with the mouse	do this
A word	Double-click the word
A sentence	Press and hold [Ctrl] and click in the sentence
A paragraph	Triple-click in the paragraph, or double-click in the selection bar next to the paragraph
A line of text	Click in the selection bar next to the line
An entire document	Press and hold [Ctrl] and click anywhere in the selection bar, or triple-click in the selection bar
A vertical block of text	Press and hold [Alt] and drag through the text
A large amount of text	Place the insertion point at the beginning of the text, move to the end of the desired selection, then press and hold [Shift] and click

Word 97

Getting Help with the Office Assistant

The Word program includes an online Help system that provides information and instructions on Word features and commands while you are using Word. You can get as little or as much information as you want, from quick definitions to detailed procedures. The **Office Assistant** is just one way to find help while working in Word. Using this animated assistant is an easy way to display Help windows and discover new features. Other Help commands are on the Help menu. ▸ In the next lesson, Angela will save, print, and close the document. Before she does this, she will use the Office Assistant to learn more about saving a document.

1. **Click the Office Assistant button 🔲 on the Standard toolbar**
   The Office Assistant appears, as shown in Figure A-11. Your animated assistant may look different depending on which assistant is selected on your computer. If this is the first time the Office Assistant has been used on your computer, you will see the message "preparing Help file for first use."

2. **Type saving documents under Type your question here, and then click Search**
   In this area you can type key words or whole questions for which you would like more information.

3. **Click Search**
   The Office Assistant offers various topics related to saving documents from which you can choose.

4. **Click the Save a document option button**
   A Help window opens detailing various save features.

5. **Scroll through the Help window and read about saving documents**
   At the bottom of the Help window you will find a list of related topics from which you can choose. These topics will give detailed instructions on performing certain operations.

6. **Position the pointer over the topic Save a new, unnamed document, until the pointer changes to 🖑 and click**
   A new Help window opens displaying the steps necessary for saving a document. When the pointer changes to 🖑 once you've placed the pointer over a word or button, you can click to display more information.

7. **Click the Save button 🔲 in the Help window**
   A message appears describing the function of this button.

8. **Click outside of the Help window in the letter document**
   The Save button message is hidden, but the Help window is still visible. The letter document is active again. A window is active when the title bar is highlighted. An inactive window will have a dimmed title bar. Compare your screen to Figure A-12.

9. **Click the Close button 🗙 in the Help window, and then click the Close button in the Office Assistant window**

FIGURE A-11: Office Assistant in Word document

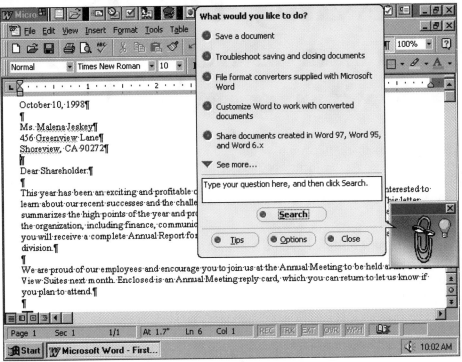

FIGURE A-12: Visible Help window

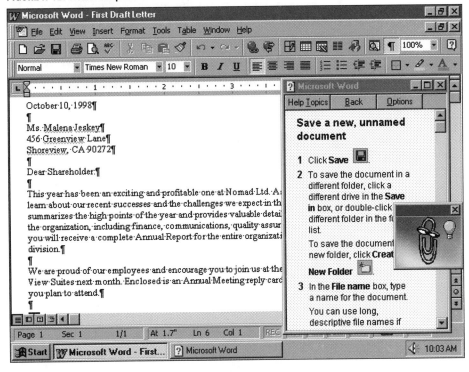

More about using Help

You can also use commands on the Help menu when searching for Help information. Click Help on the menu bar, then click Contents and Index. The Help Topics dialog box will open. You can use the Contents tab to choose from various Help topics or you can use the Find and Index tabs to search for key words that you provide. You can also use the What's This pointer ℝ? to find information. Click What's This on the Help menu, then click the What's This pointer over buttons, formatting, and features. To turn off the pointer, click What's This on the Help menu again.

Word 97

Previewing, Printing, Closing a Document, and Exiting Word

Once you have saved your document, you can print one copy of the document using the Print button on the Standard toolbar. After you have finished working in a document and it has been saved and printed, you can close the document and exit Word. ━━━ Angela has finished working with her letter for now. She would like to save, print, and close the document before exiting Word. Angela will use the directions in the Help window to save her document.

Steps

1. Click the **Print Preview button** 🔍 on the Standard toolbar
   The document appears in the Preview window, as shown in Figure A-13. The size of the page you see depends on the number and size of pages displayed the last time the Print Preview command was issued.

2. Click the **Close button** on the Print Preview toolbar to return to your document

3. Click the **Save button** 💾 on the Standard toolbar to save your document

4. Click the **Print button** 🖨 on the Standard toolbar
   The Print button prints the current document to the default printer connected to your computer. If you are not connected to a printer, ask your technical support person or instructor for assistance. You are now ready to close your document.

5. Click **File** on the menu bar, then click **Close**
   When you close a document that has changes you have not saved, Word asks if you want to save your changes. If you get a message asking if you want to save changes, click Yes. The documents closes.

6. Click **File** on the menu bar, then click **Exit**
   The Exit command closes the Word program and returns you to the Windows desktop.

QuickTip

Clicking the Close button on the right end of the menu bar closes the document. Clicking the Close button on the right end of the title bar exits the program.

Print Preview
toolbar

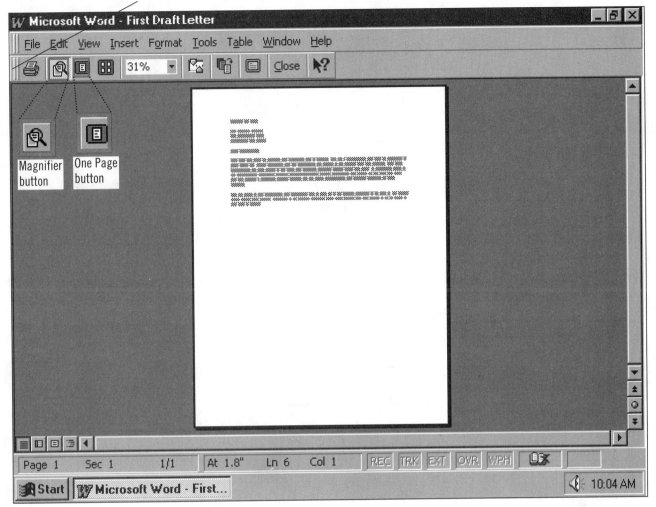

Magnifier
button

One Page
button

Practice

► Concepts Review

Label each option in the Save As dialog box shown in Figure A-14.

FIGURE A-14

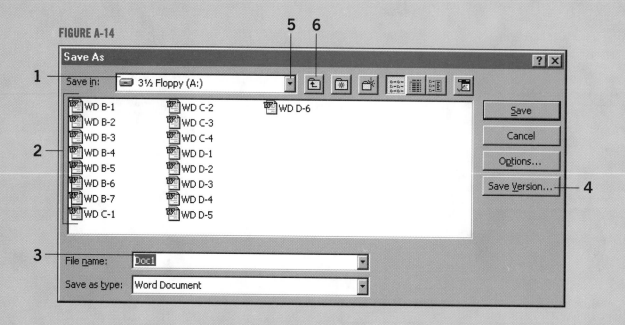

Match each of the following terms with the statement that best describes its function.

7. **Standard toolbar**
8. **Formatting toolbar**
9. **Document window**
10. **Ruler**
11. **Status bar**
12. **Deleting**
13. **Inserting**
14. **AutoText**

a. Displays area in which you enter text

b. Identifies location of insertion point and command status

c. Contains buttons for easy access to general commands such as Open and Print

d. Removing the text to the right or left of the insertion point

e. Displays tab settings, paragraph and document margins

f. Typing text between existing text

g. Contains buttons for easy access to commands that affect the appearance of text in a document

h. Standard text and expressions you can insert instead of typing

Select the best answer from the list of choices.

15. Word processing is most similar to:
   a. Performing financial analysis
   b. Filling in forms
   c. Typing
   d. Forecasting mortgage payments

16. To display another part of a document, you:
   a. Click in the Moving toolbar
   b. Scroll with a scroll bar
   c. Drag the ruler
   d. Select the Close box

17. You can get Help in any of the following ways, except:
   a. Clicking the Help box in a dialog box
   b. Double-clicking anywhere in the document window
   c. Clicking the Help button on the Standard toolbar
   d. Clicking Help on the menu bar

18. What keys do you press to move the insertion point to the first character in a document?
   a. [Ctrl][Home]
   b. [Home]
   c. [Alt][PgUp]
   d. [Shift][Tab]

19. The Close command on the File menu:
   a. Closes Word without saving any changes
   b. Closes the current document and, if you have made any changes, asks if you want to save them
   c. Closes all currently open Word documents
   d. Closes the current document without saving changes

20. To leave the Word program window, you must:
   a. Close all open documents or lose your work when you close Word
   b. Click the Exit button on the Standard toolbar
   c. Click the Close command on the File menu, which closes documents and closes Word
   d. Click the Exit command on the File menu, which closes documents and closes Word

21. Which of the following methods is not a way to select text?
   a. Clicking in the selection bar
   b. Dragging across the text
   c. Double-clicking a word with the left mouse button
   d. Dragging text to the selection bar

22. Which key do you press to remove text to the left of the insertion point?
   a. [Backspace]
   b. [Delete]
   c. [Cut]
   d. [Overtype]

▶ Skills Review

1. Launch Word, then identify the parts of the window.
   a. Click the Start button on the Windows desktop taskbar.
   b. Point to Programs.
   c. Click Microsoft Word.
   d. Identify as many elements of the Word window as you can without referring to the unit material.

2. Explore the Word program window.

a. Click each of the menus and drag the mouse button through all the commands on each menu. To close a menu without making a selection, drag the mouse away from the menu, then release the mouse button.

b. Point to each of the buttons on the toolbars, and read the ScreenTips and descriptions.

c. Click Tools, then click Options. In the Options dialog box, click the Edit tab and make sure that the first three options are selected. Click any of these three check boxes that are not selected.

d. Click OK to close the dialog box.

3. Enter and save text in a new document.

a. At the insertion point, type a short letter to a local business describing your interest in learning more about the company.

b. Don't type the inside address or a closing yet. For a greeting, type "To Whom It May Concern:". (If the Office Assistant appears offering Help in writing your letter, click Cancel.)

c. Be sure to state that you are looking for a position in the company.

d. Mention that you have been encouraged to investigate opportunities at the company by counselors, instructors, and alumni.

e. Request a copy of the company's annual report to understand the scope of the company's business. For a closing, type "Sincerly," then press [Enter] twice. Notice that Word corrects your typing for you.

f. Save the document on your Student Disk as Information Letter.

4. Insert and delete text.

a. Place the insertion point at the beginning of the document.

b. Insert today's date and press [Enter] twice.

c. Type the name of the company contact and press [Enter]. Use whatever contact name you want.

d. Type the company name and press [Enter]. Use whatever company name you want.

e. Type the company address and press [Enter].

f. Type the city, state, and postal code, then press [Enter].

g. Press [Enter] twice, then type your name and press [Enter].

h. Type your street address and press [Enter].

i. Type your city, state, and postal code and press [Enter] again.

j. Type your phone number.

k. Use [Backspace] to delete your phone number. Press [Enter] once more.

5. Select and replace text.

a. Select the text "To Whom It May Concern:", then type "Dear" followed by the name of the recipient of the letter; for example, Mr. Martin.

b. Select the last word of the document, then press [Delete] to delete the entire word.

c. Click the Undo button to restore the original text.

d. Use selecting and replacing techniques to correct any mistakes in your letter.

6. **Explore Word Help.**
   a. Click the Office Assistant button on the Standard toolbar.
   b. Type "Print" under What would you like to do?.
   c. Click Search.
   d. Click the option button next to Print a document.
   e. Click Print a range of pages.
   f. Click Options, Print Topic.
   g. Click the What's This? button, then click Properties.
   h. Click Cancel.
   i. Click the Close button in the Help window.
   j. Click the Close button in the Office Assistant window to close this Help option.

7. **Print and close the document and exit Word.**
   a. Save the document, and then click the Print button on the Standard toolbar.
   b. Click File on the menu bar, then click Close.
   c. Click No if you see a message asking if you want to save your changes.
   d. Click File on the menu bar, then click Exit.

▶ Independent Challenges

1. Using the Contents and Index command on the Help menu, learn more about Keyboard shortcuts. Use the Show Me button in the Help windows to see an animated demonstration of the features. Print the Help windows as you go using the Print Topic command on the Options menu. Figure A-15 displays an example of one of the windows that you can print.

FIGURE A-15

Keys for working with documents	
To	**Press**
Create a new document	CTRL+N
Open a document	CTRL+O
Close a document	CTRL+W
Split a document	ALT+CTRL+S
Save a document	CTRL+S
Quit Word	ALT+F4
To	**Press**
Find text, formatting, and special items	CTRL+F
Repeat find	ALT+CTRL+Y
Replace text, specific formatting, and special items	CTRL+H
Go to a page, bookmark, footnote, table, comment, graphic, or other location	CTRL+G
Go back to a page, bookmark, footnote, table, comment, graphic, or other location	ALT+CTRL+Z
Browse a document	ALT+CTRL+HOME
To	**Press**
Cancel an action	ESC
Undo an action	CTRL+Z
Redo or repeat an action	CTRL+Y
To	**Press**
Switch to page layout view	ALT+CTRL+P
Switch to outline view	ALT+CTRL+O
Switch to normal view	ALT+CTRL+N
Move between a master document and its subdocuments	CTRL+\

2. As a co-chair for the Lake City High School 1993 class reunion planning committee, you are responsible for recruiting classmates to help with reunion activities. Using Figure A-16 as a guide, draft a letter to the 1993 graduates asking for volunteers to aid the four reunion committees: entertainment, hospitality, meals, and transportation. For the inside address, use any name and address you wish. Save this document as "1993 Letter". Be sure to insert today's date and salutation. (If the Office Assistant appears offering Help in writing your letter, click Cancel.)

FIGURE A-16

June 25, 1998

Ms. Sandy Carter
8899 Lakeshore Boulevard
Minneapolis, MN 56789

Dear Sandy:

As a member of the Lake City High School class of 1993, I often think of the people who made our school such a rewarding experience for me. Of course, there are the close friends I made and kept throughout the years, but also I think about the people I somehow lost track of since graduation. The instructors, students, and administrative staff all contribute to the richness of the memories.

Now is your opportunity to play an important role in helping bring Lake City High School memories alive not only for yourself, but for your fellow classmates as well. As the co-chair of the 1998 Reunion planning committee, I am looking for ambitious, organized alumni who are interested in working on various reunion activities.

We need people for the following areas: meeting coordination for all committees, computer consulting to help us use technology to work efficiently, meals and entertainment planning for the three-day event, and logistics coordination for getting everyone to Lake City and lodging them once they return to campus. All committees need as many volunteers as possible, so you are sure to be able to work in any area you choose.

If you are interested and available to work five hours a month for the next 10 months, please let me know. You can leave me a message at (555)555-4321. I look forward to hearing from you soon.

[your name]
Lake City High School Reunion 1993
Co-Chair

3. As a recent graduate, you are scouring the planet for job opportunities. Log on to the Internet and use your browser to go to http://www.course.com. From there, click Student On Line Companions, and then click the Microsoft Office 97 Professional Edition—Illustrated: A First Course page, then click on the Word link for Unit A. Click on the link that takes you to a list of employment opportunities. After downloading a file of interesting positions, create a cover letter that describes your qualifications or the qualifications such a position would require. Use Figure A-17 as a guide for the content of this letter. Save the document as "Job Letter". Be sure to insert today's date and an inside address and salutation. (If the Office Assistant appears offering Help in writing your letter, click Cancel.)

FIGURE A-17

June 7, 1998

Ms. Kelly Grand
Hewlett Packard
HP Circle W406
Cupertino, CA 98007

Dear Ms. Grand:

I am interested in working as a Senior Programmer for your organization. I am an expert programmer with over 10 years of experience to offer you. I enclose my resume as a first step in exploring the poossibilities of employment with Hewlett Packard.

My most recent experience was designing an automated billing system for a trade magazine publisher. I was responsible for the overall product design, including the user interface. In addition, I developed the first draft of the operator's guide.

As a Senior Programmer with your organization, I would bring a focus on quality and ease of use to your system development. Furthermore, I work well with others, and I am experienced in project management.

I would appreciate your keeping this inquiry confidential. I will call you in a few days to arrange an interview at a convenient time for you. Thank you for your consideration.

Sincerely,

[your name]

4. As a co-chair for the Lake City High School class of 1993 planning committee, you have received a telephone message from a classmate volunteering to serve on the entertainment committee. Use the Letter Wizard, which appears after you type a salutation and press [Enter], to create a thank you letter to this volunteer that provides details about the entertainment committee members, meeting place, and schedule. Enter your letter preferences in each of the Letter Wizard dialog boxes. For the inside address, use any name and address you wish. Save the document with the name "Thank You Letter". Be sure to insert today's date and an inside address and salutation. Compare your letter to the one shown in Figure A-18.

FIGURE A-18

September 15, 1996

Mr. Oliver Randall
Vice President/Marketing
InterSysData Corp.
4440 Pacific Boulevard
San Francisco, CA 94104

Dear Mr. Randall:

Thank you for volunteering to participate on the entertainment committee for the Lake City High School 1990 class reunion. We are looking forward to working with you on these events.

So that you can arrange your time accordingly, please block out the first Thursday of each month for the next six months for planning meetings. All meetings will take place at 7:30 p.m. at the Comfort Corner Coffee Shop in Middleburg (on Highway 95, next to the Burger Palace drive-in). Our first meeting will be next month; please come prepared to discuss your ideas for entertainment events at the reunion.

Please let me know by noon on the meeting date if you are unable to attend any of these meetings.

[your name]
Lake City High School Reunion 1990
Co-Chair

Visual Workshop

You are currently planning an International Communications conference and have been contacting independent consultants to deliver short presentations. Type a thank you letter to a consultant who has agreed to demonstrate new online features to conference attendees. Be sure to misspell some words so you can observe the automatic corrections provided by Word. You can view AutoCorrect entries with the AutoCorrect command on the Tools menu. Try to use as many inserting, selecting, and replacing techniques as possible. Save the document as "International Voices". Compare your document to Figure A-19. You can either use the Letter Wizard or create your own letter from scratch.

FIGURE A-19

September 15, 1996

Ms. Jennifer Swanson
789 Jasmine Lane
Rapid Water, MN 55067

Dear Ms. Swanson,

Thank you for accepting our offer to demonstrate new online features at this fall's International Voices Conference. The conference will take place on October 3 at The Ocean View Suites Hotel, from 9:00am to 7:00pm.

As we discussed on the telephone, your demonstrations will include various Internet and online features that will be released in the upcoming year. Our hope is that these demonstrations will show participants how these new features will enhance the present communications between international businesses. My understanding is that you will provide all equipment necessary for your demonstrations. Please contact me, however, if you have any additional audio or video requirements.

We have scheduled your one hour presentation to be the final activity of the conference. Please plan to join us for dinner and informal discussion afterward. We look forward to your participation in this exciting event!

Sincerely,

[your name]
Conference Coordinator
International Voices

Editing
and Proofing Documents

Objectives

► **Plan a document**
► **Open a document and save it with a new name**
► **Copy text**
► **Move text**
► **Correct spelling and grammatical errors**
► **Find and replace text**
► **Preview a document**
► **Print a document**

In this unit, you will save a document with a new name so that the original document is unchanged. Using a variety of copying and moving techniques, you will learn how to make fast work of reusing and rearranging text in a document. You will also use Word's proofing tools to find and correct misspelled words and grammatical errors. In addition, Word's find and replace capabilities enable you to locate specific occurrences of text and replace each instance consistently throughout a document. After proofreading a document, you can preview it, make any necessary adjustments, then print it.   At Nomad Ltd, Angela drafted a letter to Nomad shareholders that will serve as a cover letter to the annual report. Angela would like to copy text from another document to add to the letter and proof this letter before printing it.

Planning a Document

Although Word makes it easy to modify documents after you have created them, it is always a good idea to plan the document. Planning involves identifying the audience and purpose, developing the content and organization, and then matching the tone to all these elements. After identifying the audience and the purpose of the document, which form the foundation of the plan, determine what you want to say. Once you have listed the main ideas of the document, it's important to organize these ideas into a logical sequence. When you begin writing, use a tone that matches the audience, purpose, content and organization. For example, the tone in an announcement to a company picnic will be different from a business letter requesting payment for an overdue invoice. Finally, make the document visually appealing, by using formatting that emphasizes the ideas presented. If you are working on a document for someone else, it is a good idea to verify your plan with your supervisor before you continue. ◆ Angela wants to inform shareholders of an upcoming Annual Meeting and provide an overview of the year's highlights.

Steps 1234

1. Identify the intended audience and purpose of the document

Jot down general ideas for each of these elements, as shown in Figure B-1.

2. Choose the information and important points you want to cover in the document

You write down your ideas for the document.

3. Decide how the information will be organized

Because the information about the meeting is most important, you decide to present it first. The company highlights are included next. Later, if you decide to rearrange the structure of the document, you can use Word's editing features to move, copy, and cut text as needed.

4. Choose the tone of the document

Because the document is being sent to corporate shareholders, you will use a businesslike tone. In addition, it has been a good year at Nomad Ltd, so you will also use a positive, enthusiastic tone intended to encourage shareholders to feel good about their investments in the company. You can edit the document as needed until you achieve exactly the tone you want.

5. Think about how you want the document to look

To best communicate this information to your readers, you plan to use a straightforward business letter format for the document. The letter will include lists, directions, and a signature block. Each part will require special formatting to distinguish it from the rest of the letter. If you change your mind about the format of the document, you can make adjustments later.

6. After you have completed the planning you'll want to verify the document plan with your supervisor.

You can save much time later and avoid confusion about key elements before you begin the document. Be sure to clarify any elements you are unsure about. The planning stage is a good point at which to clarify your plan.

FIGURE B-1: A possible document plan

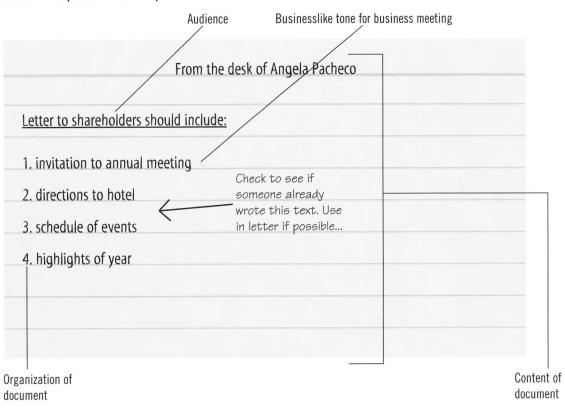

Audience   Businesslike tone for business meeting

From the desk of Angela Pacheco

Letter to shareholders should include:

1. invitation to annual meeting

2. directions to hotel   Check to see if someone already wrote this text. Use in letter if possible...

3. schedule of events

4. highlights of year

Organization of document   Content of document

Creating new documents using wizards and templates

You can use Word's document wizards and templates to create a variety of professionally-designed business documents, including resumes, memos, faxes, and business letters. These wizards and templates take into account the planning techniques described above to create documents that are consistent in tone, purpose, and formatting. All you do is provide the text. To create such a document, click the New command on the File menu, and double-click the icon for the type of document you want to create. You can use either a wizard (which guides you through a series of dialog boxes regarding your preferences for the document) or you can use a template in which you replace placeholder text with your own text. Either method gives you a great head start in developing attractive and effective documents.

Word 97

Opening a Document and Saving it with a New Name

Using text from existing documents saves you time and energy. To prevent any changes to the original document, you can open it and save it with a new name. This creates a copy of the document, leaving the original unchanged. ✐ Earlier Angela reviewed a document created by a colleague at Nomad Ltd. This document contains additional text Angela wants to use in the shareholder letter she created earlier. So that she does not alter the original documents, Angela opens the documents and saves both with new names.

Steps 123 4

Time To

✔ Start Word 97

1. **Click the Open button** 📂 **on the Standard toolbar**
   Word displays the Open dialog box, as shown in Figure B-2. The Look in list box displays the name of the drive or folder you accessed the last time you saved or opened a file. Table B-1 describes the buttons in this dialog box.

2. **Click the Up One Level button** 🔼 **until you see the drive where you save your files for this book**
   The name of the drive containing your Student Disk appears in the large box.

3. **Double-click the drive to display its contents**
   The Look in box displays the drive containing your Student Disk and the lesson files appear in the large box.

4. **Click the document named WD B-1 in the file list box, then click Open**
   The document WD B-1 appears in the document window. To keep this original file intact, you will save it with a new name, Shareholder Letter.

5. **Click File on the menu bar, then click Save As**
   The Save As dialog box opens, in which you can enter a new name for the document. Make sure the Save in list box displays the drive where you want to save your files.

6. **In the File name text box, type Shareholder Letter, then click Save**
   The document is saved with the new name, and the original document is closed. You can now safely use Shareholder Letter without changing the original document. You now need to open and save another document before beginning revisions.

QuickTip

You can double-click a file-name in the Open dialog box to open the document. This is faster than clicking the filename then clicking Open.

7. **Repeat steps 1–6, opening the document WD B-2 and saving the document as Report**
   The document is saved with the new name, as shown in Figure B-3, and the original document is closed. The Shareholder Letter is still open in a document window behind the newly saved Report document.

FIGURE B-2: Open dialog box

Look in list box

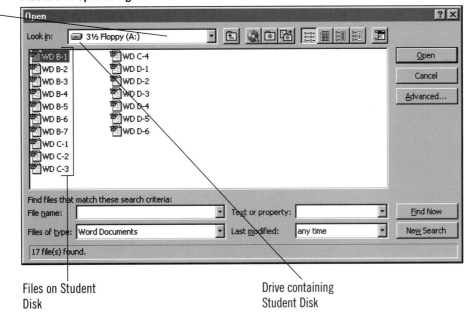

Files on Student
Disk

Drive containing
Student Disk

FIGURE B-3: Saved document

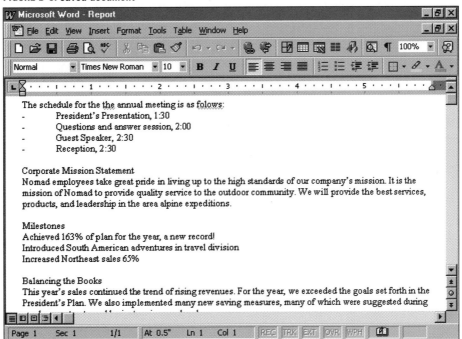

TABLE B-1: Open dialog box buttons

button	description
	Moves up one folder (the folder that contains the current folder)
	Displays icon and document name in a list
	Displays detailed information about the document, including its name, its size, its type (folder or type of file), and the date it was last modified
	Displays additional document details, including the author's name, the date created, who last saved the document, the program in which the document was created, the number of revisions, and the number of pages and words
	Displays a small picture of the document's contents to help you identify the document

Copying Text

You can copy existing text that you want to reuse in a document. You can use the Copy command or Copy button to copy text to the Clipboard so that the text is available to be pasted in other locations in the document. The Clipboard (available in any Windows program) is a temporary storage area in computer memory for text and graphics. You can also drag selected text to a new location using the mouse. Dragging is a great way to copy text when both the text and its new location are visible in the window at the same time. ◣▬▬ Next Angela will copy text from her colleague's document to her shareholder letter. Angela displays both documents at once, in separate windows, so that she can work in both documents at the same time.

QuickTip

Display paragraph marks by clicking the Show/Hide button ¶ on the Standard toolbar.

1. Click Window on the menu bar, then click Arrange All
Both documents appear in the program window, as shown in Figure B-4. You want to copy all the text from the Report document to the Shareholder Letter.

2. With the pointer in the selection bar of the Report document, triple-click the left mouse button
Triple-clicking in the selection bar selects the entire document.

CourseHelp

The camera icon indicates there is a CourseHelp available with this lesson. Click the Start button, point to programs, point to CourseHelp, then click Word 97 Illustrated. Choose the CourseHelp that corresponds to this lesson.

3. Click the Copy button 🗐 on the Standard toolbar
The selected text is copied to the Clipboard. By placing text on the Clipboard (with either the Cut or Copy command), you can insert the text as many times as you want. You want to place this text before the last sentence in the Shareholder Letter.

4. Click in the Shareholder Letter document window to make it active, then place the insertion point in front of the first sentence in the paragraph before the signature block

5. Click the Paste button 🗐 on the Standard toolbar
The copied text is inserted. It remains on the Clipboard until you copy or cut new text. To make it easier to work in the document, maximize the Shareholder Letter document window.

Time To

✔ Save

6. In the Shareholder Letter document window, click the Maximize button, ☐ then scroll to the top of the document
You can see more of the document at once with the window maximized. Compare your document to Figure B-5.

FIGURE B-4: **Two open documents in the Word program window**

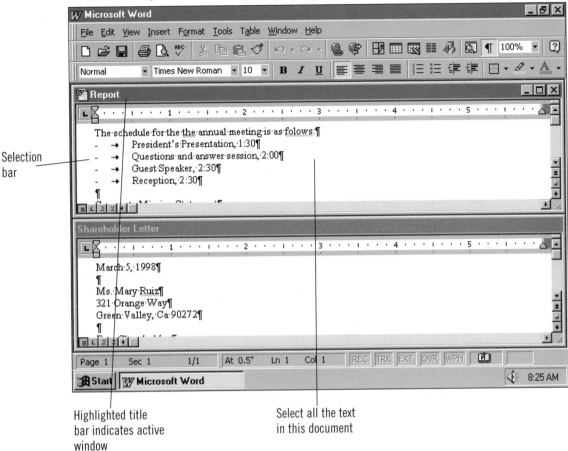

Selection bar

Highlighted title
bar indicates active
window

Select all the text
in this document

FIGURE B-5: **Completed document**

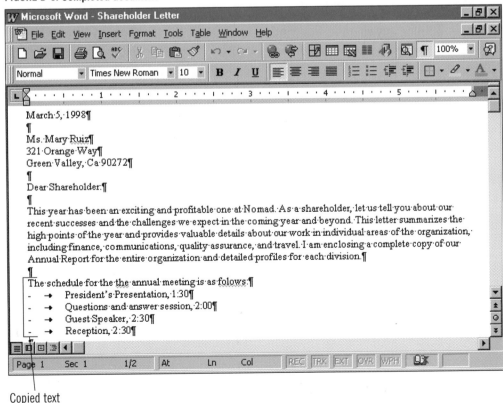

Copied text

Word 97

Moving Text

You can also move text from its current location and place it in new locations, even in other documents. You can use the Clipboard by cutting the text in one location and pasting it in new locations. You can also drag selected text to a new location using the mouse. Be sure to view the CourseHelp for this lesson before completing the steps. 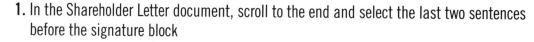 Next Angela will move text to a new location within her Shareholder Letter, using the cut and paste method. She will also move text by dragging it to a new location.

CourseHelp

The camera icon indicates there is a CourseHelp available with this lesson. Click the Start button, point to programs, point to CourseHelp, then click Word 97 Illustrated. Choose the CourseHelp that corresponds to this lesson.

QuickTip

If you want to copy selected text rather than move it when you drag, press and hold [Ctrl] first. The pointer changes to the Copy pointer when you copy text by dragging.

1. In the Shareholder Letter document, scroll to the end and select the last two sentences before the signature block

2. Click the Cut button ✂ on the Standard toolbar
   The cut text is removed from the document and placed on the Clipboard.

3. Scroll through the document until you see the schedule for the annual meeting, and then place the insertion point in the first line below the last event (Reception, 2:30)

4. Click the Paste button 🖺 on the Standard toolbar
   The sentences are inserted. Next use the dragging method to move text to the new location.

5. Select the first sentence of the text you just moved

6. Press and hold the mouse button over the selected text until the pointer changes from ↖ to ↘, *do not release the mouse button*

7. Drag the mouse up, placing the vertical bar of the pointer in the first line of text above the schedule

8. Release the mouse button
   The sentence is inserted.

9. Click anywhere in the window to deselect the highlighted text
   Compare your document to Figure B-6. The sentence has been moved.

10. Click the Save button 💾 on the Standard toolbar

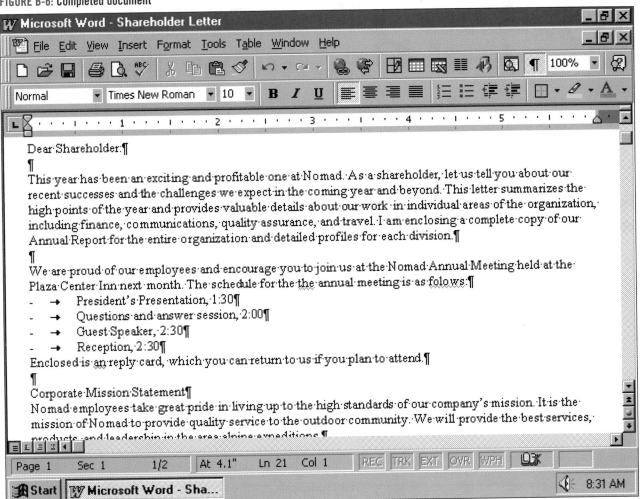

Word 97

Viewing CourseHelp

The camera icon on the opposite page indicates there is a CourseHelp available for this lesson. CourseHelps are on-screen "movies" that bring difficult concepts to life, to help you understand the material in this book. Your instructor received a CourseHelp disk and should have installed it on the machine you are using.

Because CourseHelp runs in a separate window, you can start and view a movie even if you're in the middle of completing a lesson. Once the movie is finished, you can click the Word program button on the taskbar and continue with the lessons, right where you left off.

Correcting Spelling and Grammar Errors

Word's Spelling and Grammar command identifies and corrects spelling mistakes and repeated words (such as "the the"). When you use this command, Word highlights any word that is not in its standard dictionary and displays suggested spellings from which you can choose. This command also allows you to review your document for grammatical errors such as mistakes in punctuation, sentence fragments, or agreement errors. ◄ Angela will proofread her Shareholder Letter using the Spelling and Grammar command to correct any spelling or grammatical errors.

QuickTip

The buttons in the Spelling and Grammar dialog box change depending on the type of error.

1. Press [Ctrl][Home] to move to the top of the document, then click the Spelling and Grammar button [ABC✓] on the Standard toolbar

Clicking this button is the same as choosing Spelling and Grammar from the Tools menu. The Spelling and Grammar dialog box opens, as shown in Figure B-7. The dialog box identifies the word "Ruiz" as a possible misspelling. The highlighted word is a proper noun, so you can ignore this occurrence.

2. Click Ignore in the Spelling and Grammar dialog box

Next, the dialog box indicates that "the" word the is repeated.

3. Click Delete to delete the second occurrence of the word the

The Spelling command next identifies "folows" as a misspelled word. Suggested spellings appear in the Suggestions list. The spelling that most closely resembles the misspelled word is highlighted in the Suggestions list. You can choose any one of the suggested spellings.

4. Click Change in the Spelling dialog box

The highlighted text in the Suggestions list replaces the misspelled word. Next, the Spelling and Grammar dialog box suggests using the word "a" in place of "an." To learn more about the error, you view an explanation.

5. Click the Office Assistant button [?] in the Spelling and Grammar dialog box

The Office Assistant displays an explanation of the rule that applies to this error.

6. After reading the explanation, click the Close box [X] in the right corner of the Office Assistant window

According to the information in the explanation, you decide that a change is necessary.

7. Click Change

The word "a" is substituted for the incorrect word "an." The Spelling and Grammar command finishes searching for errors.

8. Click OK

The message box closes. Compare your corrected document to Figure B-8.

9. Save your work

FIGURE B-7: Spelling and Grammar dialog box

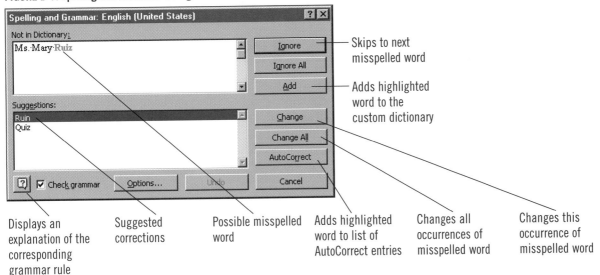

Skips to next
misspelled word

Adds highlighted
word to the
custom dictionary

Displays an
explanation of the
corresponding
grammar rule

Suggested
corrections

Possible misspelled
word

Adds highlighted
word to list of
AutoCorrect entries

Changes all
occurrences of
misspelled word

Changes this
occurrence of
misspelled word

FIGURE B-8: Proofed document

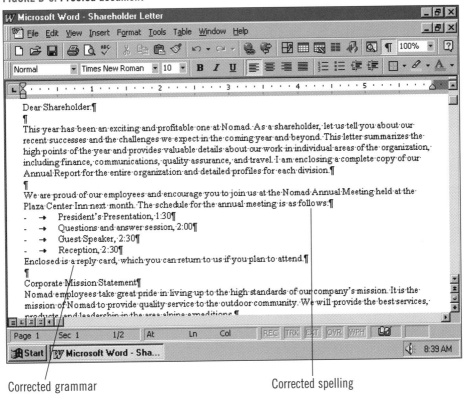

Corrected grammar

Corrected spelling

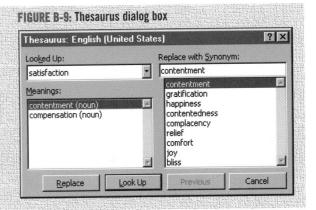

Using the Thesaurus

You can use the Thesaurus to look up synonyms of overused or awkward words in your document. Select the overused word, click Tools on the menu bar, point to Language, then click Thesaurus. The Thesaurus dialog box opens, listing synonyms of the selected word. This dialog box also displays antonyms for appropriate words. Choose a desired word in the Replace with Synonym list and click Replace to replace the selected word in your document.

FIGURE B-9: Thesaurus dialog box

Finding and replacing text

Sometimes you need to find and replace text throughout a document. For example, you might need to make a product name change, company name change, or change an abbreviation to a full name. In a long document, doing this manually would be time-consuming and prone to error. Word's Replace command automates this process, locating each occurrence of the text you want to replace. You can replace all occurrences at once or choose to replace specific occurrences individually. Word's Find command is also a useful searching tool. ✒ Angela's letter refers to the company name as simply Nomad. However, Angela believes the letter will sound more professional if she uses the company's full name, Nomad Limited. She'll use the Replace command to correct all instances of the company name at one time.

1. **If necessary, press [Ctrl][Home] to move to the top of the document, then click Edit on the menu bar, then click Replace**
   The Find and Replace dialog box opens with the Replace tab selected, as shown in Figure B-10. There are many ways to specify the text for which you want to search. See Table B-2 for a summary of search and replace options that are available when you click More. Unless you click the More button, you will not see these additional options.

2. **In the Find what box, type Nomad**
   You need to replace all occurrences of "Nomad" with "Nomad Limited" so that the correct company name will appear in the letter.

3. **Press [Tab] to move to the Replace with box, then type Nomad Limited**

4. **Click Replace All**
   Word changes all occurrences of "Nomad" to "Nomad Limited" in the document. A message appears telling you the number of occurrences (6) of the text in the document that were changed.

5. **Click OK**
   The message box closes and you return to the Find and Replace dialog box.

6. **Click Close**
   The dialog box closes and you return to the document. Compare your document to Figure B-11.

7. **Save your work**

Using the Find command

The Find command on the Edit menu allows you to locate specified text. If after finding the text, you decide you want to replace this and other occurrences, you can click the Replace tab. If you want to choose the individual occurrences of text to change, click Find Next in the Replace dialog box to locate the next occurrence. Then click Replace to change it or click Find Next again to skip to the next occurrence.

FIGURE B-10: Find and Replace dialog box

Click to display additional find and replace options

FIGURE B-11: Document after changes

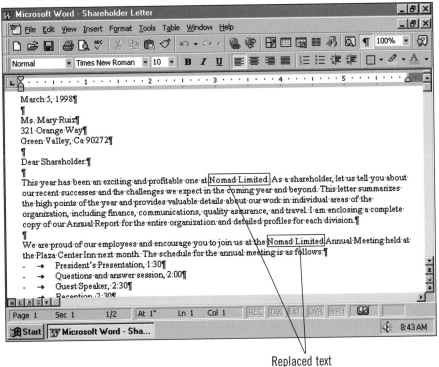

Replaced text

TABLE B-2: Replace options

replace option	description
Find What	Identifies the text to be replaced
Replace With	Identifies the text to use as a replacement
Search	Specifies the direction of the search from the current position of the insertion point: Down, Up, All (default)
Match Case	Locates only text with uppercase and lowercase letters that match exactly the entry in the Find what box
Find Whole Words Only	Locates only words that are complete and are not included as part of a larger word
Use Pattern Matching	Searches for a group of characters located at the beginning of specified text, at the end of specified text, or within specified text
Sounds Like	Locates words that sound like the text in the Find what box, but have different spellings
Find All Word Forms	Replaces all forms of a word. For example, specifying "find" in the Find what box locates "find," "finds," "found," and "finding" and replaces each with the comparable form of the replacement word.
No Formatting	Removes any formatting specifications noted in the Find what or Replace with box
Format	Displays a list of formatting specifications to find and replace
Special	Allows you to search for and replace special characters, such as a tab character or a paragraph mark

Previewing a Document

After proofreading and correcting your document, you can print it. Before you do, it is a good idea to display the document using the Print Preview command. In print preview, you can easily check the overall appearance of your document. You can also get a close-up view of the page and make final changes before printing. Next, Angela previews the document before printing it.

1. **Click the Print Preview button** 🔍 **on the Standard toolbar**
   The document appears in the Preview window. The size of the page you see depends on the number and size of pages displayed the last time the Print Preview command was issued. You want to see both pages of the document.

2. **Click the Multiple Pages button** ⊞ **on the Print Preview toolbar and drag to show two pages, as shown in Figure B-12**
   As you view the document, you notice that something is missing in the signature block. Get a close-up view of this part of the letter to examine it more carefully.

3. **Move the pointer over the page until it changes to** 🔍 **, then click near the signature block of the letter**
   The document is magnified, allowing you to read and edit the text. For example, you can change the abbreviation "VP" to a more official title, "Vice President." You can make this change without first returning to the document window.

4. **If necessary, click the Magnifier button** 🔍 **on the Print Preview toolbar**
   The Magnifier pointer changes to I. Now you can edit the text.

5. **Select the text VP, then type Vice President**
   While you are near the end of the document, you add some additional text.

6. **Place the insertion point in the line just above the text "Sincerely" and press [Enter] to create a new blank line**

7. **Type the following sentence, then press [Enter]**
   We hope to see you at the upcoming Annual Meeting.
   You can see that the letter spills only a few lines onto the second page. You would like the letter to fit on one page, which is a change you can make in Print Preview.

8. **Click the Shrink to Fit button** 🔲 **on the Print Preview toolbar**
   The text is adjusted to fit on one page. Next, you display the full page of the document.

9. **Click the One Page button** 🔲 **on the Print Preview toolbar to see the full page of the document and compare your document to Figure B-13**
   With the document complete, you can now save the document and print it without returning to the document window.

10. **Save your document.**

FIGURE B-12: **Two pages in Print Preview**

Print Preview toolbar

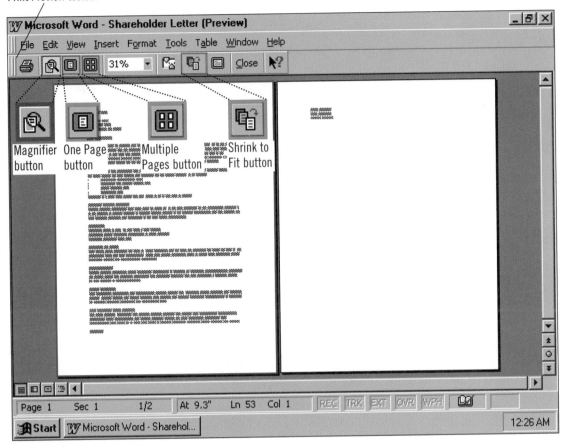

FIGURE B-13: **Document fit to one page**

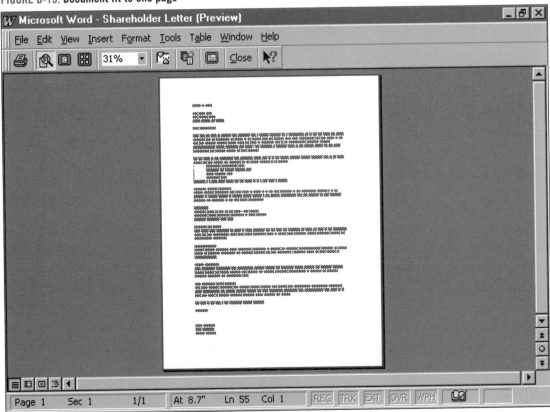

Word 97

Printing a Document

After proofreading and correcting a document, you're ready to print it. Printing a document is as simple as clicking the Print button on the Print Preview toolbar or the Standard toolbar. However, to take advantage of many printing options, use the Print command on the File menu. See Table B-3 to learn more about printing options. Angela uses the Print command to print two copies of her letter. In general, it is a good practice to save your document before printing it (to prevent loss of work if there are printer problems, for example). However, Angela saved her work at the end of the previous lesson, so she can continue without saving.

1. Click **File** on the menu bar, then click **Print**

The Print dialog box opens, as shown in Figure B-14. In this dialog box, you can specify the print options you want to use when you print your document. The name of the printer and the options you have available might be different, depending on the kind of printer you have set up with your computer.

2. In the Number of copies box, type **2**

If applicable, you can submit the second copy of the document to your instructor. In general, avoid using the printer as a copier to produce multiple copies of larger documents.

Trouble?

If you are not connected to a printer, ask your technical support person or instructor for assistance.

3. Click **OK**

The Print dialog box closes and Word prints your document. You may notice a printer icon at the bottom of the screen while the document prints. Compare your document to Figure B-15.

4. Click the **Close button** on the Preview toolbar

You leave Print Preview and return to the document window.

5. Press and hold down **[Shift]**, click **File** on the menu bar, then click **Close All**

Your document no longer appears in your document window and the other document that was open closes as well.

6. If you see a message box asking if you want to save changes, you can click **Yes**

7. Click **File** on the menu bar, then click **Exit** to close the Word

TABLE B-3: Printing options

print options	description
Name	Displays the name of the selected printer
Properties	Displays dialog box which specifies other options that vary based on the features available with your printer, such as the size or type of paper loaded in the printer, and the resolution of the graphics in the document (if any).
Print to File	Prints a document to a new file instead of a printer
Page Range	All: prints the complete document Current page: prints the page with the insertion point or the selected page Selection: prints selected text only Pages: prints user-specified pages (separate single pages with a comma, a range of pages with a hyphen)
Number of Copies	Specifies the number of copies to print
Collate	Prints all pages of the first copy before printing subsequent copies, (not available on all printers)
Print What	Prints the document (default), or only comments, annotations, styles, or other text associated with the document
Print	Specifies the print order for the page range: All Pages in Range, Odd Pages, Even Pages

Click to select a
new printer

FIGURE B-14: **Print dialog box**

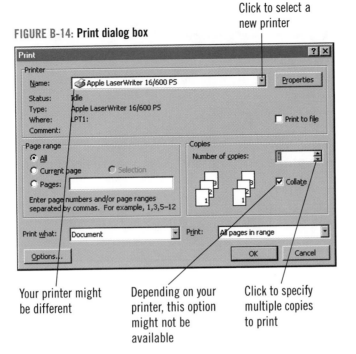

Your printer might
be different

Depending on your
printer, this option
might not be
available

Click to specify
multiple copies
to print

FIGURE B-15: **Shareholder Letter**

March 5, 1998

Ms. Mary Ruiz
321 Orange Way
Green Valley, Ca 90272

Dear Shareholder:

This year has been an exciting and profitable one at Nomad Limited. As a shareholder, let us tell you about our recent successes and the challenges we expect in the coming year and beyond. This letter summarizes the high points of the year and provides valuable details about our work in individual areas of the organization, including finance, communications, quality assurance, and travel. I am enclosing a complete copy of our Annual Report for the entire organization and detailed profiles for each division.

We are proud of our employees and encourage you to join us at the Nomad Limited Annual Meeting held at the Plaza Center Inn next month. The schedule for the annual meeting is as follows:
-         Presidentís Presentation, 1:30
-         Questions and answer session, 2:00
-         Guest Speaker, 2:30
-         Reception, 2:30
Enclosed is a reply card, which you can return to us if you plan to attend.

Corporate Mission Statement
Nomad Limited employees take great pride in living up to the high standards of our companyís mission. It is the mission of Nomad Limited to provide quality service to the outdoor community. We will provide the best services, products, and leadership in the area alpine expeditions.

Milestones
Achieved 163% of plan for the year, a new record!
Introduced South American adventures in travel division
Increased Northeast sales 65%

Balancing the Books
This yearís sales continued the trend of rising revenues. For the year, we exceeded the goals set forth in the Presidentís Plan. We also implemented many new saving measures, many of which were suggested during employee retreats and brainstorming weekends.

Communications
Nomad Limited developed office publishing department to produce all corporate communications including the annual report, the corporate newsletter, and corporate catalogs. We also completed a yearlong search for new director of communications.

Quality Assurance
This department normalized and implemented Product Testing and Standards review process. QA installed Product Testing Center. QA started working with guiding and outdoor leadership organizations to field-test all products including outerwear and recreational gear.

New Directions Travel Division
The travel division purchased two national guiding services and another with international connections. Combined, these organizations will deliver services through the New Directions subsidiary. This diversification will allow us to offer new tours in exciting locations, including South America and Africa.

We hope to see you at the upcoming Annual Meeting.

Sincerely,

Chris Peterson
Vice President
Nomad Limited

Practice

▶ Concepts Review

Label each of the elements of the Spelling and Grammar dialog box in Figure B-16.

FIGURE B-16

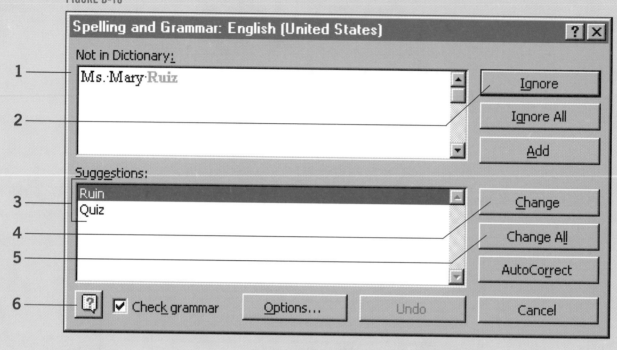

Match each of the following commands or features with the statement that best describes its function.

7. Copy command
8. Paste command
9. Spelling and Grammar command
10. Thesaurus command
11. Cut command
12. Replace command
13. Find command

a. Locates each occurrence of specified text
b. Reviews a document for correct spelling, punctuation, and usage errors
c. Lists synonyms and antonyms
d. Removes text from the document and places it on the Clipboard
e. Copies text to the Clipboard
f. Locates each occurrence of specified text and replaces all occurrences or those occurrences you specify
g. Copies text from the Clipboard into a document

14. **To place text on the Clipboard, you must first**
   a. Click the Copy button
   b. Click the Cut button
   c. Click the Paste button
   d. Select the text

15. **To display two open documents at once, you use which menu and command?**
   a. Click Window on the menu bar, then click Arrange All
   b. Click Window on the menu bar, then click Split
   c. Click Window on the menu bar, then click New Window
   d. Click File on the menu bar, click Print Preview, then click Multiple Pages

16. **Which option is NOT available in the Spelling and Grammar dialog box when a spelling error is identified?**
   a. Add the word to the dictionary
   b. Add an AutoCorrect entry
   c. Select a synonym for the word
   d. Choose a suggested spelling

17. **Which statement does not describe the Spelling and Grammar command?**
   a. Provides a way to learn about a grammatical error
   b. Suggests revisions to make a sentence correct
   c. Revises your document based on the style of the document
   d. Checks for spelling errors

18. **Which tool will identify as misspelled the word "your" when the word "you're" should be the correct word?**
   a. The Spelling and Grammar command
   b. The Preview command
   c. The Thesaurus command
   d. The AutoCorrect command

19. **Using the Find and Replace command you can do all of the following EXCEPT:**
   a. Check for all usages of the passive voice in your document.
   b. Search the document for specified text in a certain direction only.
   c. Replace all occurrences of a word or words with another word.
   d. Find all of the different forms of a word.

20. **In print preview, how do you get a close-up view of a page?**
   a. Click the Print Preview button.
   b. Click the Close button.
   c. Click the page with the Magnifier pointer.
   d. Click the One Page button.

21. Which of the following is NOT true about printing?

   a. You can choose to print only the current page of a document.

   b. You can print a range of pages in a document.

   c. You can print all the open documents from the Print dialog box.

   d. The Print button automatically prints your document without displaying the Print dialog box.

 # Skills Review

1. Open a new document and save it with a new name.

   a. Open the document named WD B-3, then save it as "Road Map."

   b. Insert today's date at the top of the document.

   c. Add an extra line after the date.

   d. Edit the signature block to contain your name.

2. Copy and move text.

   a. Using the mouse, copy the text "Open Roads, Inc." from the first sentence to the last line in the signature block.

   b. Using the Clipboard, move the last two sentences of the first body paragraph to the paragraph mark under the text "How does it work?"

3. Correct spelling and grammatical errors.

   a. Click the Spelling and Grammar button on the Standard toolbar.

   b. Correct any spelling and grammatical errors.

   c. Click OK after Word has finished searching for spelling and grammar errors.

   d. Save your changes.

4. Find and replace text.

   a. Click Edit, then click Replace.

   b. Type "Inc." in the Find what box.

   c. Type "Intl." in the Replace with box.

   d. Click Replace All to substitute the new company name.

   e. Click OK, then click Close.

   f. Save your changes.

5. Preview a document.

   a. Click the Print Preview button on the Standard toolbar.

   b. Click the One Page button.

   c. Click the page near the signature.

   d. Click the Magnifier button on the Print Preview toolbar.

   e. Select Account Representative, then type "Corporate Sales."

   f. Click the One Page button on the Print Preview toolbar.

   g. Click Close to return to normal view.

6. Print a document.
   a. Save your document.
   b. Click File, then click Print.
   c. In the copies box, type "2."
   d. Click OK.
   e. Click File, then click Close.
   f. Click File, then click Exit.

▶ Independent Challenges

1. As the co-chair for the Lake City High School class of 1993 reunion planning committee, you are responsible for recruiting classmates to help with reunion activities. Open the draft letter WD B-4 and save it as "Lake City Reunion Letter". Using Figure B-17 as your guide, use Word's proofing tools to make the following changes to the letter. To complete this independent challenge:

1. Use the Find command to locate the word "ambitious," and then use the Thesaurus to substitute another word of your choice.
2. Preview the document and edit the signature block to display your name.
3. Check the spelling and grammar in the document. Ignore your name if Word identifies it as a possible misspelled word.
4. In Print Preview, modify the title in the signature block.
5. Save your changes and print the document.

FIGURE B-17

September 17, 1998

Mr. Chris Randall
Randall and Associates
4440 Pacific Boulevard
San Francisco, CA 94104

Dear Chris:

As a member of the Lake City High School class of 1993, I often think of the people that made our school such a rewarding experience for me. Of course, there are the close friends I made and kept throughout the years, but also I think about the people that I somehow lost track of since graduation. The instructors, students, and administrative staff all contribute to the richness of the memories.

Now is your opportunity to play a important role in helping bring Lake City High memories alive not only for yourself, but for your fellow classmates as well. As the co-chair of the Lake City High Reunion 1998 planning committee,

I am looking for resourceful, organized alums that are interested in working on various reunion activities. We need people for the following areas: meeting coordination for all committees, computer consulting to help us use technology to work efficiently, meals and entertainment planning for the three-day event, and logistics coordination for handling getting everyone to Lake City and lodging them once they return to campus. All committees need as many volunteers as they can get, so you are sure to get to work in any area you choose.

If you are interested and available to work five hours a month for the next 10 months, please let me know. You can leave me a message at (555) 555-4321. I look forward to hearing from you soon.

Angela Pacheco
Lake City High Reunion 1998
Co-Chair

2. As an account representative for Lease For Less, a company that leases various office equipment such as fax machines and large copiers, you previously drafted a proposal describing the corporate discount program to a current customer. Open the document named WD B-5 and save it as "Discount Proposal." Using Figure B-18 as your guide, use Word's proofing tools to make the following changes to the letter. To complete this independent challenge:

1. Check the spelling and grammar in the document.
2. Use the Find command to locate the word "sequential."
3. Use the Thesaurus to look up an alternative word for "sequential" and replace it with a word of your choice.
4. Add the company before the text "Discount Proposal" at the top of the document.
5. Preview the document and edit the "From" line to display your name, followed by your title "Account Representative".
6. Save your changes and print the document.

3. You are the fund-raising coordinator for a nonprofit organization called Companies for Kids. In response to a potential corporate sponsor, you have previously drafted a short letter describing the benefits of being a sponsor. Open the document named WD B-6 and save it as "Kids Fund Raising." Using Figure B-19 as your guide, use Word's proofing tools to make the following changes to the letter. To complete this independent challenge:

1. Move the last sentence of the first paragraph to the start of the second paragraph.
2. Check the spelling and grammar in the document. Insert spaces between periods and the start of the next sentence as needed.
3. Use the Replace command to locate all occurrences of the word "valuable" and replace it with "important" throughout.
4. Preview the document and edit the signature block to display your name. Also, add the title "Companies for Kids" and your title to the signature block.

FIGURE B-18

LEASE FOR LESS DISCOUNT PROPOSAL

TO: MS. SANDY YOUNGQUIST
FROM: KIM LEE, ACCOUNT REPRESENTATIVE
SUBJECT: DISCOUNT PRICING
DATE: SEPTEMBER 17, 1998
CC: MARION WEST, SALES DIRECTOR

Thank you for your inquiry about a corporate discount for our temporary office services company. Enclosed is the information you requested. In addition, I have also include the premier issue of *EasyLeasing*, our exclusive newsletter.

You must use our services for at least 100 days each year, for two consecutive years to be eligible for the corporate discount. As a corporate customer, you will receive a 20% discount on general office temps and a 30% discount for our professional personnel. As your account representative, I would be pleased to discuss your temporary requirements with you. I will call you to arrange a time when we can meet.

FIGURE B-19

Companies for Kids Needs Your Help!

September 17, 1998

Celia Warden
Goff Associates
567 Ash Lane
Spring Lake, MN 55667

Dear Ms. Ward:

To complete our mission of collecting toys, clothing, and various necessary materials for children in local shelters, we would like to request your important assistance.

We depend largely on local businesses to help fund our efforts. Your company's time, services, and donations will benefit children in need. You can choose to donate time and services. Each weekend *Companies for Kids* sends out a number of teams to collect clothing and toys from the community. We desperately need organized teams to help us in this effort. Your company may also choose to make monthly donations, which will be put towards furnishing the shelters and paying various staff members that touch the lives of these children daily.

No matter how your company decides to participate in this program, you will no doubt benefit the lives of all the children who enter these shelters. I hope we can look forward to Goff Associates's participation in this important community program.

Sincerely,

Daniel Montreux
Companies for Kids
Fund Raising Coordinator

5. Save your changes and print the document.
6. Log on to the Internet and use your browser to go to http://www.course.com. From there, click Student On Line Companions, and then click the link to go to the Microsoft Office 97 Professional Edition—Illustrated: A First Course page, then click on the Word link for Unit B and locate the United Way home page. After reviewing the text and tone of a few pages, insert into your letter a few phrases or sentences that you think are especially effective and then paste them into the document. Edit the text as required to reflect the name of the Companies for Kids organization.

4. As a co-chair for the Lake City High School class of 1993 planning committee, you have received a telephone message from a classmate volunteering to serve on the entertainment committee. Open the thank you memo named WD B-7 and save it as "Volunteer Thanks Memo." Using Figure B-20 as your guide, use Word's proofing tools to make the following changes to the letter. To complete this independent challenge:

1. Move the last sentence of the second paragraph to the start of the second paragraph. ✓
2. Check the spelling and grammar in the document. ✓
3. Ignore the classmate's name if Word identifies it as a possible misspelled word.
4. Use the Replace command to replace all occurrences of the year "1980" with "1993." ✓ *1 occurrence*
5. Preview the document and edit the "From:" line to display your name and title. ✓
6. Save your changes and print the document.

title :VTpre-business student

Replace Comm: Edit Replace

FIGURE B-20

Memo

To:	Mr. Chris Randal
	Randal Associates
	4440 Pacific Boulevard
	San Francisco, CA 94104
From:	Andy Ortega, Lake City High, Class of 1993 Reunion Co-Chair
Date:	September 17, 1998
Re:	Entertainment Committee

Thank you for volunteering to participate on the entertainment committee for the Lake City 1993-class reunion. We are looking forward to working with you on these events.

Please let me know by noon on the meeting date if you are unable to attend any of these meetings. So that you can arrange your time accordingly, please block out the first Thursday of each months for the next six months for planning meetings. All meetings will take place at 7:30 p.m. at the Corner Coffee Shop in Lake City (on Highway 95, next to the Big Eight drive-in). Our first meeting will be next month; please come prepared to discuss your ideas for entertainment events at the reunion.

► Visual Workshop

As the conference coordinator for International Voices' upcoming conference, you are in charge of organizing the details for the informal dinner that will complete the Communications Conference. Use the Letter Wizard to type a letter to the banquet caterer at the conference site. Use Figure B-21 as a guide when selecting options in the wizard dialog boxes to decide how the banquet letter should look. Save the document with the name "Conference Dinner." Use the Spelling and Grammar command to identify any errors you may have made. Experiment with the Thesaurus. Try moving and copying text to arrange the letter more logically. Preview the document and make required edits. Finally, print the document, then close it and exit Word.

FIGURE B-21

October 24, 1998

Ms. Leslie Ryden
Banquet Caterer
Lakeside Center
North Bay, MN 55509

Dear Ms. Ryden:

I would like to take this opportunity to reaffirm how delighted we are to be conducting this fall's Communications Conference at the Lakeside Center on January 4. We at International Voices believe it is the perfect setting for our conference objectives.

As you requested, here are my ideas for the informal dinner that will wrap-up the day's events. I would be interested in having a low-fat, healthful cuisine for this meal. Since we will not be serving any alcoholic beverages, perhaps we could offer an array of fruit juices and sparkling mineral waters. Regarding floral decorations, I particularly liked your idea of international flags drawn by children. I believe this finishing touch will contribute to a wonderful, relaxing environment.

I hope these general guidelines will be helpful to you as you develop your menu and price proposal. I look forward to confirming our plans by late October.

Sincerely,

[your name]
[title]
[company name]

Formatting
a Document

Objectives

► **Apply font effects using the toolbar**
► **Apply special font effects**
► **Align text with tabs**
► **Change paragraph alignment**
► **Indent paragraphs**
► **Change paragraph spacing**
► **Create bulleted and numbered lists**
► **Apply borders and shading**

Using Microsoft Word's formatting capabilities, you can change the appearance of text on the page to emphasize important points and make the text easier to read. You can change the appearance of characters and words by applying **font formatting**, and you can change the appearance of entire paragraphs to improve the appearance of your documents. **Paragraph formatting** refers to the spacing, indentation, and alignment of text in paragraphs. ✎ Angela needs to format a Company Report of accomplishments to Nomad Ltd shareholders. Using a variety of methods, she will change the character and paragraph formatting to emphasize the important topics and ideas.

Applying Font Effects Using the Toolbar

You can emphasize words and ideas in a document by applying special effects to text, such as making text darker (called **bold**), slanted (called **italics**), or underlined. These options are available on the Formatting toolbar. See Figure C-1 for the buttons on the Formatting toolbar that you can use to format text. ✎▬▬ Angela wants to draw attention to the name of a newsletter described in the Company Report and to the headings, so she applies special formatting to these words.

1. Start Word

2. Open the document named WD C-1 and save it as Company Report
   First locate the text you want to emphasize.

3. In the first body paragraph, select the text NomadNotes, then click the Italic button *I* on the Formatting toolbar
   Deselect the text to see that it now appears italicized. To give special emphasis to the headings for each topic, apply bold formatting to them.

4. Select the first line in the document, International Communications, click the Bold button **B** on the Formatting toolbar, and then deselect the text
   The text now appears in bold. You decide to emphasize this text even more using a sans serif font.

5. Select the text again, click the Font list arrow on the Formatting toolbar, then scroll to and click Arial
   The text appears in the Arial font. The fonts available in the Font list box depend on the fonts installed on your computer. Next, increase the font size of the heading.

6. With the same text still selected, click the Font Size list arrow on the Formatting toolbar, then click 14
   The physical size of the text is measured in points (pts). A point is 1/72". The bigger the number of points, the larger the font size. The selected text appears in 14 point type. Because you want all headings to be formatted this way, copy the formatting to the other occurrences.

7. With the same words still selected, double-click the Format Painter button 🖌 on the Standard toolbar
   Double-clicking this button allows you to copy the same formatting multiple times. You can also click the Format Painter button once to copy formatting only once. Notice that the pointer changes to 🖌I.

8. Drag the 🖌I across each of the remaining five headings in the document: New Director and Ideas, In-House Publishing, Newsletter Update, Catalog Redesigned, Shareholder Meeting
   The font effects of the formatted text are copied to the text you select. Scroll toward the top of the screen and compare your document to Figure C-2.

9. Click 🖌 to deactivate the Format Painter, then save the document
   Notice that the Format Painter button is no longer indented.

FIGURE C-1: Text formatting buttons on the Formatting toolbar

Font
Font list arrow
Bold
Underline
Font size box
Font size list arrow
Italic

FIGURE C-2: Formatted document

Format Painter

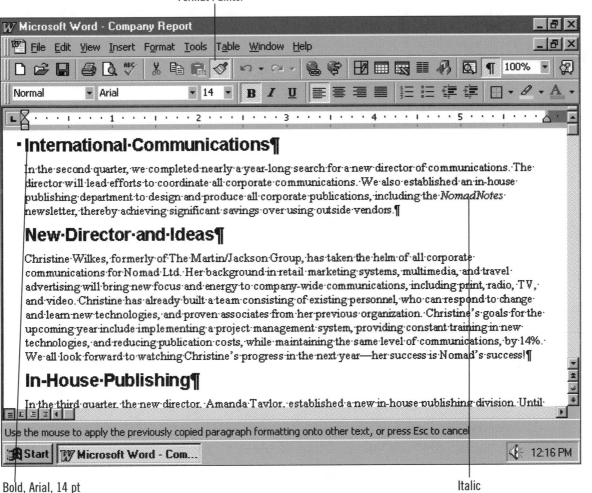

Bold, Arial, 14 pt
Italic

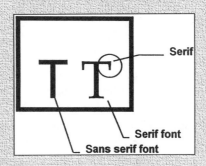

CLUES TO USE

Serif vs. sans serif fonts

Serifs are the small strokes at the ends of a character, as shown in Figure C-3. A **serif font**, such as Times New Roman, has a small stroke at the ends of its characters. Simple fonts without serifs, such as Arial, are known as **sans serif fonts**. Typically, sans serif fonts are used for headings in a document, and serif fonts are used for the body text.

FIGURE C-3: Serif vs. sans serif fonts

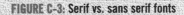

Serif
Serif font
Sans serif font

Applying Special Font Effects

Font formatting options are also available with the Font command. For example, you can apply several different kinds of underlining, as well as format text to appear in all capital letters. The Font tab in the Font dialog box also includes special options such as applying shadow, engraved, or outline effects to text. The Animation tab provides additional font effects that can be used to emphasize text when viewed on screen. ◢━━━ Angela wants to apply formatting to the name of the newsletter to draw even more attention to this new offering. She will use the options with the Font command to accomplish this.

Steps 123 4

1. In the first body paragraph, double-click the text NomadNotes to select it
With the text selected, you can format it.

2. Click Format on the menu bar, then click Font
The Font dialog box opens, as shown in Figure C-4. Distinguish the name of the newsletter from the surrounding text by having it appear in a larger font.

3. In the Size list, select 11
The name of the newsletter appears in 11 point type. In the Preview area of the dialog box, you can see a sample of the font formatting changes. Next, experiment with other font effects.

4. In the Effects section, click the Engrave check box
Notice in the Preview area that this option formats the text so the text has an engraved appearance. However, the text does not show up clearly, so change the color.

5. Click the Color list arrow, then select Black
The text appears in black in the Preview area. Try the Outline effect.

6. In the Effects section, click Outline
The text now appears outlined in the Preview area. With the Outline formatting, your text no longer needs to be italicized.

7. In the Font style list, click Regular
The text is no longer italicized. Now close the dialog box.

Time To
✔ Save

8. Click OK, then deselect the text
View the formatting applied in the document, as shown in Figure C-5.

CLUES TO USE

Applying special effects using the Character Spacing and Animation tabs

To adjust character spacing, click Font on the Format menu and choose the desired option on the Character Spacing tab. You can adjust the spacing between the individual characters. For example, you can create dramatic text effects by expanding the space between characters with the Expanded option. On this same tab, you can adjust the width of individual characters, making the characters themselves narrower or wider as needed to achieve the effect you want. You can also draw attention to text using animated text effects—text that moves or flashes—for documents that will be read online. You can highlight the headline using animated font effects such as a blinking background or red dotted lines moving around the selected text. The animated effects can only be seen online and do not appear in the printed document. Click the Animation tab in the Font dialog box to see the animation effects you can use in an online document.

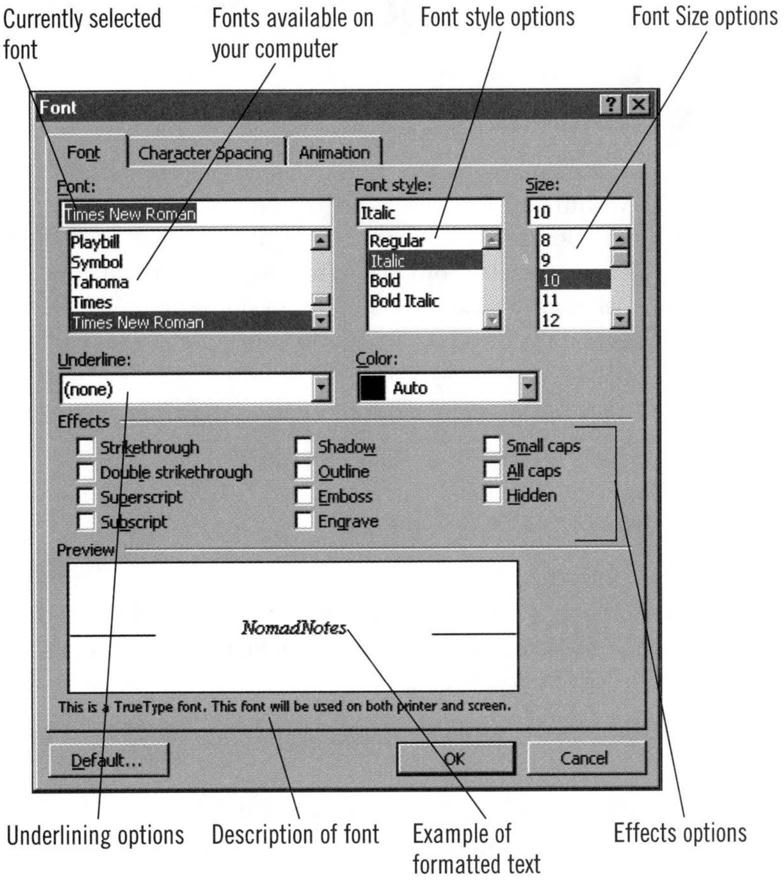

FIGURE C-4: Font dialog box

Currently selected font

Fonts available on your computer

Font style options

Font Size options

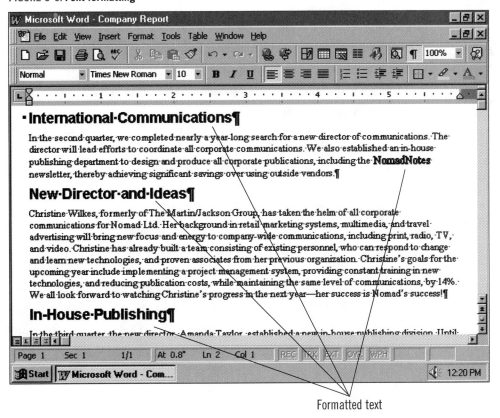

Underlining options

Description of font

Example of formatted text

Effects options

FIGURE C-5: Font formatting

Aligning Text with Tabs

Numerical information (such as tables of financial results) are often easier to read when you align the text with tabs. Use tabs rather than the spacebar to align your text because tab settings are faster, more accurate, and easier to change. When you press the Tab key, the insertion point moves to the next tab stop. By default, tab stops are located at every half inch, but you can use the horizontal ruler to create and modify tab stops. Table C-1 describes the four different types of tabs. 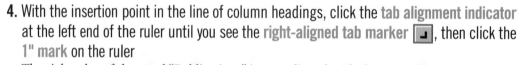 In her document, Angela wants to add a list identifying estimated cost savings.

Steps

1. **Place the insertion point after the period that follows the word vendors at the end of the first body paragraph, then press [Enter]**
   Pressing [Enter] creates a new blank line. This line will contain the column headings in the cost savings list. Next type the heading for the first column.

2. **Press [Tab], then type Publications, and press [Tab] again**
   A tab character appears before and after the word and the insertion point moves to the right to the 1½" mark on the ruler, as shown in Figure C-6. Next type the remaining headings, separating each one by pressing [Tab].

3. **Type 1997 Cost per Issue, press [Tab], type 1998 Cost per Issue, press [Tab], then type Savings per Issue**
   Currently, the headings are aligned with the default tab stops located every half inch on the horizontal ruler. To space the headings evenly, create new tab stops on the ruler.

Trouble?

You can remove a tab stop by dragging it off the ruler.

4. **With the insertion point in the line of column headings, click the tab alignment indicator at the left end of the ruler until you see the right-aligned tab marker [⌐], then click the 1" mark on the ruler**
   The right edge of the word "Publications" is now aligned with the new tab stop. Format the remaining columns to be left-aligned.

Trouble?

If you see no change in the alignment of the column headings, it means that the text was already aligned at the default tab stop. Placing a tab stop there anyway ensures the proper alignment, even if the amount of text in the line changes.

5. **With the insertion point still in the line of column headings, click the tab alignment indicator until you see the left-aligned tab marker [L], then click the 1½", 3", and 4¼" marks on the ruler**
   Left-aligned tab stops appear at the locations you clicked. To adjust a tab stop, just drag it with the mouse. Next add additional lines.

6. **Press [End] to place the insertion point at the end of the line, then press [Enter]**
   The tab stops you created for the previous paragraph are still in effect in the new paragraph. Now you can enter additional text for your list.

7. **Type the following information in the document, press [Tab] as indicated, and remember to press [Enter] at the end of each line except after the last line**
   [Tab] Newsletter   [Tab] 3.785   [Tab] 2.89   [Tab] .895 [Enter]
   [Tab] Catalog   [Tab] 8.43   [Tab] 6.546   [Tab] 1.884 [Enter]
   [Tab] Annual Report [Tab] 11.32   [Tab] 9.78   [Tab] 1.54

Time To

✔ Save

8. **Select all the text in the columns, drag the last left tab stop (currently at 4¼" on the horizontal ruler) to the 4½" mark, then deselect the text**
   All the text aligned with this stop is moved. Compare your screen to Figure C-7.

FIGURE C-6: Working with tabs

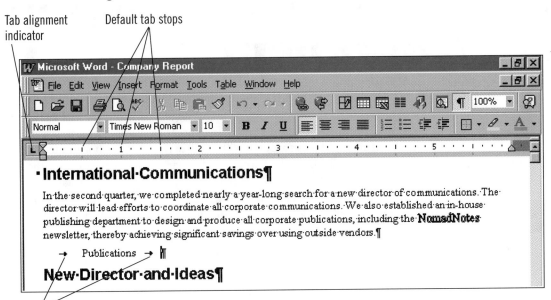

Tab alignment indicator

Default tab stops

Nonprinting tab marks

FIGURE C-7: Using tabs

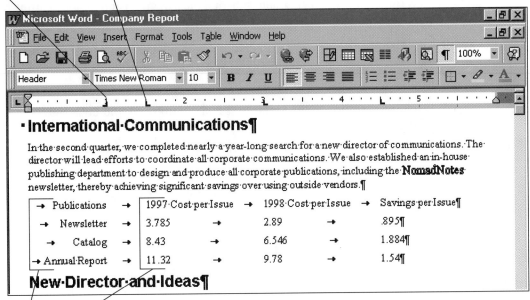

Right-aligned tab stop

Left-aligned tab stop

Text aligned with right-aligned tabs

Text aligned with left-aligned tabs

TABLE C-1: Different types of tabs

alignment	description	Button
Left	Text aligns at the left and extends to the right of the tab stop	
Center	Text aligns at the middle of the tab stop, extending an equal distance to the left and right of the stop	
Right	Text aligns at the right and extends to the left of the tab stop	
Decimal	Text aligns at the decimal point. Text before the decimal extends to the left; the text after the decimal extends to the right	

Changing Paragraph Alignment

Another way to change the appearance of text in a document is to change the alignment of paragraphs. By default your text is left-aligned. However, you can center a paragraph (usually done in a title, or in menus or invitations), or you can right-align a paragraph so that its right edge is even with the right margin (usually seen in dates and signatures of letters). You can also justify a paragraph so that both the left and right edges are even with both margins (as in reports or textbooks). All these alignment options are available on the Formatting toolbar or with the Paragraph command on the Format menu, as shown in Figure C-8.  Angela wants the title to stand out, as well as to convey that the document is a first draft. She will use the buttons on the Formatting toolbar to improve the appearance of the document by changing the alignment of specific paragraphs.

1. Place the insertion point in the first line, **International Communications**, then click the **Center button** ▤ on the Formatting toolbar
   The first line is centered evenly between the left and right margins of the page. Note that you do not need to select the text in a paragraph to apply paragraph formatting. Next, add a second line of text to the title.

2. Press **[End]** to place the insertion point at the end of the current line, then press **[Enter]**
   This inserts a new blank line that is centered between the left and right margins. When you press [Enter], the new paragraph "inherits" the paragraph and font formatting from the previous paragraph.

3. Type **First Draft**
   The text is centered automatically as you type. Next, use justified formatting to give the report a more formal appearance.

4. Place the insertion point in the first body paragraph and click the **Justify button** ▤ on the Formatting toolbar
   This formatting creates even left and right edges of the paragraph. Continue formatting each of the remaining body paragraphs.

5. Repeat step 4 in each of the remaining five body paragraphs
   Compare your document to Figure C-9. Next align the closing text at the end of the document so that it is aligned at the right margin.

6. Press **[Ctrl] [End]** to place the insertion point at the end of the document, then click the **Align Right button** ▤ on the Formatting toolbar
   This formatting places the right edge of the text "Nomad Ltd" at the right margin. Include the month and year as part of the closing.

7. Press **[Enter]** and type **Sept**, press **[Enter]**, press **[Spacebar]** and then type **1998**
   The AutoComplete feature allows you to type the first few characters of a word and a tag above the text displays the word that Word will insert if you press [Enter]. Notice that the text in the new line remains right-aligned. Compare the end of your document to Figure C-10.

8. Save the document

FIGURE C-8: **Paragraph dialog box**

Click here to
display paragraph
alignment options

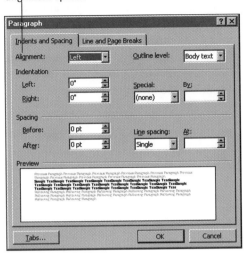

FIGURE C-9: **Paragraph formatting changes**

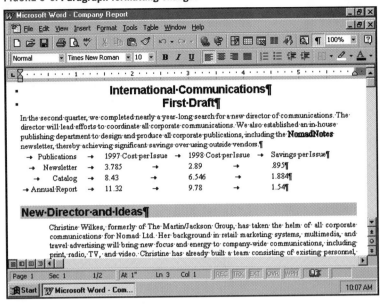

FIGURE C-10: **Additional formatting changes**

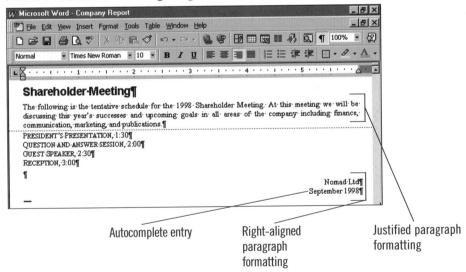

Autocomplete entry

Right-aligned
paragraph
formatting

Justified paragraph
formatting

Indenting Paragraphs

One way to add structure to the appearance of a document is to increase the white space by changing the indentation of individual paragraphs. When you indent a paragraph you are changing the width of each line in the paragraph. You can modify the indentation from the right or left edge of the document, or both. You can indent paragraphs using three methods: with the buttons on the Formatting toolbar, the Paragraph command on the Format menu, and the horizontal ruler. Angela would like to indent several paragraphs in her document to reflect the structure of her document. For example, she wants subtopics to be indented under main ideas.

1. **Place the insertion point in the paragraph under the heading** New Director and Ideas **and click the** Increase Indent button  **on the Formatting toolbar**
   Clicking the Increase Indent button indents the left edge of the paragraph to the first tab stop. To give your document structure, make the "In-House Publishing" heading a subtopic under the heading "New Director and Ideas."

2. **Place the insertion point in the heading** In-House Publishing **and click**
   Next change the left and right indentation of the next heading and two body paragraphs using the Paragraph command.

3. **Select the body paragraph under the heading** In-House Publishing **through the body paragraph under** Newsletter Update, **click** Format **on the menu bar, and then click** Paragraph
   The Paragraph dialog box appears. Make sure the Indents and Spacing tab appears foremost in the dialog box.

4. **In the Indentation area, click the** up arrow **in the** Left box **until you see** 1" **and in the** Right box **click the** up arrow **until you see** 0.5"

5. **Click** OK, **then deselect the text**
   Word changes the left and right indentation for these paragraphs, as shown in Figure C-11

6. **Select the heading** Catalog Re-designed **and the body paragraph that follows, drag the** First Line Indent marker **on the ruler to the half-inch mark** Dragging the first line indent marker indents only the first line of text in a paragraph. To have all the lines in the paragraph be indented the same amount, adjust the indentation for the remaining lines of the paragraph.

7. **Drag the** Hanging Indent marker **to the half-inch mark**
   Dragging the hanging indent marker indents the remaining lines of the paragraph (the first line of the paragraph does not move). Although this formatting indents all the lines in these paragraphs in the same way, they are not indented enough to identify the text as a subtopic.

8. **Drag the** Left Indent marker **to the 1" mark**
   Dragging this marker indents all the lines of the paragraph at once. The next heading, body paragraph, and list should also be indented.

9. **Select the heading** Shareholder Meeting **through the end of the list, and then drag the** Left Indent marker **to the half-inch mark**

10. **Select all the text from** Catalog Re-designed **through the last body paragraph, and drag the** Right Indent marker **to the 5.5" mark, then deselect the text**
    You have completed changing the indentation of the paragraphs in the document. Compare your document to Figure C-12.

Trouble?

Word hides settings in a dialog box when you have selected text that includes different format settings for the same feature.

Time To

✔ Save

FIGURE C-11: Indented paragraphs

First Line Indent marker

Hanging Indent marker

Left Indent marker

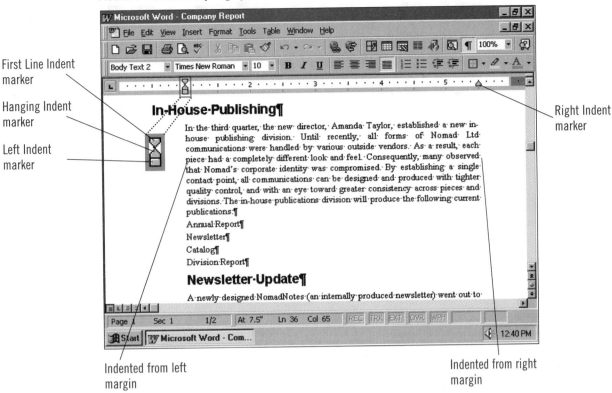

Right Indent marker

Indented from left margin

Indented from right margin

FIGURE C-12: More indented paragraphs

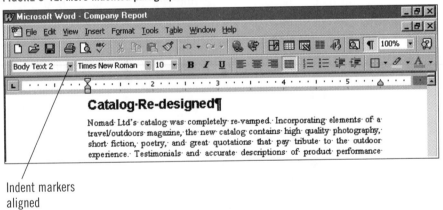

Indent markers aligned

Using Hanging Indent Paragraph Formatting

Sometimes you want a paragraph formatted so that the first line of paragraph is not indented as much as the text in the remaining lines. This formatting is known as a **hanging indent**, as shown in Figure C-13. Hanging indent formatting is usually seen in product or features lists or in glossaries. Notice the arrangement of the indent markers on the horizontal ruler and the indentation of the first and remaining lines of the paragraph. You can create a hanging indent by dragging the hanging indent marker on the horizontal ruler.

FIGURE C-13: Hanging indent

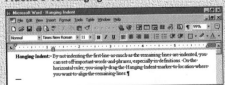

Changing Paragraph Spacing

Another way to make a document easier to read is to increase the amount of spacing between lines. For example, increase the line spacing in documents where you expect readers to add written comments (as in thesis papers or draft versions of a document). Line spacing options are available with the Paragraph command on the Format menu. You can also increase the amount of space between paragraphs to better separate ideas in paragraphs.  Angela would like to provide space in this draft document for comments from her colleagues in the Marketing Department. She'll increase the line spacing and the spacing before and after the list of publications for written feedback.

Steps 1 2 3 4

1. Select the entire document by pressing [Ctrl][A]

2. Click Format on the menu bar, then click Paragraph
   The Paragraph dialog box opens where you can change the line spacing from the default single-gle spacing.

3. Click the Line spacing list arrow, click 1.5 lines, then click OK
   The dialog box closes and the paragraphs appear with 1.5 line spacing between the lines. So that the list below the "In-House Publishing" heading is easier to read, you can increase the space after the list.

4. Place the insertion point in the line Annual Report, right-click the mouse, click Paragraph in the pop-up menu, and then click the Indents and Spacing tab
   Using the right mouse button is a handy way to format paragraphs.

5. Click the up arrow next to the Spacing After box three times until you see 18 pt in the box
   Each time you click the arrow, the value in the box increases by 6 points. As you click, notice that the Preview area of the dialog box displays the effect of your changes.

6. Click OK
   The space between the list and the following body paragraph increases. Next increase the space before the tabbed list.

7. Place the insertion point in the first line of the tabbed list, click Format on the menu bar, then click Paragraph

8. Click the up arrow next to the Spacing Before box twice until you see 12 pt in the box and click OK
   Compare your screen to Figure C-14. You have finished adjusting paragraph spacing for now.

Time To

✔ Save

FIGURE C-14: Increased spacing in a document

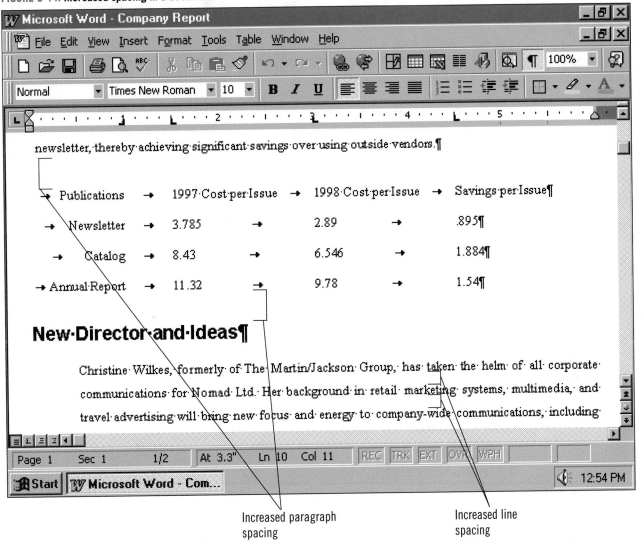

Increased paragraph spacing

Increased line spacing

Creating Bulleted and Numbered Lists

When you group paragraphs in a list, you can create a bulleted list. In a bulleted list, each paragraph in the list is preceded by a **bullet**, a small symbol such as a circle or square. With the Bullets button on the Formatting toolbar, you can insert a bullet in front of each item in a list. When you want to show items in a sequence, a numbered list best reflects the order or priority of the items. To create a simple numbered list (starting with the numeral "1"), you can use the Numbering button on the Formatting toolbar. You can also use the Bullets and Numbering command on the Format menu to specify additional bullet and numbering formatting options. Angela decides to draw attention to the lists in her document by formatting them with bullets and numbering.

1. Select the list of four publications starting with **Annual Report**, click the **Bullets button** on the Formatting toolbar, and then deselect the text
   A bullet character appears in front of each item in the list as shown in Figure C-15. Next change the type of bullet shape.

2. Select the four items in the list, click **Format** on the menu bar, then click **Bullets and Numbering**
   The Bullets and Numbering dialog box opens, as shown in Figure C-16. In this dialog box, you can choose from seven different bullet styles. You can also change any of the seven styles to use whatever shape you prefer. Change to the arrow style.

3. Click the third box in the second row and click **OK**
   The list appears as a bulleted list with a small arrow in front of each line.

4. Click the **Increase Indent button** on the Formatting toolbar until the bullets are aligned with the text in the previous paragraph
   Next add numbering to the schedule at the end of the document.

5. Select the four items in the meeting schedule at the end of the document, then click the **Numbering button** on the Formatting toolbar
   The schedule is now a numbered list. Because you would like to view alternate numbering formats, use the Bullets and Numbering command available on a pop-up menu.

6. If necessary, select the four lines of the schedule, then right-click the selected text
   A pop-up menu appears, from which you can select the Bullets and Numbering command.

7. Click **Bullets and Numbering** on the pop-up menu, then click the **Numbered tab**, if necessary, in the dialog box
   The Numbered tab in the Bullets and Numbering dialog box displays additional numbering options. To impart a more formal tone to the text, choose a Roman numeral format.

8. In the first row, click the **Roman numeral** (the fourth) option and click **OK**
   The bullets in the list change to Roman numerals.

9. Click the **Increase Indent button** until the numbers are aligned with the text in the previous paragraph, then deselect the text
   Compare your document to Figure C-17.

Time To

✓ Save

FIGURE C-15: Bulleted list

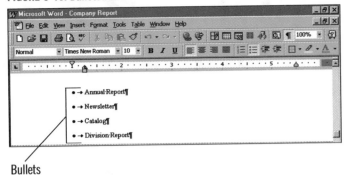

Bullets

FIGURE C-16: Bulleted tab in Bullets and Numbering dialog box

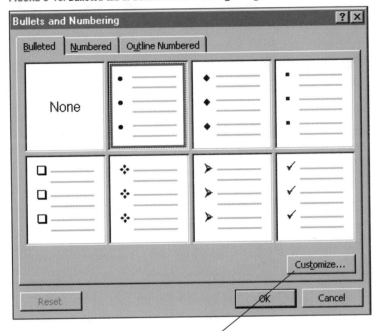

Click to create your
own bullet style

FIGURE C-17: Numbered list

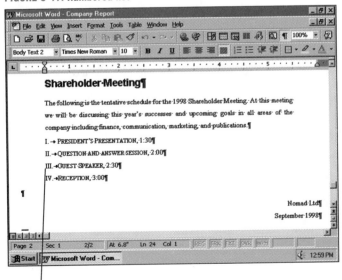

Roman numerals

Applying Borders and Shading

Borders add visual interest to paragraphs of text. **Borders** are lines you can add to the top, bottom, or sides of paragraphs. Preset border settings make it easy to create a box around a paragraph. You can also use shading to offer even more visual interest to paragraphs of text. **Shading** is a background color or pattern you add behind the text of a paragraph. With the Tables and Borders toolbar you can apply borders and shading options you use most often, or you can use the Borders and Shading command to select from additional border and shading options. Angela wants to use borders and shading to emphasize the title and main topics in the document. First, she'll add a double-lined box around the title to give the document a more formal appearance.

Trouble?

If you see the Office Assistant, click the Cancel button in the Office Assistant window to work without the Office Assistant.

1. Click the Tables and Borders button ⊞ on the Standard toolbar
The Tables and Borders toolbar appears. The pointer changes to ✎ .

2. Click the Draw Table button ✎ on the Tables and Borders toolbar to deactivate the Draw Table feature for now
You can move the toolbar anywhere you want by dragging it to a new location. The document now appears in Page Layout view, as shown in Figure C-18. Now you can select the text you want to format.

3. Select the first two lines (the title) of the document
Next select the style of border you want to apply.

4. Click the Line Style list arrow on the Tables and Borders toolbar and scroll to select the double line

QuickTip

You can quickly remove a border for a selected paragraph by verifying that the line style matches the border you want to remove and then clicking the button that corresponds to the line you want to remove.

5. Click the Outside Border button ⊞ on the Tables and Borders toolbar
A double-line box border surrounds the text, spanning the width of the margins. Next emphasize the main headings in the document by adding shading.

6. Select the New Director and Ideas heading and the paragraph mark, then click the Shading Color list arrow
Change the shaded background to gray.

7. Click Gray 25% (the third option in the second row)
The text appears with a gray background. To apply the same shading to the other main headings in the document, repeat the last command to selected text.

QuickTip

A fast way to repeat the previous command is to press [F4].

8. For each of the remaining four headings, select the heading and its paragraph mark and click Edit on the menu bar, and then click Repeat Shading Color
The other main headings are formatted with shading. You have finished formatting your document for now, so hide the Tables and Borders toolbar.

9. Click the Close button ✕ on the Tables and Borders toolbar
The Tables and Borders toolbar is no longer displayed. Compare your document to Figure C-19.

10. Save your work, then close and exit Word.

FIGURE C-18: Tables and Borders toolbar

Tables and
Borders toolbar

Line Style list
arrow

Shading Color
list arrow

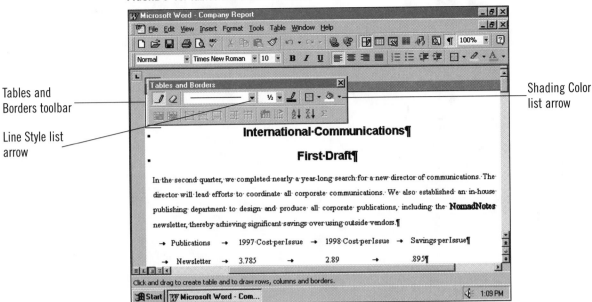

FIGURE C-19: Gray shading in a document

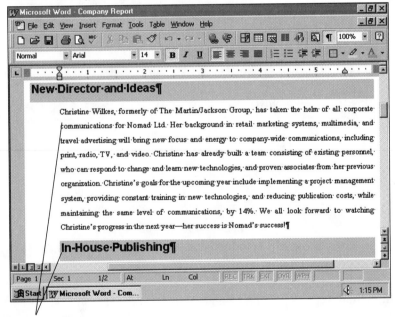

Light gray shading
applied

Creating borders with the Borders and Shading command

The Tables and Borders toolbar provides the most frequently used border and shading options. However, even more border and shading options are available with the Borders and Shading command on the Format menu. This command displays the Borders and Shading dialog box. On the Borders tab, you can select box and shadowed box preset borders, as well as specify the color of the border. You can also indicate how far away from the text the border should appear. On the Shading tab, you can specify the color of both the foreground and background of the shaded area. This feature allows you to customize the intensity of the shading you apply to text.

Practice

► Concepts Review

Label each of the formatting elements shown in Figure C-20

FIGURE C-20

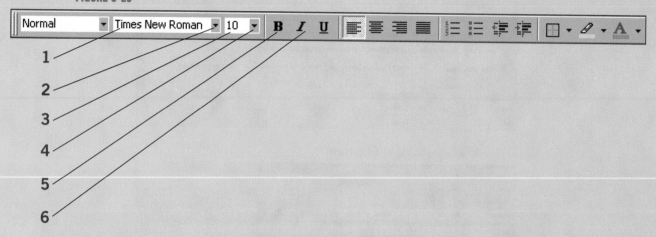

1
2
3
4
5
6

Match each of the following terms with the statement that best describes it or its function.

7. Font
8. Bold
9. Font effect
10. Bullets
11. Numbering
12. Borders
13. Paragraph formatting

a. Character formatting such as hidden text and small caps
b. The design set of characters
c. Text which appears darker
d. Used to reflect a sequence of events or importance in a list
e. Symbols or graphics preceding items in a list
f. Lines added to paragraphs of text
g. Changes the line spacing, alignment, and space between paragraphs

Select the best answer from the list of choices.

14. **Which paragraph formatting feature is not available on the Formatting toolbar?**
    a. Paragraph alignment
    b. Line spacing
    c. Decrease indentation
    d. Increase indentation

15. **To add a specific amount of space between paragraphs, the best solution is to:**
    a. Press [Enter] until you get the amount of space you want
    b. Use the Spacing Before and After options in the Paragraph dialog box
    c. Adjust the top margin for each paragraph
    d. Use the Line Spacing options in the Paragraph dialog box

16. **Which of the following automatically adds a bullet to selected text?**
    a. Right-clicking in a bulleted list
    b. Clicking Format on the menu bar, then clicking Bullets and Numbering
    c. Clicking the Bullets button on the Formatting toolbar
    d. Pressing [Ctrl][B] on the keyboard

17. A hanging indent refers to formatting in which:
- **a.** The text in the first line is not indented as much as the remaining lines of a paragraph
- **b.** All lines of a paragraph are indented more than the paragraph above it
- **c.** All lines of a paragraph are aligned under the same tab stop
- **d.** The text in the first line is indented more than the remaining lines of a paragraph

18. You can choose alternative bullet graphics from which of the following dialog boxes?
- **a.** Bullets and Numbering
- **b.** Change Bullets
- **c.** WingDings
- **d.** Symbol

19. Which button do you click when you want to apply shading to text?
- **a.** Borders
- **b.** Tables and Borders
- **c.** Borders and Shading
- **d.** Shading

20. You can access the shading feature by
- **a.** Clicking Format on the menu bar, then clicking Paragraph
- **b.** Clicking the Border button on the Formatting toolbar
- **c.** Clicking the right mouse button in a paragraph
- **d.** Clicking Format on the menu bar, then clicking Borders and Shading

▶ Skills Review

1. Apply font effects using the toolbar.
- **a.** Launch Word.
- **b.** Open the document named WD C-2, then save the document as "Shipping Letter".
- **c.** Select the text "RoadMap" and click the Italic button on the Formatting toolbar.
- **d.** With the text still selected, click the Underline button. Then click the Italic button to remove the italic formatting.
- **e.** With the text still selected, click the Font list arrow and choose Arial.
- **f.** Click the Font Size box on the Formatting toolbar and type "10.5" and press Enter.
- **g.** Repeat Steps c-f for the second occurrence of the word RoadMap.

2. Apply special font effects using the Font command.
- **a.** Select the first occurrence of "Open Roads, Inc."
- **b.** Click Font on the Format menu, choose Arial, then 12 pts, then Bold.
- **c.** In the Effects area, click the Outline box and All caps box, then click OK.
- **d.** With the text still selected, double-click the Format Painter button on the Standard toolbar. With the Format Painter pointer, select each occurrence of the company name, "Open Roads, Inc." in the document.
- **e.** Click the Format Painter button on the Standard toolbar.

3. Align text with tabs

a. Place the insertion point in the blank line above "Our Promise to You..." and press [Enter].

b. Press [Tab] then type "Weight"; press [Tab] then type "Cost", then press [Enter] to create a new blank line.

c. Press [Tab] then type "Under 1 lb"; press [Tab] then type "5.25", then press [Enter] to create a new blank line.

d. Press [Tab] then type "1 - 10 lbs"; press [Tab] then type "10.75".

e. Select all three lines of the list and place a left-aligned tab stop at the 2" mark.

f. With the same three lines selected, click the tab alignment indicator at the left end of the ruler until you see the decimal tab marker.

g. Place a decimal-aligned tab stop at the 4.5" mark.

h. Press [End] to place the insertion point at the end of the last item, then press [Enter].

i. Press [Tab] and type "More than 10 lbs", press [Tab] and type "14.50", save your changes.

4. Apply paragraph formatting

a. Press [Ctrl][Home] to place the insertion point at the beginning of the document.

b. Type today's date and press [Enter].

c. Place the insertion point in the date line, then click the Center button on the Formatting toolbar.

d. Select the text of the signature block. Click Format on the menu bar, then click Paragraph. In the Indentation area, scroll the Left up arrow until you see 4.5". Click OK to return to your document.

e. Select all of the body paragraphs (including the list).

f. Click Format on the menu bar, then click Paragraph.

g. In the Line Spacing area, choose 1.5 lines, then click OK.

h. Select the "Generate pre-printed. . . ." line, and then click Paragraph on the Format menu.

i. In the After box, click the up arrow until you see 12, then click OK.

j. Select the three body paragraphs, from "Thank you. . ." to ". . . you have."

k. Click the Justify button on the Formatting toolbar.

l. Be sure to select the placeholder "[Your Name]" and replace it with your name.

m. Save your changes.

5. Create bulleted and numbered lists

a. Select the list of three items starting with "track the location. . ." and ending with "generate pre-printed. . . ."

b. Click the Numbers button on the Formatting toolbar, then click to deselect the text.

c. Select the same three lines of text and right-click the selected text.

d. Click the Bullets and Numbering command on the pop-up menu, then click the Bulleted tab.

e. Choose a bullet pattern you like, then click OK.

6. Apply borders and shading

a. Click Toolbars on the View menu, then choose Tables and Borders.

b. With the insertion point in the line containing the date, choose the 1½ pt line from the Line Style box on the Tables and Borders toolbar.

c. Click the Bottom Border button on the Tables and Borders toolbar.

d. Select the list of shipping prices, starting with the line containing "Weight" and "Cost."

e. Choose the ¾ pt line from the Line Style box on the Borders toolbar.

f. Click the Outside Border button on the Tables and Borders toolbar.

g. Select the first line of the list and choose the 1½ pt line from the Line Style box on the Borders toolbar.

h. Click the Bottom Border button on the Tables and Borders toolbar.

i. Select the paragraph under the heading in the middle of the document, and choose 25% shading from the Shading box on the Tables and Borders toolbar.

j. Click Toolbars on the View menu, then choose Tables and Borders to hide the Tables and Borders toolbar.

k. Save your changes to the document, print the document, and exit Word.

► Independent Challenges

1. As a committee member assigned to plan the Carson Associates Family Weekend, you have been asked to design the announcement for the Carson Classic golf tournament. Another committee member has begun the document by entering some of the tournament information. Open the document WD C-3 and save it as "Golf Classic". Using Figure C-22 as your guide, enhance the appearance of the document using font and paragraph formatting.

To complete this Independent Challenge:

1. Center the title of the document, and change the font to Arial, Bold, Italics, 18 pt.

2. Add 25% Gray shading to the title.

3. Center the paragraph after the title.

4. Add the information about time and location in a list in the center of the document using tabs. Press [Tab] before and after the word "Where".

5. Place a right tab stop at the 1½" mark and a left tab stop at the 2" mark for the tournament information.

6. Center the heading "Schedule". Format this heading in Bold, Arial.

7. Add numbers to the schedule of events. Left align this list.

8. Place a 1½ pt line above the line "Complete and send the attached...".

9. Preview the document and click the Shrink to Fit button if the document does not appear on one page.

10. Save, and print the memo, then close it.

FIGURE C-21

CARSON ASSOCIATES

ANNUAL

GOLF TOURNAMENT

Dust off your clubs and sharpen your spikes for the

Annual Carson Associates Golf Classic! Compete for

valuable prizes and the admiration of your peers.

Where:	Shoreside Greens Golf and Country Club
When:	June 23rd Shot Gun start at 7:30 a.m.
Who:	Mixed foursomes
How Much:	See below

Schedule

1. 1st Foursome tee time 7:15am and every 15 minutes after

2. Social Hour at the 19th Hole

3. Lunch is served at 1:30 p.m.

4. Awards ceremony begins at 2:00 p.m.

Complete and send the attached order form (along with your check) to:

[your name]

CARSON CLASSIC CO-CHAIR

P.O. Box 567

Lake City, MA 03411

2. As coordinator for the Carson Associates Golf Classic, you have been asked to create a certificate to be awarded to the golfer with the longest drive. Open the document WD C-4 and save it as "Golf Certificate". Enhance the appearance of the certificate using font and paragraph formatting. After completing the certificate, access the World Wide Web to plan a golfing vacation in Arizona.

To complete this Independent Challenge:

1. Center all the text.
2. Format the title with 36 pt, bold, italicized, Comic Sans Ms font. In the Font dialog box, apply the shadow effect.
3. Use 1.5 line spacing in all paragraphs.
4. Use 24 pt font on all the text except the title and the text "Longest Drive". Use 36 pt font on this text.
5. Use 12 pt line spacing before and after the date and before the line "for the." Use 12 pt line spacing before and after the line "Presented".
6. Place a 1½ pt line under the line "Recipient" for writing the winner's name.
7. Type your name and title at the bottom of the award. Right align this text and Format it at 24points.
8. Place a ½ pt border above your name for your signature.
9. Drag the Indent marker to the 2" mark.
10. Preview, save, and print the certificate, then close it.
11. Log on to the Internet and use your browser to go to http://course.com. From there, click Student On Line Companions, and then click the link to go to the Microsoft Office 97 Professional Edition-Illustrated: A First Course page, then click on the word link for Unit C.

3. As co-chair for the Lake City High School class of 1993 reunion, you need to draft a memo to the planning committee members informing them of the place and times of committee meetings. Since you are unsure of how to format this memo, you will use the Memo Wizard which will request information about your memo and will format it for you. After the memo is created, you can adjust the formatting to your own preferences. You will save this memo as "Reunion Memo".

To complete this Independent Challenge:

1. Create a new document using the Memo Wizard on the Memo tab in the New dialog box. Choose the Professional memo style.
2. After you answer the questions on each page of the Wizard dialog boxes, then click Next.
3. Enter "Reunion Memo" for the Title.
4. Enter the date, your name, and the topic "Meeting dates". Clear the CC check box.
5. Clear all boxes except Writer's initials and page numbers on the next two pages. Click Finished on the last page.
6. Format the title with Arial, Bold, 14 pt font. Underline the title with a 1½ pt line.
7. Center the title.
8. Create appropriate paragraph text and meeting dates and times.
9. Format the document attractively with borders, shading, bullets, and paragraph formatting a double-line 1½ pt border and 20% gray shading and 6 pt After paragraph formatting.
10. Preview, save, and print the memo, then close it.

4. As an account representative for Lease For Less, a company that rents various office equipment such as fax machines and large copiers, you need to draft a letter explaining the corporate discount program to a current customer. Instead of formatting your letter from scratch, you can use one of Word's letter templates to automatically format parts of the letter for you. You can modify the formatting after the letter is complete. Save this document as "Discount Letter". Use Figure C-22 as a guide to complete the letter.

To complete this Independent Challenge:

1. Use the Professional Letter Template on the Letter tab in the New dialog box.
2. Type the company name and format it with 100% Black shading.
3. Type the return address. Format the Font Size to 9 pt.
4. Type the customer name, address, and body of the letter.
5. Add the bulleted list at the bottom of the letter. Choose any bulleted style you like. Then indent the bulleted list to the 1" mark.
6. Format the Bulleted list to have 6 pt spacing after each line. (Hint: Select all lines at one time.)
7. Add the company name to the signature.
8. Format the letter and company name font in Bold and Shadowed.
9. If you are asked to save changes to the wizard, click No.
10. Preview, save, and print the document, then close it.

FIGURE C-22

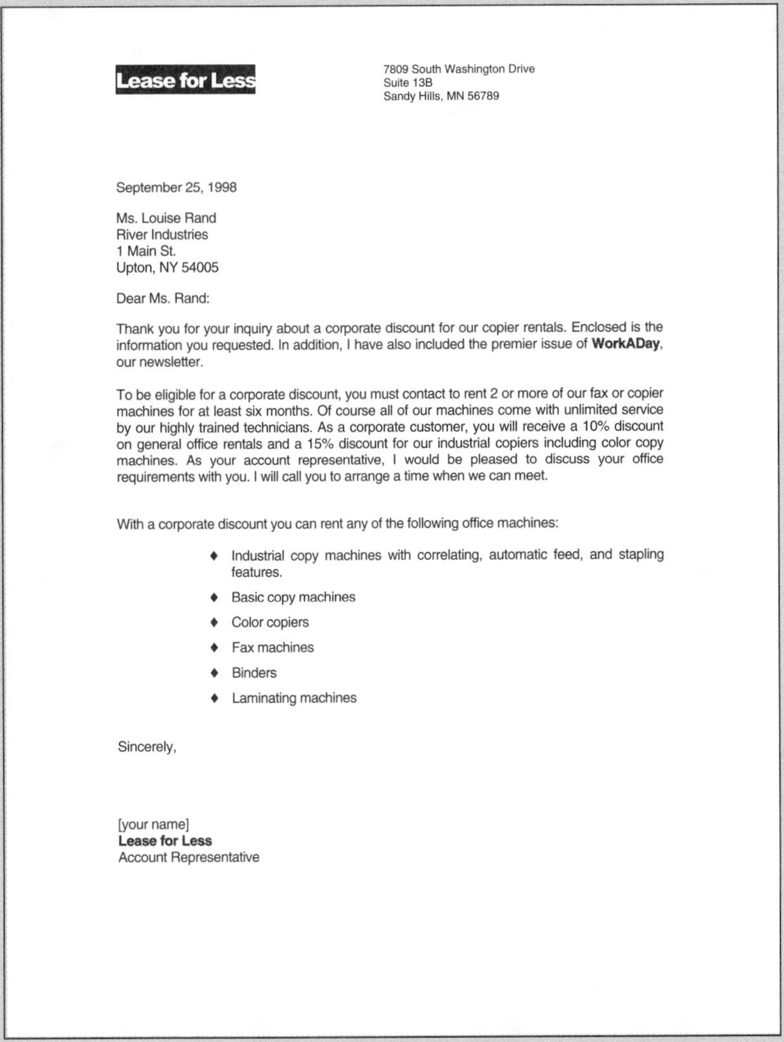

Lease for Less

7809 South Washington Drive
Suite 13B
Sandy Hills, MN 56789

September 25, 1998

Ms. Louise Rand
River Industries
1 Main St.
Upton, NY 54005

Dear Ms. Rand:

Thank you for your inquiry about a corporate discount for our copier rentals. Enclosed is the information you requested. In addition, I have also included the premier issue of **WorkADay**, our newsletter.

To be eligible for a corporate discount, you must contact to rent 2 or more of our fax or copier machines for at least six months. Of course all of our machines come with unlimited service by our highly trained technicians. As a corporate customer, you will receive a 10% discount on general office rentals and a 15% discount for our industrial copiers including color copy machines. As your account representative, I would be pleased to discuss your office requirements with you. I will call you to arrange a time when we can meet.

With a corporate discount you can rent any of the following office machines:

- Industrial copy machines with correlating, automatic feed, and stapling features.
- Basic copy machines
- Color copiers
- Fax machines
- Binders
- Laminating machines

Sincerely,

[your name]
Lease for Less
Account Representative

▶ Visual Workshop

As fundraising coordinator for Companies for Kids, you have been asked to create a letter to local company owners asking for donations of money and time. Use the Letter Wizard and choose the Elegant letter style to create your letter. After entering text, modify the formatting to improve the appearance of the letter even further. Save the document as "Elegant Kids Letter". Using Figure C-23 as a guide, complete the formatting for the document. Preview, save, and print your document before closing it.

FIGURE C-23

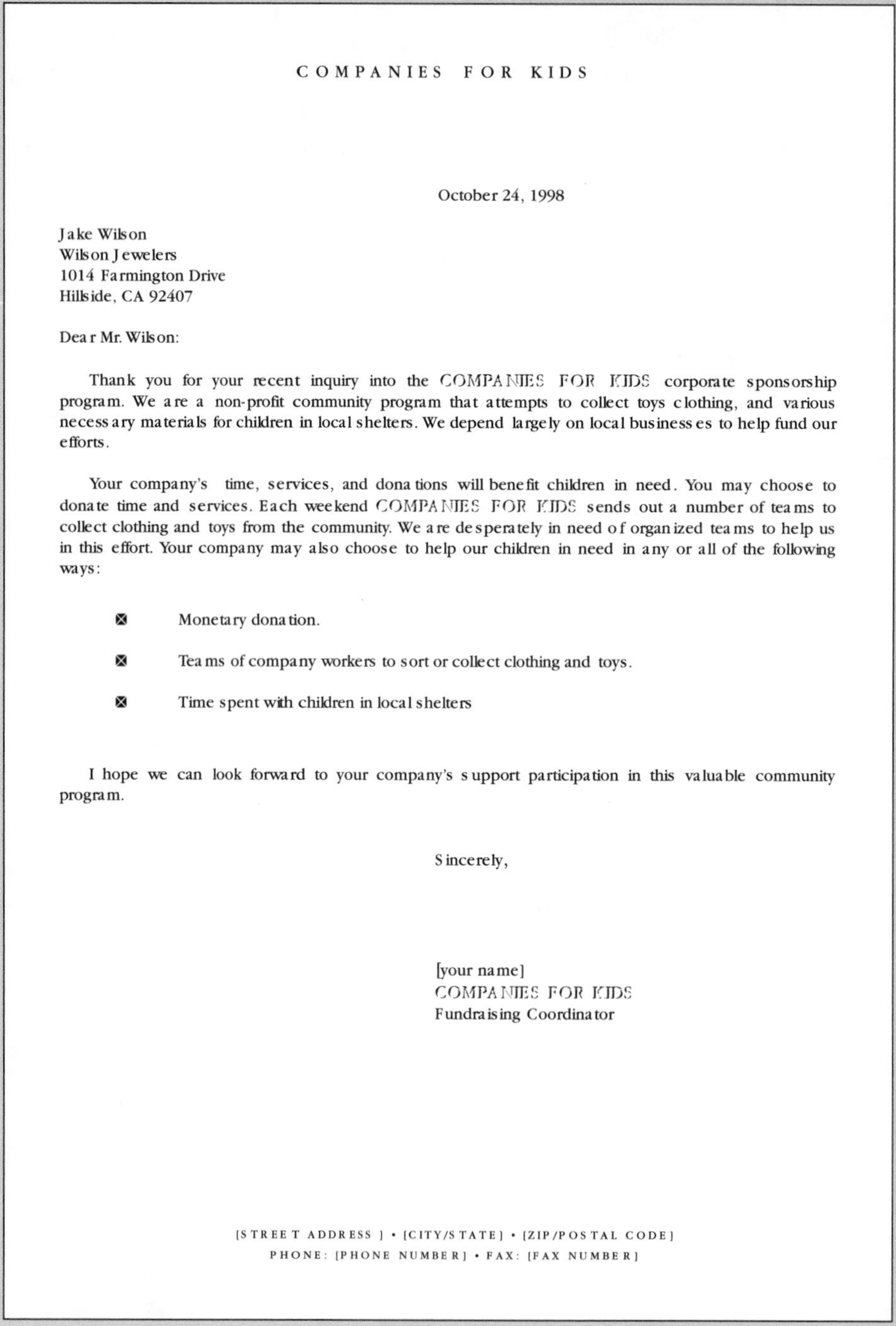

COMPANIES FOR KIDS

October 24, 1998

Jake Wilson
Wilson Jewelers
1014 Farmington Drive
Hillside, CA 92407

Dear Mr. Wilson:

Thank you for your recent inquiry into the COMPANIES FOR KIDS corporate sponsorship program. We are a non-profit community program that attempts to collect toys clothing, and various necessary materials for children in local shelters. We depend largely on local businesses to help fund our efforts.

Your company's time, services, and donations will benefit children in need. You may choose to donate time and services. Each weekend COMPANIES FOR KIDS sends out a number of teams to collect clothing and toys from the community. We are desperately in need of organized teams to help us in this effort. Your company may also choose to help our children in need in any or all of the following ways:

- ⊠ Monetary donation.

- ⊠ Teams of company workers to sort or collect clothing and toys.

- ⊠ Time spent with children in local shelters

I hope we can look forward to your company's support participation in this valuable community program.

Sincerely,

[your name]
COMPANIES FOR KIDS
Fundraising Coordinator

[STREET ADDRESS] • [CITY/STATE] • [ZIP/POSTAL CODE]
PHONE: [PHONE NUMBER] • FAX: [FAX NUMBER]

Working
with Tables

Objectives

► **Create a new table**
► **Convert text to a table**
► **Insert and delete rows and columns**
► **Calculate data in a table**
► **Sort information in a table**
► **Format a table**
► **Use the Draw Table button**
► **Modify a table with the Tables and Borders toolbar**

In this unit you'll learn how to format text in a table. A **table** is text arranged in a grid of rows and columns. With Word, you can add or delete information in a table without having to manually reformat the entire table. You can sort and calculate information that appears in a table and quickly make attractive tables using preset table formats. You can also customize your tables to fit your exact needs by drawing rows and columns exactly where you would like them. Tables are an excellent tool for displaying data normally found in lists or columns. ✐ Nomad Ltd has acquired an adventure travel company called Alpine Adventures. With the acquisition, Angela would like to improve the appearance of Alpine's newsletter. Because the newsletter includes pricing information, Angela uses tables to present this information to readers.

Creating a New Table

To create a blank table, you can use the Insert Table button on the Standard toolbar. Or you can use the Insert Table command on the Table menu. ✎ Angela thinks it might help potential customers decide which tour to take if they know the number of participants and general age group for each tour. She will present this information in a table.

Steps 1234

29.8.99

1. Launch Word

2. Open the document named WD D-1 and save it as Package Tours 1998
   Begin by placing the insertion point near the end of the document.

3. Scroll to the end of the document and place the insertion point in front of the paragraph mark above the heading Time to Leave?
   Now you can create your table.

4. Click the Insert Table button ▦ on the Standard toolbar, then drag in the grid to select three rows and five columns, as shown in Figure D-1, and then click the mouse
   A blank table appears in the document. To see the entire width of the table, you might need to adjust the magnification.

5. Click in the Zoom box on the Standard toolbar, type 95 and then press [Enter]
   Compare your table to Figure D-2. A **cell** is the intersection of a row and column. Inside each cell is a **cell marker**, which identifies the end of the contents in the cell. The end of each row is identified with an **end-of-row marker**. **Borders** surround each cell so you can see the structure of the table. Neither the cell markers nor the end-of-row markers appear when you print the document. Next, you enter the information you want in the table.

6. In the first cell, type Tour, then press [Tab]
   Pressing [Tab] selects the next cell in a table. Pressing [Shift][Tab] selects the previous cell. You continue entering text in the table.

7. Type Under 20, press [Tab], type 20-34, press [Tab], type 35-50, press [Tab], type Over 50 and press [Tab]
   Pressing [Tab] at the end of a row selects the first cell in the next row. You continue entering text in the table, pressing [Tab] after each cell.

8. Type the following text in the table as indicated below (for now, *do not press [Tab] at the end of the last row*)

Country Culture	15	20	25	45
Pastoral Idyll	20	35	30	15

   At the end of the last row, you decide to add a new row to the bottom of the table.

9. Press [Tab] to create a new row, and type the following text in the table as indicated below *(do not press [Tab] at the end of the last row)*

Mountain Top	45	35	15	5

   Compare your table to Figure D-3.

Time To
✔ Save

▶ WD D-2 **WORKING WITH TABLES**

FIGURE D-1: **Dragging to specify rows and columns**

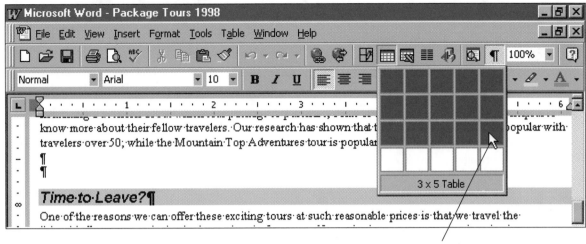

Drag to specify
rows and columns

FIGURE D-2: **New table in a document**

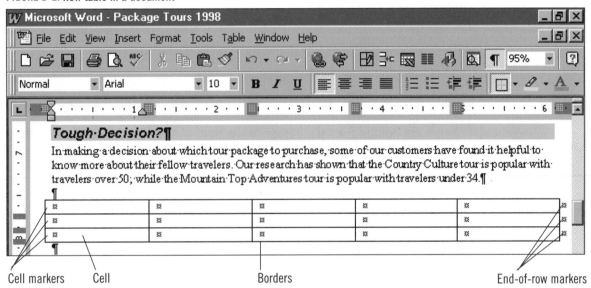

Cell markers   Cell   Borders   End-of-row markers

FIGURE D-3: **Completed table**

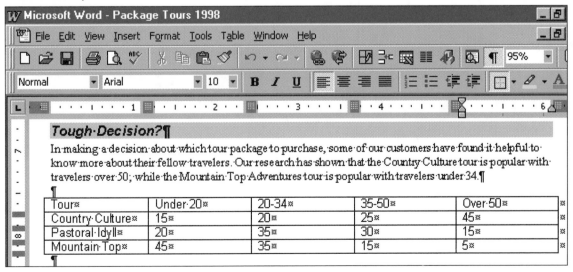

Tour	Under 20	20-34	35-50	Over 50
Country Culture	15	20	25	45
Pastoral Idyll	20	35	30	15
Mountain Top	45	35	15	5

Converting Text to a Table

You can convert existing text into a table by selecting the text and then using the Insert Table button on the Standard toolbar. The text you are converting to a table must be formatted with tabs, commas, or paragraph marks so that Word can interpret the formatting and create the table. Angela wants to convert the text about tour prices to a table so that readers will be able to quickly identify pricing information.

1. Scroll to the top of the document, and select the four lines that begin with Tour and end with Country Culture

   Because this text is already formatted with tabs, you can convert it to a table.

2. Click the Insert Table button  on the Standard toolbar

   Clicking this button is the same as choosing Insert Table from the Table menu or the Convert Text to Table command on the Table menu.

3. Deselect the highlighted table

   The selected text appears in a table format, as shown in Figure D-4. Because one column is too narrow for the text to fit appropriately, you need to adjust the column width.

4. Position the pointer over the border to the right of the column heading Lodging until the pointer changes to ◄╫►, then drag to the right slightly so that the heading appears on one line

   Notice how the height of the row automatically adjusts to accommodate the amount of text that is in the tallest cell in the row. You can also customize the size of the row to a specific height.

5. Select the text Tour in the first cell of the first row, then type Twelve-day Package Tour

   The row height adjusts to accommodate the text you type, but notice that the column width does not adjust automatically.

6. Place the insertion point in the empty cell below Trains and type 50

   The last price in this column is also missing, so you move to the last cell and enter the new price.

7. Press [Alt][PgDn] to move to the last cell in the fourth column, then type 75

   This keyboard shortcut moves you quickly to the last cell in a column. Your table is revised, as shown in Figure D-5, so you save your work.

Trouble?

If the width of only one cell in the column changes when you adjust the column width, deselect the cell, then click the Undo button 🔁 on the Standard toolbar. You must deselect the cell before adjusting the column width, if you want to adjust the width of the entire column.

Time To

✔ Save

FIGURE D-4: Text converted to a table

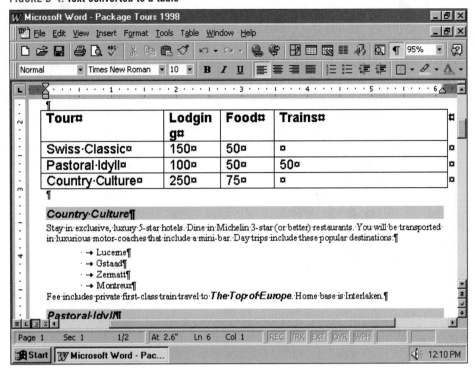

FIGURE D-5: Completed table

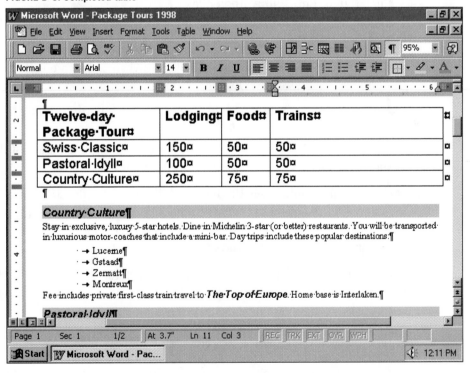

Adjusting row height

To establish a specific row height you can use the Cell Height and Width command on the Table menu. This command displays a dialog box in which you can specify a fixed height for rows. Use this feature when you want to make all the rows in a table the same height. You may also use the Cell Height and Width command to make all columns in a table the same width.

Inserting and Deleting Rows and Columns

You often need to change the number of rows or columns so that you can add or remove information. You can quickly add or delete rows and columns using the commands on the Table menu or use the commands on the pop-up menu for tables.  Nomad Ltd has determined that Alpine Adventures should discontinue the Swiss Classic tour and add a new budget-oriented tour. Angela will delete the row containing the Swiss Classic information, add a row for the new tour, and also add a Total column that displays the total price of each tour.

 **Steps**

1. Place the insertion point in the Swiss Classic row of the first table, then click the **right mouse button**

   The pop-up menu for tables appears. This menu contains the commands you are most likely to use when working in a table.

2. Click **Delete Cells...**

   The Delete Cells dialog box opens. In this dialog box, you can specify the cells you want to remove from the table. Delete the row for the discontinued tour.

3. Click **Delete Entire Row**, then click **OK**

   This command deletes the row containing the insertion point. Now, add a new row.

4. Click the **Insert Rows button** 🔳 on the Standard toolbar

   Notice that the Insert Table button and name changes based on what is currently selected. Next enter the information for the new tour.

5. Type **Mountain Top**, press **[Tab]**, then type the following numbers in the cells in the new row: 75   0   20

   Before adding a new column to the end of the table, you must adjust the width of the last column so that the new column will fit on the page.

6. Position the pointer over the border to the right of the last column until the pointer changes to ◄╫►, drag to the left to the **5"** mark on the horizontal ruler

   Next, you create a new column at the end of the table for the total price of each tour. To do so, you must first select the end-of-row markers to the right of the last column in the table.

7. At the top-right of the table, position the pointer above the end-of-row marker, and when the pointer changes to ↓, click the **left mouse button** as shown in Figure D-6

   This selects the column of end-of-row markers.

8. Click **Table** on the menu bar, then click **Insert Columns**

   A new blank column appears at the right end of the table. You can also click the Insert Columns button 🔳 on the Standard toolbar to insert a new column (again the Insert Table button will change based on what is selected). Word places the insertion point in the first cell of the new column when you begin typing.

9. Leaving the column selected, type **Total**

   Compare your document to Figure D-7.

QuickTip

To quickly delete an entire row or column using the keyboard, select the row or column, then press [Shift][Delete] or [Ctrl][X]. To remove only the text from a selected row or column, press [Delete].

 **Time To**

✔ Save

FIGURE D-6: Adding a column to the end of the table

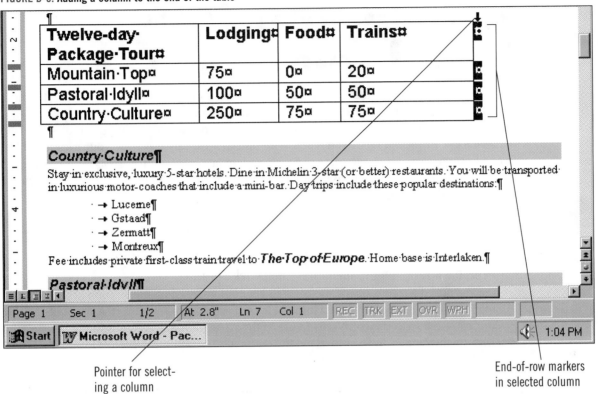

Pointer for select-
ing a column

End-of-row markers
in selected column

FIGURE D-7: Completed table

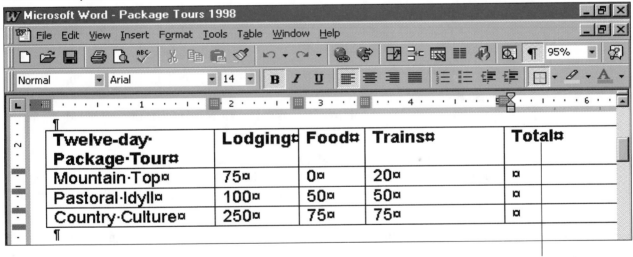

New column and text

Using the selection bar in tables

The area to the left of each row in a table contains the selection bar. Clicking in the selection bar to the left of a row selects that row in the same way clicking in the selection bar to the left of a line of text selects the entire line. In addition, each cell in the table contains its own selection bar. You can click the selection bar to the left of text in a cell to select an individual cell.

Calculating Data in a Table

Your table can include calculations based on the numbers in rows and columns. The Formula command allows you to perform calculations on data in a table. Built-in formulas make it easy to quickly perform standard calculations (such as totals or averages). Using formulas prevents mathematical errors and helps you work more quickly. You can also enter your own formulas. In addition, you can also change data in a table and update calculations. ✐ To provide the tour price for each tour, Angela uses the Formula command and a built-in formula to calculate the total cost per day for each tour.

Steps

1. **Place the insertion point in the cell below the Total cell in the first table of the document, click Table on the menu bar, then click Formula**
   The Formula dialog box opens, as shown in Figure D-8. Based on the location of the insertion point in the table, Word suggests a formula in the Formula box—in this case, the built-in SUM formula—and suggests which cells to use in the calculation, the columns to the left. Because these are the values you want to use in this calculation, accept the suggested formula.

2. **Click OK**
   The dialog box closes and the sum of the values in the row appears in the current cell. To calculate the other total values in this column, repeat the last command by pressing [F4].

3. **Press [↓] to move the insertion point to the next cell in the Total column, then press [F4]**
   [F4] is a function key located at the top of your keyboard that repeats the action you just performed. Function keys are used for shortcut commands. After you press [F4], the sum of the values in this row appears in the cell.

4. **Press [↓] to move the insertion point to the last cell in the Total column, then press [F4]**
   The sum of the values in this row appears in the cell. Next, update the cost of lodging for the Country Culture tour to reflect a new lower rate of 200.

5. **Select the last value in the Lodging column, 250, then type 200**
   The new value, 200, replaces the previous value of 250. When you change values used in a calculation, Word does not automatically update the total to reflect a new value, so you need to recalculate the values in the table.

Time To
✔ Save

6. **Select the last value in the Total column, 400, press [F9] and then deselect the cell**
   Word recalculates the total, and "350" appears in the cell, as shown in Figure D-9. Pressing [F9] updates calculations in a table.

FIGURE D-8: Formula dialog box

```
Formula                                    ? X
Formula:
=SUM(LEFT)

Number format:
[                                      ▼ ]

Paste function:          Paste bookmark:
[              ▼ ]        [            ▼ ]

          [  OK  ]        [ Cancel ]
```

Suggested formula

FIGURE D-9: Completed table

Microsoft Word - Package Tours 1998

File Edit View Insert Format Tools Table Window Help

Normal ▼ Arial ▼ 14 ▼ **B** *I* U ... 95% ▼

Twelve-day Package Tour¤	Lodging¤	Food¤	Trains¤	Total¤
Mountain·Top¤	75¤	0¤	20¤	95¤
Pastoral·Idyll¤	100¤	50¤	50¤	200¤
Country·Culture¤	200¤	75¤	75¤	350¤

Recalculated total

CLUES TO USE

Creating your own calculations

To enter your own calculation in the Formula dialog box, you refer to cells in the table using cell references. A cell reference identifies a cell's position in the table. Each cell reference contains a letter (A, B, C and so on) to identify its column and a number (1, 2, 3 and so on) to identify its row. For example, the first cell in the first row is A1, and the second cell in the first row is B1, as you can see in Figure D-10. You can create a formula to multiply, divide, add, and subtract the values of individual cells. Multiplication is represented by an asterisk (*); division is represented by a slash (/). For example, the formula to determine the total price for twelve days of the Country Culture tour would be =E4*12.

FIGURE D-10: Cell references

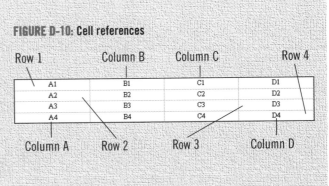

Row 1	Column B	Column C	Row 4
A1	B1	C1	D1
A2	B2	C2	D2
A3	B3	C3	D3
A4	B4	C4	D4

Column A   Row 2   Row 3   Column D

Sorting Information in a Table

Sometimes the information in a table is easier to interpret if the rows are sorted to appear in a particular order. For example, you might sort a department telephone directory by name, or a project plan by date. You can sort by a single column or by multiple columns. For each column, you can sort in **ascending** or **descending** order. Ascending order (the default) arranges rows from smallest to largest for numbers and from A to Z for text. Descending order arranges rows from largest to smallest for numbers and from Z to A for text. ⬛➤ To arrange the rows in a logical order, Angela sorts the table so that the most expensive tour appears first and the least expensive tour appears last.

1. **Place the insertion point anywhere in the table**
   You do not need to select the entire table to perform a sort.

2. **Click Table on the menu bar, then click Sort**
   The Sort dialog box opens, as shown in Figure D-11. In this dialog box, you can specify how you want your table sorted. The Sort by list contains the headings for all the columns in the table and displays the heading for the first column by default. Instead, sort the table by the information in the Total column.

3. **Click the Sort by list arrow, then click Total in the list of columns**
   Choose the option to display the tours starting with the most expensive and ending with the least expensive.

4. **Click the Descending radio button in the Sort by section**
   This button sorts rows from the largest value to the smallest value. Next, indicate that you do not want the first row (the column headings) included in the sort.

5. **In the My list has section, make sure the Header row option button is selected**
   This button ensures that the first row of the table (containing the column headings) is not sorted along with the other rows in the table.

6. **Click OK**
   The dialog box closes, and the table is sorted based on the values in the Total column. Deselect the text and compare your document to Figure D-12.

7. **Save the document**

FIGURE D-11: Sort dialog box

First column heading appears by default | Click to display list of column headings in table | Sorts information from smallest to largest value | Sorts information from largest to smallest value

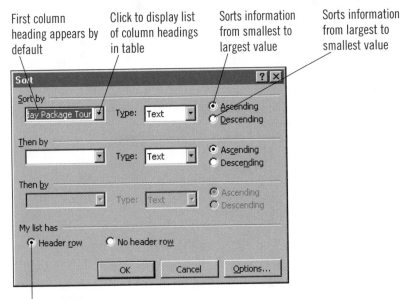

Specifies that first row is not included in the sort

FIGURE D-12: Sorted table

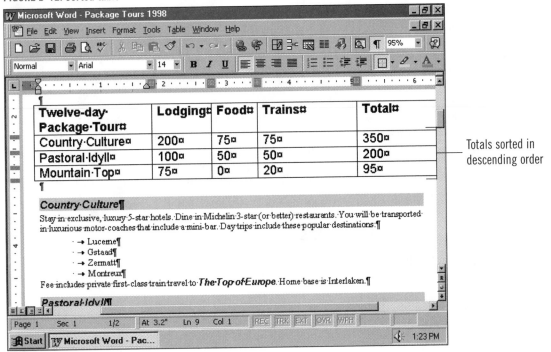

Totals sorted in descending order

Sorting by more than one column

By sorting your table by more than one column, you can better organize information. For example, if you sort a table by a column containing last names, the rows containing the same last name are grouped together. To sort the rows within each group, select a second column by which to sort, such as one containing first names. You can sort by values in up to three different columns using the Sort by box and the two Then by boxes.

Formatting a Table

In the same way you can add borders and shading to paragraphs, you can improve the appearance of a table by adding borders and shading to rows and columns. Although you can use the buttons on the Tables and Borders toolbar to apply shading and borders to individual rows and columns, Word's Table AutoFormat command provides a variety of preset table formats from which you can choose.  Now Angela will use the Table AutoFormat command to apply attractive borders and shading to the table she created.

Steps

QuickTip

For best results, you should always sort a table before formatting it with Table AutoFormat because the borders applied to a row also move when the position of a row changes after sorting. This could cause the table to be formatted inappropriately.

1. With the insertion point in the table, click Table on the menu bar, then click Table AutoFormat

The Table AutoFormat dialog box opens, as shown in Figure D-13. In this dialog box, you can preview different preset table format settings. You can also identify the parts of the table to which you want to apply specific formatting. For example, use a simple grid format for your table.

2. In the Formats list, scroll the list of formats, then click Grid 3

The Preview box shows how the Grid 3 option formats a table. To emphasize the information in the Total column, apply special formatting to the last column.

3. In the Apply special formats to section, click the Last Column check box

In the Preview box, notice that the last column of the sample table appears in bold.

4. Click OK

The dialog box closes and the table appears with new formatting. Notice that the Table AutoFormat command also adjusted the columns so that the table fits attractively between the margins. Next, you would like to emphasize the column headings.

5. Select the first row (the column headings), then click the Bold button **B** on the Formatting toolbar

The column headings appear in bold. Next, center the numbers in the table for easier reading.

6. Select the cells that contain numbers, then click the Center button ≣ on the Formatting toolbar

The numbers in these cells appear centered in the columns.

7. Deselect the table, then save the document

Compare your table to Figure D-14.

FIGURE D-13: Table AutoFormat dialog box

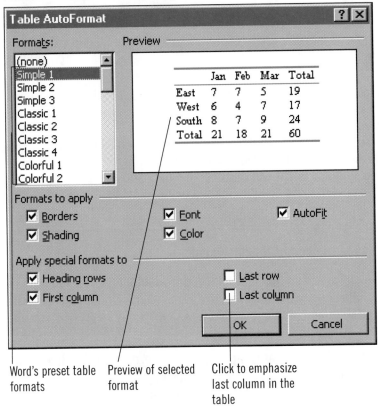

Word's preset table formats | Preview of selected format | Click to emphasize last column in the table

FIGURE D-14: Completed table

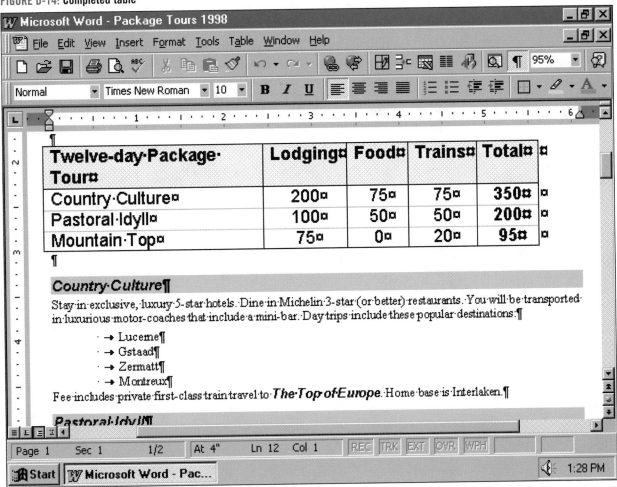

Using the Draw Table Button

Sometimes you may not want a simple table with the same number of cells in each row or column. For example, you might want a table with only one cell in the header row or an extra cell in the last column to display an emphasized total. Word's Draw Table button allows you to customize your tables by drawing the cells exactly where you want them. Angela would like to add a table displaying the best airfares to Switzerland. She would like the top row of the table to contain only the name of the airline. To accomplish this, she will customize her table to contain only one cell in the first row.

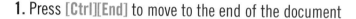

1. Press **[Ctrl][End]** to move to the end of the document

Trouble?

If you see the Office Assistant to create a table with a demonstration, click Cancel.

2. Click the **Tables and Borders button** 📰 on the Standard toolbar
The Tables and Borders toolbar is displayed, as shown in Figure D-15. Notice that the Draw Table button ✏️ on the Tables and Borders toolbar is automatically depressed and the Draw Table pointer ✏️ is displayed.

3. With the table pointer near the last paragraph mark of the document, click while dragging down and to the right, creating a cell about 4" wide and 1" tall
Use the rulers as a guide for determining the size of the cell. The first cell you draw using the Draw Table button represents the outside border of the entire table. Next create smaller cells within the first one.

4. Click on the left side of the cell about ¼" below the top line and drag the pointer straight across to the right side of the cell, and then release the mouse
Notice as you drag the pointer across the table, you can see a dotted line representing a cell border. Next you create a column in the table.

QuickTip

If you do not like the placement of a line in your table, you can erase the line using the Eraser button 🩹 on the Tables and Borders toolbar. Just click the Eraser button and then click the line you want to erase.

5. Click the bottom of the new line about 1¼" from the left edge of the table and drag down to the bottom line of the table
Compare your table to Figure D-16. Next, you add more rows to the table.

6. Click on the left side of the table about ¼" under the top cell and then drag across to the right side of the table
A new row is added to the table. Add another column that divides the right column.

7. Create another line that splits the right column at 2¼", then click the **Draw Table button** ✏️ on the Tables and Borders toolbar
Clicking the Draw Table button deactivates the table pointer. After customizing your table you are ready to add text.

Time To

✔ Save

8. Place the insertion point in the first cell of the table, then type **World Travel Airlines**, as shown in Figure D-17
In the next lesson, you will modify your table to make it more attractive.

FIGURE D-15: **Tables and Borders toolbar**

Eraser button
removes lines
between cells

Line Style

Line Weight

Borders

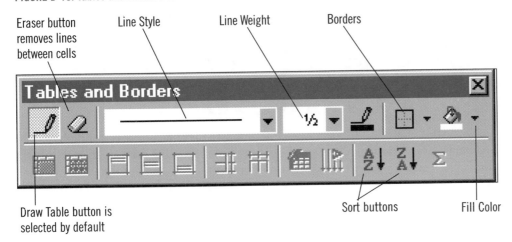

Draw Table button is
selected by default

Sort buttons

Fill Color

FIGURE D-16: **Adding a row to a custom table**

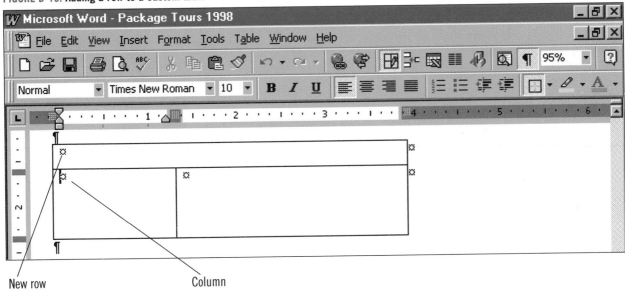

New row

Column

FIGURE D-17: **Completed table**

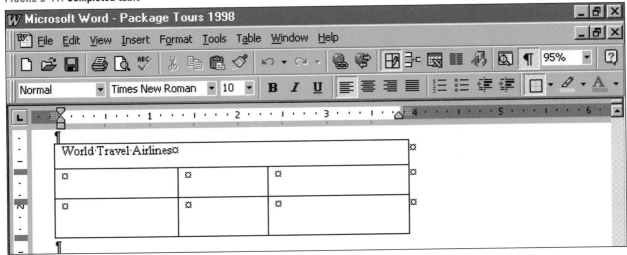

World·Travel·Airlines¤

Modifying a Table with the Tables and Borders Toolbar

You can also use the Tables and Borders toolbar to improve the appearance of your tables. This toolbar contains various buttons that can be used to format the table itself or arrange the text within the table. For example, the Distribute Columns button automatically makes selected columns equal widths.　　Angela will use the Tables and Borders toolbar to improve the appearance of her table. She will begin by splitting the cells in the table to add another column to the end of the table.

1. Select the last column of the second and third rows, and then click the Split Cells button 📵 on the Tables and Borders toolbar
   The Split Cells dialog box opens, as shown in Figure D-18. In this dialog box, you can choose to split the selected cells into additional rows or additional columns or both. In this case, split these cells into 2 rows and 2 columns.

2. Verify that the Number of rows and Number of columns boxes both display 2, then click OK
   The original cells are divided into 4 smaller cells, as shown in Figure D-19. Next, you make the width of all the columns equal.

3. Select the entire table, then click the Distribute Columns Evenly button 🏢 on the Tables and Borders toolbar
   All the columns are now the same width. Now you are ready to enter text.

4. In the new cells, type the text shown in Figure D-20 and be sure to press [Tab] at the end of the last row to create a new row of cells
   Next, center the text in the columns.

QuickTip

To select the table without selecting the end-of-row markers, select the text in the first row, then drag down and to the right.

5. Select the entire table (do *not* select the end-of-row markers), then click the Center button 📰 on the Formatting toolbar
   To improve the appearance of the table, make all the rows the same height.

6. Select all the rows in the table, if necessary, and click the Distribute Rows Evenly button 📑 on the Tables and Borders toolbar
   Now all the rows are the same height. Next you can give the table a more elegant appearance.

7. Click anywhere in the table, click the Table AutoFormat button 📔 on the Tables and Borders toolbar, and then scroll to and double-click the Elegant preset format

8. Click Table on the menu bar, and then click Cell Height and Width, and on the Row tab, click the Center option button, and then click OK
   Your table is centered on the page. Compare your table to Figure D-20.

Time To

✔ Save
✔ Preview
✔ Print
✔ Exit

9. Click the Tables and Borders button 🞥 on the Standard toolbar
   The Tables and Borders toolbar is hidden. Angela has finished working with the document for now.

FIGURE D-18: **Split Cells dialog box**

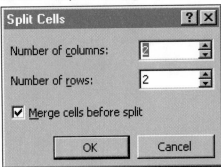

FIGURE D-19: **New cells**

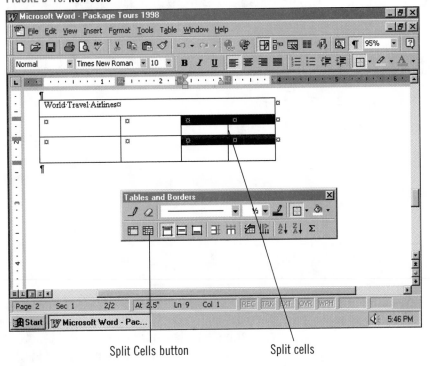

Split Cells button   Split cells

FIGURE D-20: **Completed table**

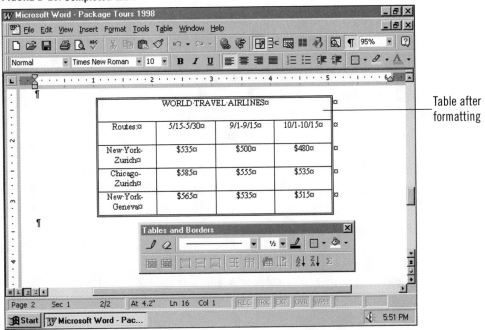

Table after formatting

Practice

► Concepts Review

Label each of the elements in Figure D-21.

FIGURE D-21

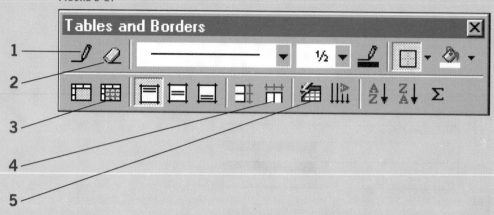

Match the number of each of the following terms with the statement that best describes its function.

6. Insert Table button

7. Table AutoFormat

8. = SUM

9. Gridlines

10. Descending order

a. Sorting from largest to smallest or from Z to A

b. Allows you to choose from preset tables

c. Creates a table from existing text

d. The built-in formula provided by Word in the Formula dialog box

e. Printing lines separating cells in a table

Select the best answer from the list of choices.

11. Which of the following statements is NOT a major benefit of using tables (rather than tabs) to align text in rows and columns?

  a. You can add and delete information without reformatting the entire table.

  b. You can format the table using the Table AutoFormat command.

  c. The status bar displays the cell reference to identify your location in the table.

  d. You can sort and calculate information in a table.

12. Which statement best describes the commands available on the pop-up menu for working in a table?

  a. The pop-up menu contains only the commands found on the Table menu.

  b. The pop-up menu contains the commands you are likely to use most often when working in a table.

  c. The pop-up menu contains Table AutoFormat settings from which you can choose.

  d. The pop-up menu contains the Formula command to insert calculations in a table.

13. Which of the following statements best describes how to delete only the text inside a row?

  a. Select the row, then press [Delete].

  b. With the insertion point in the row, click Table then click Delete Cells. Then click Delete Entire Row.

  c. Select the row, then click the Cut button.
  d. Select the row, click Edit, then click Cut.

14. To insert a column at the end of a table, you must first:
  a. Select the last column.
  b. Place the insertion point in the last column.
  c. Select the last cell in the table.
  d. Select the end-of-row markers at the right end of the table.

15. To add a new blank row to the bottom of a table, you:
  a. Place the insertion point in the last row, click Table, then click Insert Rows.
  b. Select the last row, click Table, then click Insert Rows.
  c. Place the insertion point in the last cell of the last row, then press [Tab].
  d. Select the end-of-row markers at the right end of the table, then press [Tab].

16. In which one of the following instances does the row height in a table NOT adjust?
  a. When the amount of text in a cell fits on more than one line.
  b. When you click Table, then click Cell Height and Width.
  c. When you drag a horizontal gridline between rows.
  d. When you click Cell Height and Width on the table pop-up menu.

17. When sorting a table, what is the easiest way to ensure that the header row is NOT sorted along with the other rows?
  a. In the Sort dialog box, click the Header row radio button in the My list has section.
  b. Sort the table before adding the header row.
  c. Split the table before sorting it.
  d. Use the Table AutoFormat command first.

18. Which of the following statements is NOT true of the Table AutoFormat command?
  a. You can apply special formatting to the last column.
  b. You can apply special formatting to the last row.
  c. You can see an example of the format in the Table AutoFormat dialog box.
  d. You can see an example of your table with new formatting in the Table AutoFormat dialog box.

19. Which of the following is a valid cell reference for the first cell in the third column?
  a. C1
  b. ROW1COL3
  c. 1C
  d. 3A

20. Which of the following is NOT true about sorting rows in a table?
  a. The Sort command always sorts all the rows in a table.
  b. You can sort a table by more than one column.
  c. You can specify not to sort the header row.
  d. You can choose the order in which you want rows sorted.

▶ Skills Review

1. Create a table and convert text to a table
- **a.** Launch Word, then open the document named WD D-2 and save it as "Travel Expenses".
- **b.** Select all six lines of text.
- **c.** Click the Insert Table button on the Standard toolbar.
- **d.** Select the text "Taxis", then press [Delete].
- **e.** Type "Transportation", then click Bold if necessary.
- **f.** Type "January" in the empty cell in the first row.
- **g.** Click the Save button on the Standard toolbar.

2. Insert and delete rows and columns.
- **a.** With the insertion point in the third row, click Table on the menu bar, then click Delete Cells, click Delete Entire Row, then click OK.
- **b.** Place the insertion point in the last cell of the last row of the table, then press [Tab].
- **c.** Type "Misc.", press [Tab], then type "54.88" [Tab] "73.65" [Tab] "63.49".
- **d.** Select the end-of-row markers at the right end of the table, then click the Insert Columns button on the Standard toolbar.
- **e.** In the first cell of the new column, type "Expense Total".
- **f.** Click the Save button on the Standard toolbar.

3. Calculate data in a table.
- **a.** Place the insertion point in the second cell in the Expense Total column, click Table on the menu bar, click Formula, then click OK.
- **b.** Press [↓] to move the insertion point to the next cell in the Expense Total column and press [F4].
- **c.** Repeat Step 3b for the remaining cells in the Expense Total column.
- **d.** Select the Transportation value in the January column, then type "123.50".
- **e.** Select the Transportation value in the Expense Total column, then press [F9] to update the total.
- **f.** Click the Save button on the Standard toolbar.

4. Sort information in a table.
- **a.** Place the insertion point anywhere in the table.
- **b.** Click Table on the menu bar, then click Sort.
- **c.** In the Sort by section, select Expense Total in the columns list.
- **d.** Click the Descending radio button.
- **e.** In the My list has section, make sure the Header row radio button is selected, then click OK.
- **f.** Click the Save button on the Standard toolbar.

5. Format a table.
- **a.** If the table is not already selected, click Table on the menu bar, then click Select Table.
- **b.** Click the Tables and Borders button on the Standard toolbar.
- **c.** Click the Table AutoFormat button on the Tables and Borders toolbar.
- **d.** In the Formats list, review different formats by selecting each and viewing it in the Preview section.
- **e.** In the Formats list, click Columns 5.
- **f.** In the Apply special formats to section, click the Last column check box, then click OK.
- **g.** Select all the cells that contain numbers and click the Align Right button on the Formatting toolbar.
- **h.** Add "0" to the cents place of any value that is missing the final zero.

i. Click the Save button on the Standard toolbar.

j. Click the Print button on the Standard toolbar, then close the document.

6. Use the Draw Table button.

a. Open a new document and save it as "Agenda".

b. Drag and draw a cell 2" high and 3" wide.

c. Drag a line below the top line of the table creating a cell about .25" high.

d. Repeat Step 6c creating a table with four cells total.

e. Add a vertical line in the middle of the last three cells to make two columns.

f. Enter the text below.
Agenda
8:30   Opening Ceremonies
10:00
12:00   Group Luncheon

g. Click the Save button on the Standard toolbar.

7. Modify a table with the Tables and Borders toolbar.

a. Select the empty cell in the third row.

b. Click the Split Cells button.

c. Be sure that the Number of columns box contains 2, and that the Number of rows box contains 1, then click OK.

d. Enter the text below.
Meeting A for Advisors
Meeting B for Committee Members

e. Select the first column in the table and position the pointer over the border between the first and second columns. Drag the pointer to the left until the column is about ¾" wide.

f. Select the third row and position the pointer over the border between the second and third columns. Drag the pointer to the left until the two cells are about the same size.

g. Select the table, then click the Center button on the Formatting toolbar.

h. Use the Colorful 2 format in Table AutoFormat.

i. Save, print, and close the document. Then hide the Tables and Borders toolbar and exit Word.

▶ Independent Challenges

1. As the director of marketing for ReadersPlus publishing company, you are responsible for sales projections for the new beginners reading series called "Everyone Is A Reader." You have been asked to present these projections at the upcoming sales kickoff meeting. Begin by creating a new document and saving it as "Projected Sales". Then format the document with the following changes, using Figure D-22 as a guide for how the completed document should look.

To complete this independent challenge:

1. Create a table with 5 rows and 5 columns.
2. Enter the following text:

Everyone is a Reader	West	East	Midwest	South
Anthologies Only	5000	7000	5800	7200
Supplements Only	2400	3500	4000	1100
Anthologies with guides	6800	6700	9400	8200
Complete Package	6500	7500	6300	7700

3. Adjust the last column width to be about 1".
4. Add a Total column to the right side of the chart.
5. Calculate the total for each row.
6. Format the table with the Grid 3 preset format.
7. Preview, save, print, then close the document.

FIGURE D-22

Everyone is a Reader	West	East	Midwest	South	Total
Anthologies Only	5000	7000	5800	7200	25000
Supplements Only	2400	3500	4000	1100	11000
Anthologies with guides	6800	6700	9400	8200	31100
Complete Package	6500	7500	6300	7700	28000

2. As the conference coordinator for Educational Consultants, Inc., you are in charge of tracking the costs for an upcoming Creativity Conference. You want to compare this year's conference costs with those of last year's conference. Create a new document and save it as "Conference Costs". Complete the following formatting.

To complete this independent challenge:

1. Create a table with 7 rows and 3 columns.
2. Enter the following text:

Conference Costs	1997	1998
Dinner	740	1300
Audio/video rental	270	425
Presenter fees	300	550
Decorations	500	800
Printing fees	300	420
Hall rental	800	1100

3. Adjust the last column width to be about 1".
4. Add a column to the right side of the chart.
5. Add the column heading "Difference" to the new column.
6. In the Difference column, calculate the difference between 1998 versus 1997 costs for each row. Hint: For the first row, type "=C2-B2" in the Formula dialog box. Using the [F4] key to repeat a command copies the previous formula so you cannot use [F4] to insert formulas with varying cell references.
7. Sort the table by 1997 costs, from highest to lowest.
8. Format the table with the List 5 preset format.
9. Center the columns so that they contain fee values.
10. Preview, save, print, then close the document.

3. Task References are documents which summarize commands, buttons, and keystroke shortcuts for the features you learn about in each unit. Log on to the Internet and use your browser to go to http://www.course.com. From there, click Student On Line Companions, and then click on the link to go to the Microsoft Office 97 Professional Edition-Illustrated: A First Course page, then click on the Word link for Unit D. Download the Unit D Task Reference. Although this document is already formatted as a table, you decide to customize the table. Save the final table as "Table Task Reference".

1. Sort the by the text in the first column.
2. Sort the table again, this time by the text in the third column and the first column.
3. Improve the table's appearance by applying the preset format setting.
4. Preview, save, print, then close the document.

4. As a co-chairman of the entertainment committee for the Lake City 1998 class reunion, you are responsible for calculating attendance fees for the planned events. You want to create a table showing the distribution of attendees among all the events. Another member of the committee has provided you with the number of classmates who have responded for specific events. Open the document named WD D-3 and save it as "Reunion Costs".

To complete this independent challenge:

1. Convert the tabbed text to a table.
2. Add a row to the end of the table, specifying "Variety Show" as the event with 120 attendees at $7 per person.
3. Calculate the total for each row, using a multiplication formula. (Hint: For the first row, type "=B2*C2" in the Formula dialog box. Using the [F4] key to repeat a command copies the previous formula so you cannot use [F4] to insert formulas with varying cell references.)
4. Format the table with the List 8 preset format.
5. Right align the columns that contain numerical values.
6. Preview, save, print, then close the document.

▶ Visual Workshop

As part of your responsibilities as the director of the Extreme Fitness health club, you must prepare a price list for club activities. Use the Draw Table button and other features on the Tables and Borders toolbar to create a table that identifies activities such as basketball, racquetball, aerobics classes, etc., and enter a price for each activity. Use Figure D-23 as a guide for creating your table. Use the Eraser button to delete any border lines you don't want in your table. (Hint: Use the Distribute Columns Evenly button and the Distribute Rows Evenly button to make your columns and rows even.) Format the table in any preset format desired. Save the document as "Activity Prices".

FIGURE D-23

Activity	Price	Sales	Total
Aerobics classes	$15.00	89	$1335.00
Basketball	$7.00	152	$1064.00
Raquetball	$10.00	214	$2140.00
Swimming	$10.00	345	$3450.00
Total for 1997		**800**	**$7989.00**

Formatting

Pages

Objectives

► **Control text flow between pages**
► **Adjust document margins**
► **Insert headers**
► **Insert footers**
► **Modify text in a footer**
► **Change page orientation**
► **Change formatting in multiple sections**
► **Create headers for specific pages**

In addition to formatting text and paragraphs, you can format the pages of your documents. **Page formatting** includes determining the margins between the text and the edge of the page. It also includes the size and orientation of a page. Additional formatting options allow you to specify the text flow on and between pages. Another feature allows you to add text that will appear at the top or bottom of each page in the document, in the form of headers and footers. To complete the formatting in her financial summary for Nomad Ltd, Angela Pacheco needs to adjust the document's margins, change the orientation for an additional page, and add headers and footers to her document.

Controlling Text Flow between Pages

When the amount of text in a document fills a page, Word automatically creates a page break, which places any remaining text at the start of the next new page. Sometimes this break results in a line or two appearing alone at the bottom of the page with the rest of the paragraph continuing on the next page, giving the document an awkward appearance. Using text flow features, you can control how text flows on and between pages. 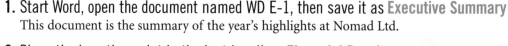 Angela would like to have the Financial Results heading appear with the paragraph that follows it.

QuickTip

Turn off spelling and grammar checking. Display paragraph marks.

1. Start Word, open the document named WD E-1, then save it as Executive Summary
This document is the summary of the year's highlights at Nomad Ltd.

2. Place the insertion point in the last heading, Financial Results
To control the flow of text affecting this heading and the next paragraph, you can use the Paragraph command.

3. Click Format on the menu bar, then click Paragraph
The Line and Page Breaks tab contains the formatting option you want to use.

QuickTip

You can quickly insert your own page break anywhere in a document by pressing [Ctrl][Enter]. In normal view, this kind of break (sometimes called a hard page break) appears as a light gray line labeled "Page Break" in your document.

4. Click the Line and Page Breaks tab
The Line and Page Breaks tab appears foremost in the dialog box. The Pagination area contains the options that affect the flow of text over the pages of the document. Table E-1 describes the text flow options. Choose the option to always keep this heading with the following paragraph.

5. Click the Keep with next check box, then click OK
The heading (and the text that follows it) appears on the next page. To get a better picture of the flow of the document, preview it.

6. Click the Print Preview button 🔍 on the Standard toolbar
The document appears in the Preview window. Next, preview all the pages of the document.

Trouble?

Do not be concerned if the amount of text you see in your own document does not match the amount of text shown in the figure. The exact amount of text you see can depend on the resolution of your monitor, or the type of printer connected to your computer.

7. Click the Multiple Pages button 🔳 on the Preview toolbar and click the second box in the first row of the grid to see the entire document
Compare your document to Figure E-1. The text in the legend that appears to run off the second page will be addressed later in this unit. If you see only one page of the document, click the Multiple Pages button again, and this time click to the first box in the second row. Click the Multiple Pages button one more time, and click to the second box in the first row.

8. Click File on the menu bar, then click Save
The document is saved. Notice that several lines of text appear on the second page. Because you want all the headings in the summary document to appear on the first page, you will adjust the margins so that the text will appear on the first page.

FIGURE E-1: New text flow in document

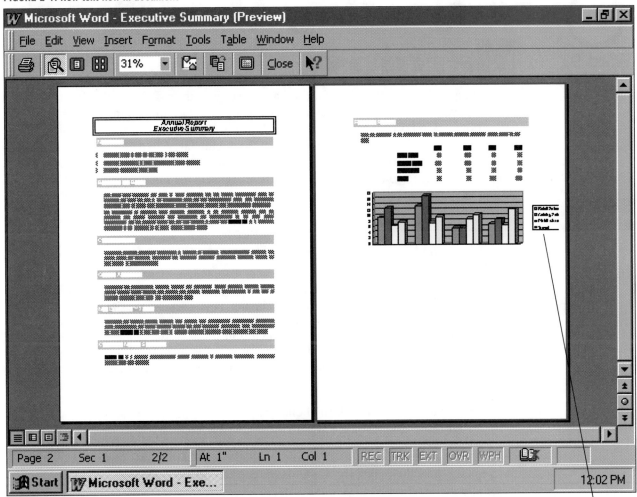

This problem will
be corrected later
in this lesson.

TABLE E-1: Pagination text flow options

choose this option	to
Widow/Orphan control	Prevent the last line of a paragraph from printing at the top of a page (widow), and the first line of a paragraph from printing at the bottom of a page (orphan)
Keep lines together	Prevent a page break within a paragraph
Keep with next	Prevent a page break between the selected paragraph and the paragraph after it
Page break before	Position the selected text at the top of the next page

Adjusting Document Margins

The white space between the edge of the text and the edge of the page is called the **margin**. When you first create a document, the default size of the top and bottom margins is 1 inch, while the left and right margins are set to 1.25 inch, as shown in Figure E-2. However, you might decide to adjust margins to improve the appearance of the document or to manipulate the amount of text on a page. You can adjust the size of individual margins on the Margins tab of the Page Setup dialog box. ✎ Angela will adjust the margins in her document, so that all the main ideas of her summary document fit on the first page.

1. **Click File on the menu bar, click Page Setup, then click the Margins tab (if it is not already foremost)**
   The Page Setup dialog box appears, as shown in Figure E-3. On the Margins tab, you can determine the size of the margins for a document. First, decrease the size of the top margin.

2. **Click the Top down arrow until .8" appears in the box, then click OK**
   This reduces the size of the top margin, but it is not enough to move all the desired text from page 2 to the first page. Change the other margins to increase the amount of text that will fit on the first page.

3. **Click File on the menu bar, then click Page Setup**
   The Page Setup dialog box opens with the Margins tab displayed.

4. **Click the Bottom down arrow until .7" appears, click the Left down arrow until 1" appears, and then click the Right down arrow until 1" appears**
   Notice that the Preview area of the dialog box reflects your changes as you make them.

5. **Click OK**
   Adjusting the margins causes Word to move the text that previously appeared on the second page onto the bottom of the first page. The part of the chart that appears to run off the second page will be addressed later in this unit. To have the entire table appear on the next page with the chart, you can apply additional text flow formatting.

6. **Click Close on the Preview toolbar**
   The document appears in the normal view; you can now apply formatting to have all the lines of the entire table stay together on the same page.

7. **Select all five lines of the table under the Financial Results heading, then click Format from the menu bar, then click Paragraph**

8. **On the Line and Page Breaks tab, click the Keep with next check box, then click OK**

9. **Click the Print Preview button 🔍 on the Standard toolbar**
   The document appears in the Preview window, as shown in Figure E-4.

10. **Click Close on the Preview toolbar**
    The document appears in the normal view.

Trouble?

Different screens at different resolutions might display the flow of text differently.

Time To

✔ Save

FIGURE E-2: **Margins in a document**

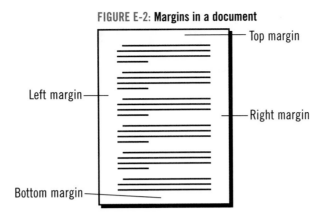

Top margin

Left margin

Right margin

Bottom margin

FIGURE E-3: **Margins tab in Page Setup dialog box**

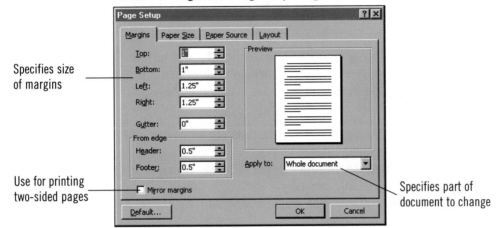

Specifies size of margins

Use for printing two-sided pages

Specifies part of document to change

FIGURE E-4: **Preview of highlights document**

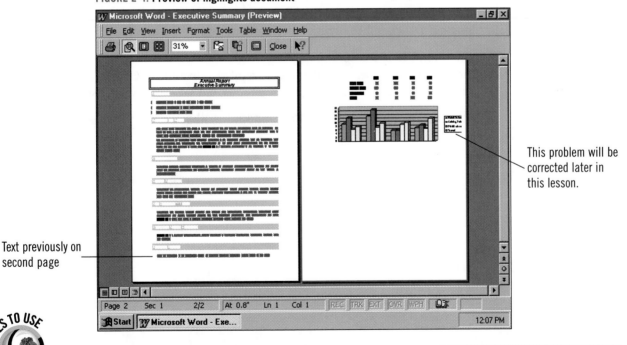

This problem will be corrected later in this lesson.

Text previously on second page

Adjusting the Margins with the Ruler

You can adjust document margins in the page layout view or in the Preview window (if the ruler is displayed) by dragging the edges of the rulers. Position the pointer at an edge of a ruler until the pointer changes to ↔, and then drag to the size you want. If you hold down [Alt] as you drag, you can see the exact margin size.

Inserting Headers

In multiple page documents the top or bottom of every page typically contains information such as the page number, title, author's name, or date. Text that appears at the top of every page is called a **header**, while text appearing at the bottom of every page is called a **footer**, which you will learn about in the next lesson. You can use both headers and footers in your document. Angela would like the title of the Executive Summary to appear at the top of every page, so she begins by selecting and cutting the text she wants to use as a header.

Steps

1. **Select the first two lines in the document including the paragraph marks (enclosed in the double-box border) and click the Cut button ✂ on the Standard toolbar**
   Cutting this text removes the bordered title from the document and places it on the Clipboard. Because this is the text you want to appear at the top of every page, open the Header area of the document.

2. **Click View on the menu bar, then click Header and Footer**
   The document appears in Page Layout view but the text is dimmed. You cannot edit the body of the document while the Header or Footer area is displayed. This command also displays the Header and Footer toolbar, as shown in Figure E-5. In the Header area, you can type the text you want to appear at the top of every page, or you can paste the text you placed on the Clipboard.

3. **Click the Paste button 📋 on the Standard toolbar**
   Clicking the Paste button inserts the text from the Clipboard into the Header area. You can drag the Header and Footer toolbar to another area of the window if it obscures your view.

4. **Scroll down to the second page**
   The header also appears on the next page of the document. Compare your document to Figure E-6. You are now ready to create a footer, but save your work first before continuing.

5. **Click the Save button 💾 on the Standard toolbar**

FIGURE E-5: Inserting headers

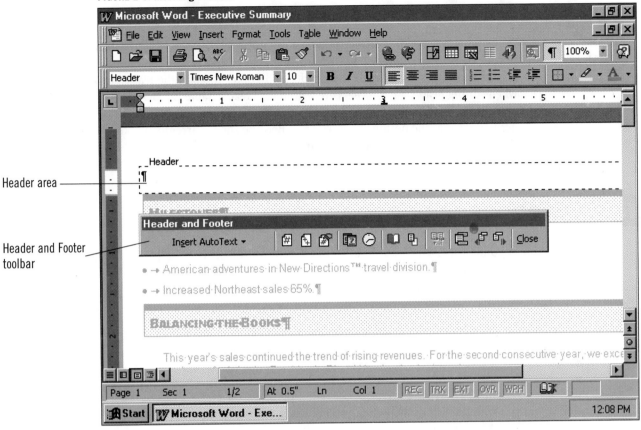

Header area

Header and Footer toolbar

FIGURE E-6: Text in a header area

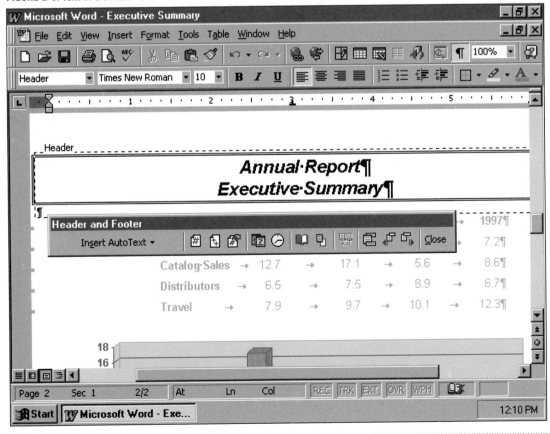

Inserting Footers

In the same way headers display information at the top of every page, footers display information at the bottom of every page. You use the Header and Footer toolbar to switch between the header and footer areas. With the Header and Footer toolbar, the features you use most often when editing headers and footers are within easy reach. Table E-2 describes each of the buttons available on the Header and Footer toolbar. ◢▬▬▬ Angela would like the date and page number to appear at the bottom of every page. Because she is currently working in the header area, she begins by switching to the footer area.

Steps 1 2 3 4

1. **Click the Switch Between Header and Footer button 🗒 on the Header and Footer toolbar**
   Clicking this button displays the Footer area, in which you can type or insert the information you want to appear at the bottom of every page.

2. **Click the Insert Date button 📆 on the Header and Footer toolbar**
   The current date appears in the footer. Use the preset tab stops already defined in the footer area to position text. You can also insert text that you want to precede the page number.

3. **Press [Tab] twice, type Page, then press [Spacebar]**
   With the text in the footer, you are ready to insert the page number.

4. **Click the Insert Page Number button 🔢 on the Header and Footer toolbar**
   Clicking the Insert Page Number button inserts an instruction so that Word automatically supplies the correct page number on each page. Compare your footer to the one shown in Figure E-7. Now examine the footer on the following page.

5. **Scroll to the next page**
   The footer also appears on the next page of the document. You have finished working with headers and footers for now, so you can close the footer area.

6. **Click Close on the Header and Footer toolbar**

7. **Click Page Layout View button 🔲 and scroll to the bottom of the page to see the footer in the document**
   Compare your document with Figure E-8. Notice that the text in the footer appears dimmed.

8. **Click the Save button 💾 on the Standard toolbar**

FIGURE E-7: Page numbers in a footer area

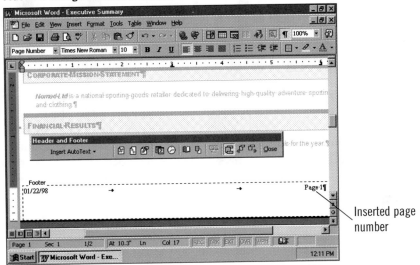

Inserted page number

FIGURE E-8: Text in a footer

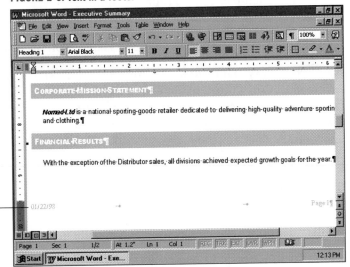

New text in the footer

TABLE E-2: Buttons on the Header and Footer toolbar

click	to
🔲	Move the insertion point between the header and footer areas
🔲	Move the insertion point to the previous header or footer area, when the document is divided into sections
🔲	Move the insertion point to the next header or footer area, when the document is divided into sections
🔲	Insert the header or footer from the previous section in the current section OR break the connection between sections, allowing different headers or footers to be created
🔲	Insert a field for sequential page numbers, starting with 1, that is updated when pages are added or deleted
🔲	Insert a field for the current date, based on the computer's clock, that is updated when the document is opened or printed
🔲	Insert a field for the current time, based on the computer's clock, that is updated when the document is opened or printed
🔲	Display the Page Setup dialog box, where you can modify the margins, paper source, paper size, and page orientation
🔲	Display or hide the document text while working in headers and footers

Modifying Text in a Footer

When you need to edit the text in a header or footer, you simply display the header or footer area again. Although you can use the Header and Footer command on the View menu, when you are in page layout view, it is quicker to double-click in the area you want to edit. For example, to edit the footer in your document (which is displayed in page layout view), double-click the footer part of the document. ✐ Next, Angela decides to display the document name along with the page number. She uses a built-in AutoText entry to accomplish this.

Steps 1 2 3 4

1. **Scroll to display the footer in the document window, then double-click anywhere in the footer**
   The footer area opens. Now, you are ready to edit the footer.

2. **Place the insertion point in front of the word Page**
   Next, insert the document name using the AutoText feature.

3. **Click Insert AutoText on the Header and Footer toolbar, as shown in Figure E-9**

4. **Click Filename, type a comma, and press [Spacebar]**
   The filename of the document appears in the footer. If you change the name of the document, Word automatically updates this information in the footer. Because it is useful to know the total number of pages in a document, you can supply this information at the end of the footer.

5. **Place the insertion point after the page number, press [Spacebar], type of, then press [Spacebar] again**

6. **Click the Insert Number of Pages button ⊞ on the Header and Footer toolbar**
   The total number of pages in the document appears in the footer, as shown in Figure E-10.

7. **Click Close on the Header and Footer toolbar**
   The Header and Footer toolbar closes. Compare your document to Figure E-11.

8. **Click the Save button ⊞ on the Standard toolbar**

FIGURE E-9: **Insert AutoText button**

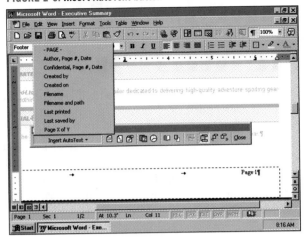

FIGURE E-10: **Number of pages in footer**

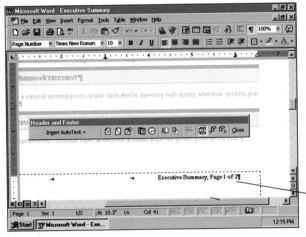

New information
in footer

FIGURE E-11: **Completed footer**

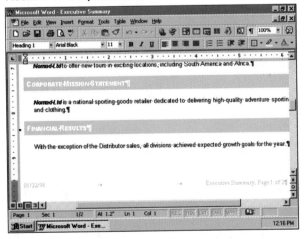

Using fields

You can use fields to insert and update information that Word retrieves from your document and your computer. A **field** is an instruction or code that tells Word what you want to insert. Word offers hundreds of fields, each inserting very specific information in the document. Some of the more common fields you might insert in a document include the document name, revision number, the date that the document was saved or printed, and information that appears in the Properties dialog box (available with the Properties command on the File menu).

Changing Page Orientation

In most of the documents you create, the page itself is oriented such that it is taller than it is wide. This orientation is called **portrait**. When you arrange text on a page that is wider than it is tall, this orientation is called **landscape**. Figure E-12 illustrates the difference between portrait and landscape orientation. ➤➤➤➤ On the second page of the document, Angela noticed that the legend in the chart is too close to the edge of the page. She would like to change the orientation for the second page. She starts by displaying the document in normal view, so she can better locate the part of the document she wants to format.

Steps 1234

1. Click the Normal View button 🗎

2. Scroll to and place the insertion point at the beginning of the text Financial Results
Only the text from this point forward will be formatted with a new orientation.

3. Click File on the menu bar, then click Page Setup
This command displays the Page Setup dialog box. The orientation settings are on the Paper Size tab.

4. Click the Paper Size tab
Clicking this tab displays the Paper Size options in the Page Setup dialog box, as shown in Figure E-13. You can display the second page of the document in landscape orientation so that all of the chart appears when it is printed.

5. In the Orientation area, click the Landscape option button, click the Apply to list arrow, then click This point forward
Clicking this button formats the contents of the second page in landscape orientation. Next, check the margins for this part of the document.

6. Click the Margins tab
Notice that the previous settings for the top and bottom margins are now the settings for the left and right margins. You can change the margins so that they are consistent through-out the document.

7. In the Top box type .8, in the Bottom box type .7, in the Left box type 1, and in the Right box type 1
Notice that the Preview area of the dialog box reflects your changes as you make them. Next, specify the part of the document you want formatted.

8. Click the Apply To list arrow and click This point forward
This selection ensures that only this part (page two and after) of the document is affected by these changes.

9. Click OK, then click the Save button 🖫 on the Standard toolbar
Although you cannot see the changes in normal view, the second page is now formatted in landscape orientation with new margins. A double dotted line labeled "Section Break (Next Page)" was automatically inserted, as shown in Figure E-14. A section break allows you to for-mat different parts of the same document with different page setup settings. Section breaks are inserted whenever you specify Page Setup options that affect only part of a document.

FIGURE E-12: Comparing page orientation

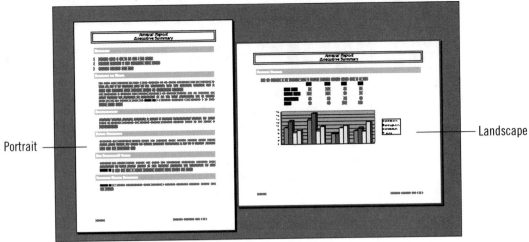

Portrait

Landscape

FIGURE E-13: Paper size options

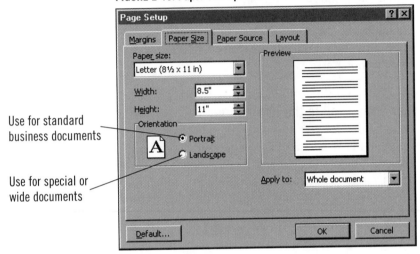

Use for standard business documents

Use for special or wide documents

FIGURE E-14: Section break in a document

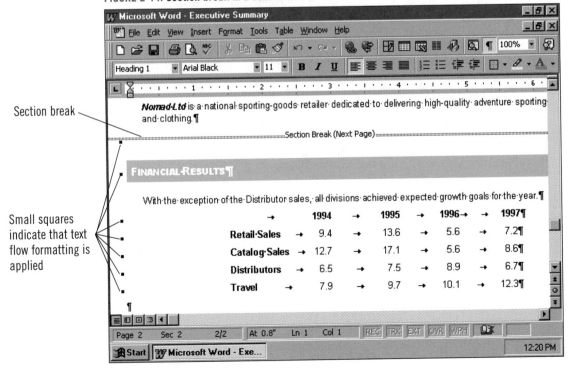

Section break

Small squares indicate that text flow formatting is applied

Changing Formatting in Multiple Sections

Whenever you format your document into sections and change the margins or orientation in different sections, you might also need to adjust the tab positions in the headers and footers. For example, suppose you inserted tabs to right-align text in a header or footer, and then you changed the width of the document by adjusting the document margins or orientation. You will want to adjust the tab position in the header or footer to match the new margins in the document, so that the text continues to be centered or right-aligned between the new margins. ✒ Angela wants to adjust the tab position in the footer for the second section to keep the page numbers aligned with the right margin.

Steps

1. Place the insertion point in the second page of the document, click View on the menu bar, then click Header and Footer

The Header area for section two appears. Because the header is centered without a tab, it is unaffected by the changes to the page orientation and requires no adjustments. But the page number in the footer was placed with tabs and needs adjustment, so you can start by displaying the footer area.

2. Click the Switch Between Header and Footer button 🖻 on the Header and Footer toolbar, then scroll to the right margin

The Footer area for section two appears. Notice also that the Same as Previous button is indented on the Header and Footer toolbar, as shown in Figure E-15. By default, each section in a document uses the same footer information as the previous section. Because of the wider orientation in section two, you want to adjust the tab position for the footer in this section, so you must break this connection between the footers.

3. Click the Same As Previous button 🖻 on the Header and Footer toolbar, then scroll to the right margin again

The button is no longer indented and the connection is broken between the two sections. Now, you can adjust the position of the right-aligned tab stop.

4. Drag the right-aligned tab in the horizontal ruler to the 9-inch mark

The page number information appears at the right margin in the footer. You have finished formatting the document for now, so you can close the Footer area.

5. Click Close on the Header and Footer toolbar

The Footer area closes and you return to the document. Before closing and printing the document, preview the document to see how it will look.

6. Click the Print Preview button 🔍 on the Standard toolbar

Examine both pages of the document. Compare your document to Figure E-16.

7. Click Close on the Preview toolbar

Return to the document window.

8. Click the Save button 🖫 on the Standard toolbar, then click the Print button 🖨 on the Standard toolbar

9. Close the document

FIGURE E-15: Second section footer area

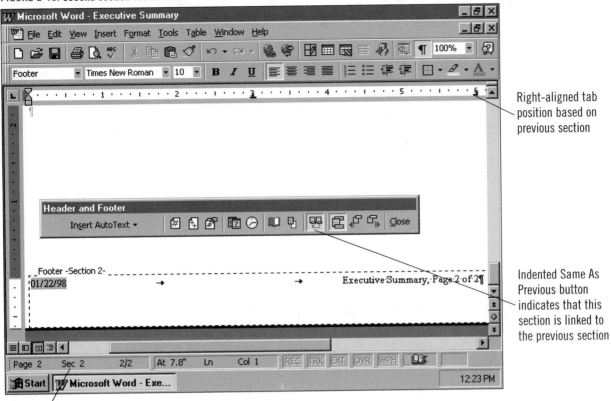

Right-aligned tab position based on previous section

Indented Same As Previous button indicates that this section is linked to the previous section

Indicates section number

FIGURE E-16: Different footers in the same document

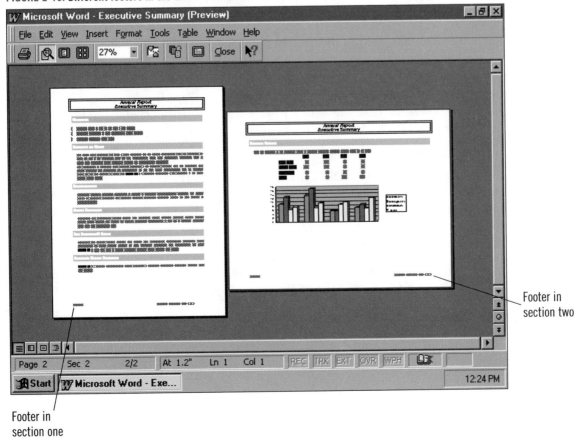

Footer in section two

Footer in section one

Creating Headers for Specific Pages

Word also offers various header and footer formatting that is especially helpful in larger documents. Often when you create a large document, it will contain a title page on which you may not want to include the headers or footers. The Layout tab on the Page Setup command allows you to specify a different header or footer for the first page of the document. This tab also allows you to create different headers and footers for the even and odd pages of a document. ✒ Angela would like to add headers to the Nomad Annual Report. Since the report will be printed with the pages facing each other in a book format, Angela would like the page numbers to appear on the outside margin of the pages.

Steps 1 2 3 4

1. Open the document named **WD E-2**, then save it as **Nomad 1998**
   This document contains a more in-depth report of activities occurring at Nomad Ltd throughout the past year. You will add to the document headers containing the page numbers.

2. Click **File** on the menu bar, then click **Page Setup**
   The Page Setup dialog box opens. On the Layout tab, you can specify the header and footer options you want for the document.

3. Click the **Layout tab**, then click the **Different first page check box** in the Headers and Footers box
   Choosing this option will allow you to exclude the page number on the title page of your document. Since the page numbers always appear on the outside of facing pages, you will need to align the numbers on the even and odd pages differently.

4. Click the **Different odd and even check box**, then click **OK**
   The Page Setup dialog box closes. You are now ready to enter the page numbers in the headers.

5. Place the insertion point in the second page, click **View** on the menu bar, then click **Header and Footer**
   The Header and Footer areas and the Header and Footer toolbar are displayed in the document window. Notice the Header area is labeled Even Page Header. All the headers and footers are now labeled Even, Odd, or First Page. You will use Insert AutoText on the Header and Footer toolbar to insert page numbering information.

6. With the insertion point left-aligned, click **Insert AutoText** on the Header and Footer toolbar, click **Page X of Y**, select the text, then press **[F9]**
   Page X of Y AutoText entry automatically inserts the page number and the total number of pages in the document, as shown in Figure E-17. You need to press **[F9]** to update the header to reflect the number of pages in the document. Next insert this same information for the odd pages of your document.

7. Scroll to the third page, with the insertion point in the Odd Page Header box, click the **Align Right button** ▤ on the Formatting toolbar, and then repeat step 6

Time To

✔ Save
✔ Print the document
✔ Exit Word

8. Click **Close** on the Header and Footer toolbar

9. Click the **Print Preview button** 🔍 on the Standard toolbar and display all four pages of the document, as shown Figure E-18. Then click **Close** on the Preview toolbar

FIGURE E-17: **Page X of Y AutoText entry**

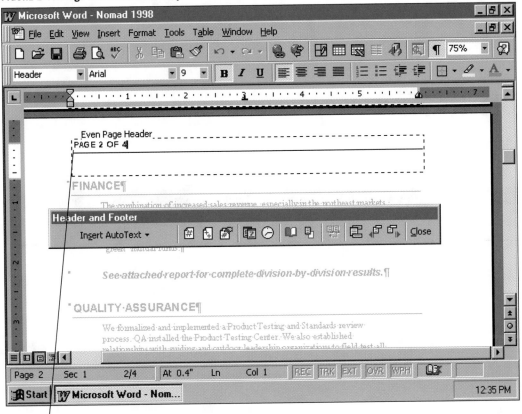

Page number and
number of pages in
document

No header on
first page

FIGURE E-18: **Entire document in Print Preview**

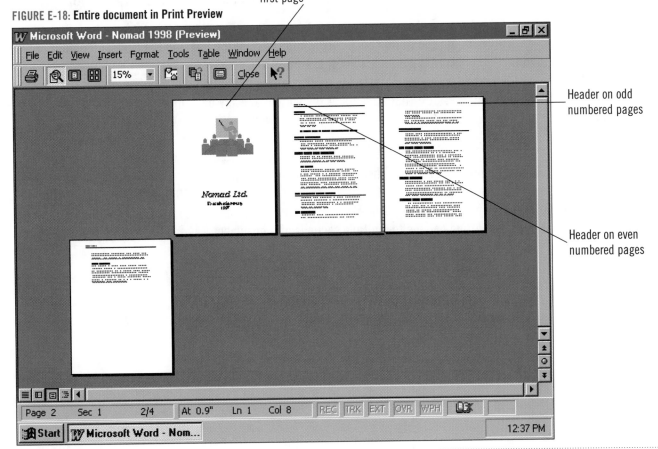

Header on odd
numbered pages

Header on even
numbered pages

Practice

► Concepts Review

Label each of the elements in Figure E-19.

FIGURE E-19

1   2   3   4   5

Match each of the following terms with the statement that best describes its function.

6. Footer
7. Header
8. Portrait orientation
9. Field
10. Margin
11. Landscape orientation

a. Text that appears at the top of every page in a document
b. The white space between the edge of the text and the edge of the page
c. A page that is wider than it is tall
d. A special instruction or code for information that Word automatically updates
e. Text that appears at the bottom of every page in a document
f. A page that is taller than it is wide

Select the best answer from the list of choices.

12. Which of the following can you NOT accomplish in the Page Setup dialog box?
    a. Adjust the margins for the top, bottom, left, and right edges of a document.
    b. Adjust the tab settings for a header and footer.
    c. Apply unique page formatting options to multiple sections of a document.
    d. Select the page orientation.

13. When you decrease the size of all margins in a document:
    a. You increase the amount of text that will fit on the page.
    b. You decrease the amount of text that will fit on the page.
    c. The amount of text that will fit on the page does not change.
    d. You are not able to add headers and footers to the document.

14. **Which of the following is NOT true about headers and footers?**
    a. Clicking View, Header and Footer displays the Header and Footer toolbar.
    b. You can insert fields in a header or footer.
    c. You can paste existing information into a header or footer without having to retype it.
    d. You can edit document text while you are working in headers and footers.

15. **Which of the following is NOT an example of a field you can enter in a header or footer?**
    a. Document name
    b. Current date
    c. Total number of pages in the document
    d. Right-aligned tab stop

16. **Which of the following is true when you create a new section with modified orientation and margin settings?**
    a. Any existing tab settings in the header and footer areas are automatically adjusted to match the new margin settings.
    b. In normal view, there is no visible indication in the document that a new section has been created.
    c. You cannot create a new section with both modified orientation and margin settings.
    d. You may have to manually adjust headers and footers so that they align properly with the new margin settings.

17. **To break the connection between a header or footer in multiple sections of a document, you:**
    a. Click the Switch Between Header and Footer button on the Header and Footer toolbar.
    b. Double-click one of the headers with the right mouse button.
    c. Click the Same As Previous button on the Header and Footer toolbar.
    d. Click the New Section button on the Header and Footer toolbar.

18. **Which of the following is a good reason to use landscape orientation in a document?**
    a. You are formatting a long document.
    b. You are creating a document with unusually wide margins.
    c. A document requires that it is printed on a page that is wider than it is tall.
    d. Landscape orientation is useful only when creating graphics.

19. **Which of the following is NOT a way to display the number of pages in a document?**
    a. Numbering button on the formatting toolbar.
    b. Insert Page Number button on the Header and Footer toolbar.
    c. NumPages field using Field command on the Insert menu.
    d. Insert Number of Pages button on the Header and Footer toolbar.

20. **Which of the following is NOT true when you format part of a document in landscape orientation?**
    a. You must change the position of the printer paper before printing the landscape page.
    b. After changing the orientation, you might need to adjust the width of the header and/or footer areas.
    c. You can see the different orientation in the print preview window.
    d. The landscape orientation option appears on the Paper Size tab in the Page Setup dialog box.

▶ Skills Review

1. Control text flow between pages.
a. Start Word and open the document named WD E-3. Save the document as "Software Letter".
b. Place the insertion point in the heading "Reference Card…"
c. Click Format on the menu bar, then click Paragraph.
d. Click the Line and Page Breaks tab to bring it forward.
e. Click the Page break before check box and click OK.

2. Adjust document margins.
a. Click the Print Preview button on the Standard toolbar and examine all pages of the document.
b. Click File on the menu bar, click Page Setup, then click the Margin tab.
c. In the Top box, click the down arrow until .7 appears in the box. In the Bottom box, click the down arrow until .7 appears. In the Left box click the down arrow until 1 appears, and in the Right box click the down arrow until 1 appears. In the Header box, click the up arrow until .8 appears. Then click OK.
d. Click Close on the Preview toolbar.

3. Insert a header.
a. Select the first line in the document (the date), be sure to include the paragraph mark, and click the Cut button on the Standard toolbar.
b. Click View on the menu bar, then click Header and Footer.
c. Click the Paste button on the Standard toolbar.
d. Scroll through the document to review your changes and save the document.

4. Insert a footer.
a. Click the Switch Between Header and Footer button on the Header and Footer toolbar.
b. Type "Page", press [Spacebar], then click the Insert Page Number button on the Header and Footer toolbar.
c. Press[Spacebar], type "of", then press [Spacebar].
d. Click the Insert Number of Pages button on the Header and Footer toolbar.
e. Click Close on the Header and Footer toolbar, then save your work.

5. Modify a footer.
a. Click the Page Layout View button, if not already in Page Layout view.
b. Double-click the footer.
c. Press [End], then press [Tab] twice and type "Continued on Next Page".
d. Drag the right-aligned tab marker to the right, to the 6.5" mark.
e. Scroll through the document to review your changes.
f. Click Close on the Header and Footer toolbar, then save your work.

6. Change page orientation.

  a. Scroll to and place the insertion point at the top of the second page.

  b. Click File on the menu bar, then click Page Setup.

  c. Click the Paper Size tab.

  d. In the Orientation area, click the Landscape radio button.

  e. Click the Apply To list arrow and click This point forward.

  f. Click the Margins tab.

  g. In the Top box, type ".7", in the Bottom box, type ".5", in the Left box type "1", and in the Right box type "1".

  h. Click the Apply To List arrow and click This point forward.

  i. Click the Layout tab.

  j. Click the Section Start arrow and choose New Page, if it is not already selected.

  k. Click OK and save your changes.

7. Use different footers in the same document.

  a. Place the insertion point in the second page of the document, click View on the menu bar, then click Header and Footer.

  b. With the insertion point in the Header area, click the Same as Previous button on the Header and Footer toolbar (to deselect it).

  c. Select the date and press [Delete].

  d. Click the Switch Between Header and Footer button on the Header and Footer toolbar.

  e. Click the Same as Previous button.

  f. Drag the right-aligned tab in the horizontal ruler to the 9" mark.

  g. Delete the text "Continued on Next Page".

  h. Type "Transport Express Inc., 1998".

  i. Click the Close button on the Header and Footer toolbar.

  j. Click the Print Preview button on the Standard toolbar and review your changes.

  k. Click Close on the Preview toolbar.

  l. Save your document and print it.

  m. Close the document and exit Word.

▶ Independent Challenges

1. The Mountain Top Tours travel company would like to create a more dramatic format to announce their upcoming tours in Switzerland. As their in-house publishing expert, you have been asked to create a new look for their brochure. Open the document WD E-4 and save it as "Mountain Landscape".

  To complete this independent challenge:

1. Format the entire document in landscape orientation.

2. Adjust the top margin to be .4" and the footer margin to .3".

3. Insert a left-aligned header with the text "DRAFT 1.0"

4. Adjust the right-aligned tab in the footer so that it is even with the new right margin.

5. Preview, save, and print the document, then close it.

2. As co-chair for the Lake City High School Reunion entertainment committee, you want to help golfers attending the golf tournament find their way to the golf course. Add a map as a second page to a draft version of the golf announcement. Open the document WD E-5 and save it as "Golf Map". Make the following changes in the document.

To complete this independent challenge:

1. Format the second page in landscape orientation.

2. Adjust the top and bottom margins to be .7 inch each for the second page only.

3. Adjust the header margin to be .4 inch and the footer margin to be .3 inch for the second page only.

4. Create a footer in each section that includes a field for the name of the file at the left margin and the date at the right margin. Adjust the right-aligned tab in the footer in the second section.

5. Preview, save, and print the document, then close it.

3. As an intern in the Communications Department for a large manufacturer of microprocessors, you have been asked to improve the appearance of the analysis document of the company's financial statement. For quick access to this information, the company has placed an electronic version of the annual report on its Web site. After exploring the report highlights, you obtain a copy of the text (much of which is already complete) and add a few finishing touches to prepare the document for printing. Because this document will be printed on two sides of each page (to save paper), you will need to create different footers for odd and even numbered pages.

To complete this independent challenge:

1. Create a new blank document in Word and save it with the name "Financial Summary".

2. Log on to the Internet and use your browser to go to http://www.course.com. From there, click Student Online Companions, then click the link for this textbook, click the Word link for Unit E, then locate the 1995 Highlights page.

3. Click the Financial Statements link and finally click the link Managements Discussion and Analysis.

4. Select all the text in the document and copy it to the Clipboard. Paste it into the new blank document. Format the entire document in 12pts and 1.5 line spacing.

5. Add a title to the top of the document and add headings (use whatever text you wish) before every second paragraph. Format each of the headings so that they are never separated from the body of the following paragraph.

6. Adjust the top and bottom margins to be 1.25".

7. Specify different headers/footers for odd and even numbered pages.

8. Center the company name in the header for all pages. For odd numbered pages create a footer that contains the name of the document at the left margin, the date in the center, and page numbering information (use the Page X of Y format) at the right margin. Reverse this order for the footers in even numbered pages.

9. Preview, save, and print the document, then close it.

4. Your company has recently created a program to help the local food pantry collect food. Through this program employees are given longer lunch hours to volunteer at the food pantry, sorting donations and stocking shelves. You would like to give a certificate to all the employees who have volunteered over the past year. Using Figure E-20 as a guideline for formatting, create a new document and save it as "Volunteer Certificate".

To complete this independent challenge:

1. Use a border and indentation to create a signature line.

2. Experiment with different fonts, font sizes, and alignment.

3. Create a new first page by inserting a hard page break. On the new first page, create a cover memo to accompany the award.

4. Change the orientation of the last page of the memo (for the certificate) to print in landscape orientation.

5. Adjust the margins as necessary.

FIGURE E-20

MEMO

DATE: 06/23/97
TO: ANDRA CARSON, VICE PRESIDENT
FROM: YOUR NAME
RE: ATTACHED CERTIFICATE

Here is my first attempt at creating an certificate that goes to all of the employees who have volunteered at the food shelf over the past year. Please share any comments or suggestions you have about the certificate. I would like to have the certificate printed and distributed by the end of the month

Enc. 1

IN APPRECIATION OF YOUR EFFORTS

Awarded to

Recipient

Food Shelf Volunteer

Presented by
Carson Associates

Wednesday, June 24, 1997

Your Name

▶ Visual Workshop

As the conference coordinator for the upcoming Decorative Ideas Conference, you have been assigned the task of finalizing the conference menu. The caterer has supplied a menu for your approval. Open the document named WD E-6 and save it as "Final Menu". Using Figure E-21 as a guide, format the document so that the menu appears on a separate page and in landscape orientation. The letter should appear in portrait orientation. Also add a header containing the date, and a footer containing the document name and a page number. Adjust margins as necessary.

FIGURE E-21

Mr. Archibald Ryden
Banquet Caterer
Pinewood Center
Grande Point, MN 55509

Dear Mr. Ryden:

Your ideas for the menu at our creativity conference are exactly what we had in mind. I took the liberty of preparing a menu card that will accompany the meal. Because I need to give the printers at least two weeks lead time, please try to get in touch by the end of the week.

Please feel free to comment on any changes made to the menu and offer suggestions as you feel necessary.

Thanks again for your prompt and attentive service.

Sincerely,

[your name]
Conference Coordinator
Decorative Consultants, Inc.

9/05/98

Decorative Conference Cuisine Menu

Hors D'Ouevres   *A savory collection of herbs and flavors on focaccia*

First Course   *Pasta with Fresh Tomato and Basil Sauce*

Main Course   *Curried Salmon with Fresh Vegetables*

Dessert   *Tarte tatin*

Bon Appetite!

Final Menu   Page 2 of 2

Formatting
with AutoFormat and Styles

Objectives

- ► **Create and apply character styles**
- ► **Use AutoFormat and the Style Gallery**
- ► **Modify styles**
- ► **Create and apply new paragraph styles**
- ► **Display style names in a document**
- ► **Move around with styles**
- ► **Replace styles**
- ► **Format as you type**

There are many formatting features available in Word that provide a variety of ways to quickly format a document the way you want. By using **styles**, which are collections of format settings you store together, you can apply combinations of format settings quickly. And with the AutoFormat feature, Word automatically applies styles and improves formatting in an entire document for you. You can also use the Style Gallery to format a document, choosing from many built-in, professionally designed business documents provided with Word. You can even opt to format as you type. ✎— Angela will use a variety of techniques to improve the appearance of a cover letter to shareholders and an executive summary for the annual report.

Creating and Applying Character Styles

Using styles can save a lot of time and reduce formatting errors. A **character style** is a stored set of font format settings. When you create a character style, you store the font format settings so that you can apply them quickly in one step, rather than applying each setting to each occurrence you want to format. Using character styles to format text ensures consistent formatting. For example, if you use bold, small caps, and italics formatting for product names in a brochure, you want all the product names to be formatted the same way. In the summary document, Angela would like to format *all* occurrences of the company name with identical format settings.

Steps 1 2 3 4

1. Start Word 97, open the document named **WD F-1** and save it as **Nomad Report**
Because the first occurrence of the company name, Nomad Ltd, is already formatted with the settings you want to use, you can create a style based on an example of existing character formatting.

2. Select the first occurrence of the company name **Nomad Ltd**, click **Format** on the menu bar, then click **Style**
The Style dialog box opens in which you can view, modify, and create new character and paragraph styles. Here, you can create a new character style.

3. Click **New**
The New Style dialog box opens, as shown in Figure F-1. In this dialog box, provide a name for the new style and specify the type of style you want to create.

4. In the Name box, type **CompanyName**
This stores the format settings of the selected text in a style called "CompanyName." You can use uppercase or lowercase characters, punctuation, and spaces in a style name. Next, indicate that you are creating a character style rather than a paragraph style.

5. Click the **Style type list arrow**, then click **Character**
Note that the Preview area shows how text will appear with the format settings, and the Description area lists the settings.

6. Click **OK** to close the New Style dialog box, then click **Apply** in the Style dialog box
The dialog box closes. You won't see any change in the selected text, because it is already correctly formatted. The CompanyName character style is applied to the text. Now you can apply this style to other occurrences of the company name in the document.

7. In the second-to-last body paragraph, select the company name, click the **Style list arrow** on the Formatting toolbar, then click **CompanyName**
The style list contains all the styles you can apply to text, including the new style you created, as shown in Figure F-2. In addition, character styles are followed by the ⓐ icon to distinguish them from paragraph styles, which are followed by a ¶.

8. Repeat Step 7 for the next occurrence of **Nomad Ltd**
Compare your document to Figure F-3.

9. Click the **Save button** 🖫 on the Standard toolbar

FIGURE F-1: New Style dialog box

Enter a new style name

Select the style type

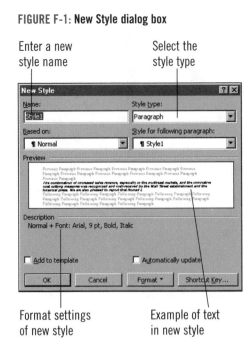

Format settings of new style

Example of text in new style

FIGURE F-2: Style list

Current style

Style arrow

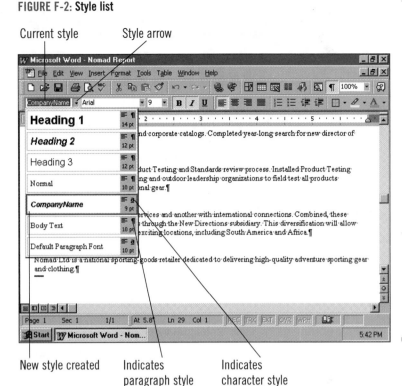

New style created

Indicates paragraph style

Indicates character style

FIGURE F-3: Character styles applied

New character style applied to company name

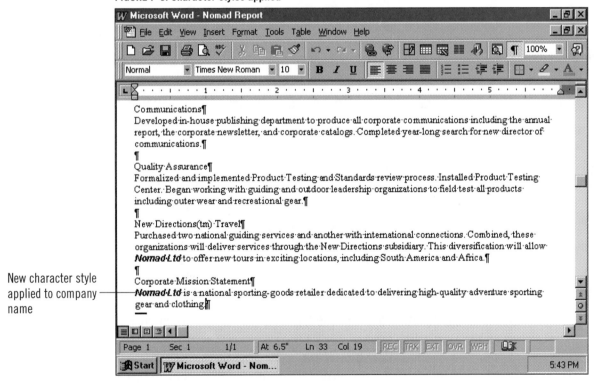

Applying styles when creating them

When you create a style based on selected text, it is important to click Apply in the Style dialog box. By clicking Apply, you apply the style name to the text, so that this text is also updated if you later decide to change characteristics of the style.

Using AutoFormat and the Style Gallery

With the AutoFormat feature, Word makes a number of changes, described in Table F-1, that improve the appearance of a document. In addition, certain paragraph styles found in the default template, Normal, are applied automatically. A **paragraph style** is similar to a character style, except that it contains format settings you can apply to paragraphs, rather than to selected words. Once styles are established in a document, you can use the Style Gallery to format your document in styles from the different templates provided. A **template** is a special document containing styles and other options you want to use in specific kinds of documents. Angela wants to add attractive formatting and paragraph styles to the summary document.

1. **Press [Ctrl][Home], click Format on the menu bar, then click AutoFormat**
   The AutoFormat dialog box opens. This dialog box offers the option of accepting or rejecting changes after the document has been formatted (you won't use that option now) or of formatting the document without first reviewing each change. This default option is a fast way to format a document.

2. **Select the Auto Format now option button, if necessary, then click OK**
   AutoFormat enhances the appearance of the document, as shown in Figure F-4. Styles are applied throughout the document. To give the document a more professional look, choose a template from the Style Gallery.

3. **Click Format on the menu bar, then click Style Gallery**
   The Style Gallery dialog box opens. In this dialog box, you can choose from the list of templates and preview your document with styles from the selected template. Select a professional template and preview the document.

4. **In the Template list box, scroll down, then click Professional Memo**
   The Preview of box displays the document in styles from the Professional Memo template.

5. **Click OK**
   Word applies the styles defined in the template as shown in Figure F-5. To see which style was applied to the headings, place the insertion point in a heading.

6. **Place the insertion point in the heading Balancing the Books**
   Notice the style name that appears in the Style list box on the Formatting toolbar indicates that the Heading 1 style is applied to this paragraph. Because of its location under the large bold title, the text "Milestones" was not correctly analyzed as a heading during the AutoFormat process. You can format it with the same style as the other headings by applying the Heading 1 style.

7. **Place the insertion point in the heading Milestones, then click the Style list arrow on the Formatting toolbar**
   The Style list box now displays the styles available in the Professional Memo template. Notice that the style names are displayed with the style's formatting characteristics.

8. **Scroll the Style list box, then click Heading 1 (the first style displayed in the Style list)**
   Compare your document to Figure F-6.

9. **Click the Save button 🖫 on the Standard toolbar**

Trouble?
Do not be concerned if this step takes a few minutes.

FIGURE F-4: Document formatted with AutoFormat

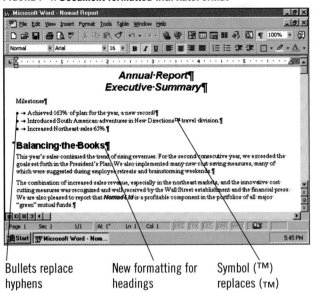

Bullets replace   New formatting for   Symbol (™)
hyphens   headings   replaces (TM)

FIGURE F-5: Reformatted document with PROFESSIONAL MEMO styles

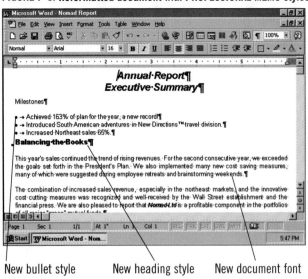

New bullet style   New heading style   New document font

FIGURE F-6: Updated style

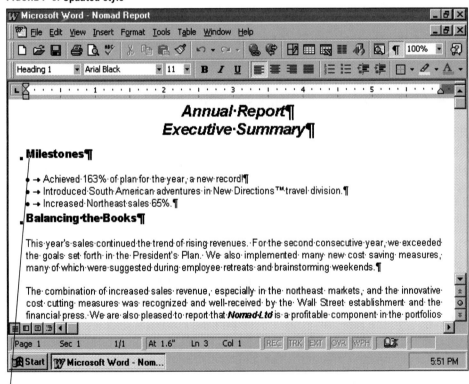

Updated Heading 1 style

TABLE F-1: Changes made by AutoFormat

change	description
Applies styles	Applies paragraph styles to all paragraphs in a document, including headings, lists, body text, salutations, addresses, etc.
Adjusts spacing	Adds and removes extra paragraph marks as needed and replaces spaces and tabs with proper indentation
Replaces symbols and characters	Replaces hyphens and other symbols used to denote a list with bullets and replaces fractions entered as "1/2" with ½ symbol and inserts the trademark, registered trademark, and copyright symbols where indicated

Modifying Styles

When you use styles to format text, you can change format settings quickly and consistently for every occurrence of the style in the document. Modifying a style changes the appearance of all text formatted in that style. You save time and make fewer mistakes because you don't need to search for each occurrence of text that has formatting you want to change. The fastest way to modify a style is to change the formatting in a selected example and reapply the style. ◀ After reviewing the style of the Milestones heading, Angela decides to change the style of the font to small caps. After modifying the font style for the first heading, she'll update the Heading 1 style to change all the text formatted with this style.

1. Select the Milestones heading

2. Click Format on the menu bar, then click Font
   The Font dialog box opens. To make the heading text more distinctive, use the font effect called "small caps".

3. Click the Small caps checkbox

4. Click the Shadow checkbox, then click OK
   Now that you have adjusted the font formatting, you decide to increase the spacing before each heading.

5. Click Format on the menu bar, then click Paragraph

6. On the Indents and Spacing tab, click the Spacing before up arrow once to 6 pts, then click OK
   The space before this paragraph is increased. Now that this heading contains the formatting you want, modify the Heading 1 style, based on the modified "Milestones" heading, to format all the headings in the document in the same way. After changing the formatting, you can update a style by reapplying it to the same text.

7. Click the Style list arrow on the Formatting toolbar, then click Heading 1
   The Modify Style dialog box opens, as shown in Figure F-7. You can either update the style based on the selected text, or reformat the selected text with the original attributes of the style. In this case, modify the style based on the currently selected text.

8. Click OK to update the Heading 1 style based on the currently selected text
   All text formatted with the Heading 1 style now appears in small caps and is shadowed throughout the document. Deselect the text and compare your document to Figure F-8.

9. Click the Save button 🖫 on the Standard toolbar

QuickTip

A fast way to apply a built-in heading style is to press [Alt][Ctrl] and the corresponding heading level. For example, to apply a Heading 1 style, press [Alt][Ctrl][1]. To apply a Heading 2 style, press [Alt][Ctrl][2], and so on.

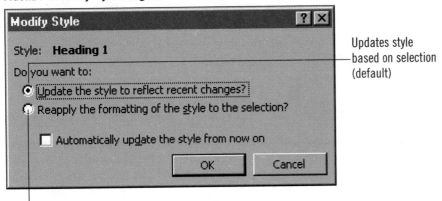

FIGURE F-7: Modify Style dialog box

Updates style
based on selection
(default)

Reapplies previous
style to selection

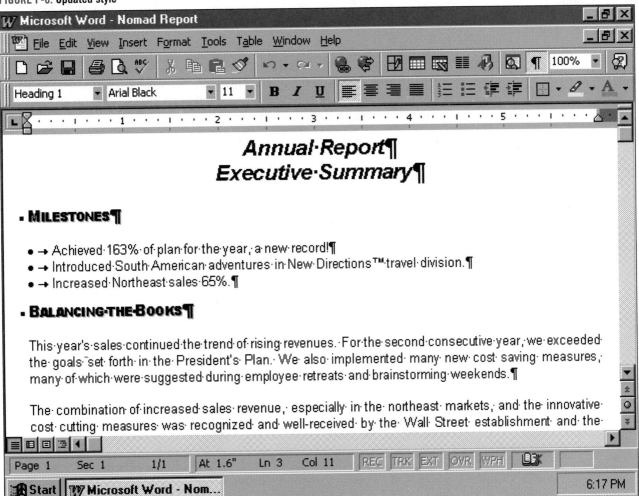

FIGURE F-8: Updated style

Creating and Applying New Paragraph Styles

You are not limited to using the paragraph styles provided by Word templates. In the same way you created a character style earlier in this unit, you can create your own customized paragraph styles. You can create a new style based on an example of selected text or you can specify the paragraph formatting you want in the Style dialog box. You can even assign a keyboard short-cut to a style.  Angela would like to create a style to format the title of the Executive Summary so that it is distinctive.

QuickTip

You can quickly apply a style by pressing [Ctrl][Shift][S] to select the Style list on the Formatting toolbar. Type the name of the style in the Style list, then press [Enter].

1. **Select the first line of the document, click Format on the menu bar, then click Style**
   With the Style dialog box open, you are ready to create a new style.

2. **Click New, and in the Style Name box type NewTitle**
   The name "NewTitle" is the name of the new style. Next, identify that you want to create a paragraph style.

3. **Click the Style Type arrow and select Paragraph, if it is not already selected**
   To use a border as part of the NewTitle style, you need to specify additional format charac-teristics next.

4. **Click Format, then click Border on the list**
   The Borders and Shading dialog box appears. This is the same dialog box that appears when you select the Borders and Shading command on the Format menu. In this dialog box you can specify the settings that will be applied as part of the new style you are creating.

5. **From the Style list, click the double line, click the Width list arrow, click 3 pt, then click the Box border style in the Setting area on the left side of the dialog box, if it is not already selected**
   A preview of the border appears in the Preview area.

6. **Click OK until you return to the Style dialog box, then click Apply**
   The first line of the title appears with a border around it. Now, you can apply the NewTitle style to the next line of the title.

7. **Place the insertion point in the next line, click the Style arrow on the Formatting tool-bar and click NewTitle**
   The next line of the title appears in the NewTitle style, as shown in Figure F-9.

8. **Click the Save button 🖫 on the Standard toolbar**

FIGURE F-9: New style in document

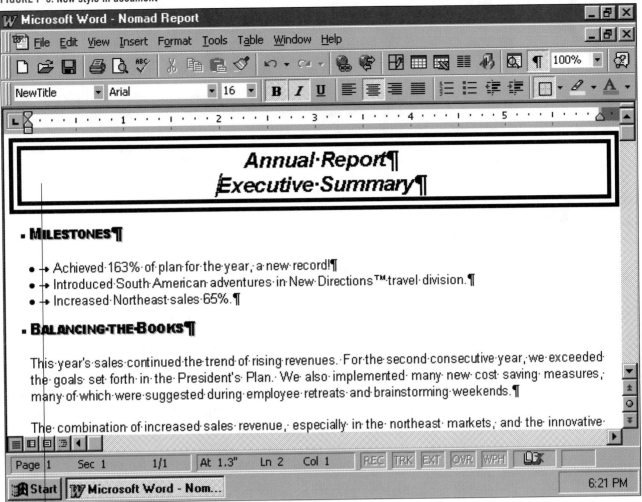

Title in new style

Assigning keyboard shortcuts to styles

To apply styles even faster, you can assign a keyboard shortcut to a style. In the Style dialog box you choose the style to which you want to assign a keyboard shortcut. Then click the Modify button. Then click the Shortcut key button. Press the combination of keys you want to use as a shortcut and click Assign. Take care not to assign a keyboard shortcut that has already been assigned to another command. If you share a computer with others, click the Save Changes in arrow and select the document you are currently editing.

Displaying Style Names in a Document

When formatting with styles it is often useful to see the name of the style applied to a paragraph. In the document's normal view, you can display the style names in the Style area at the left side of the window. You can also modify a style by double-clicking the style name in the Style area. These style names do not appear in the printed document, but you do have the option to print a separate document describing all the styles that are used. ✒ Angela would like to see the names of all the paragraph styles she is using in her document.

Steps

1. Click Tools on the menu bar, click Options, then click the View tab
The View tab appears foremost in the dialog box, as shown in Figure F-10. On this tab, you can specify the width of the Style area in the document window.

2. Click the Style area width up arrow until you see 1", then click OK
When you return to the document window, you see the names of the styles at the left edge of the window, as shown in Figure F-11. So that the Style area takes no more space than necessary, adjust the width of it.

3. Position the pointer over the vertical line that separates the Style area from the rest of the document, and when the pointer changes to ↔, drag the line so that the Style area is no wider than the longest style name
Depending on your computer system, you might need to increase or decrease the Style area. Next, make one last change to the Body Text style.

4. Scroll (if necessary) to a paragraph formatted in the Body Text style and double-click the style name in the Style area
The paragraph that is formatted in Body Text style is selected. The Style dialog box opens, so you can now modify the style.

5. Click Modify, click Format, then click Paragraph from the list
In the Paragraph dialog box, decrease the spacing after each body paragraph.

6. In the Spacing After box, click the down arrow once, changing the spacing to 6 pt, then click OK until you return to the Style dialog box
Continue by applying these changes.

7. Click Apply, then deselect the text
Clicking Apply closes the dialog box and updates the style throughout the document. Because you no longer need the Style area displayed, you can hide it.

8. Position the pointer over the vertical line that separates the Style area from the rest of the document, and when the pointer changes to ↔, drag to the left until the Style area disappears
Compare your document to Figure F-12. You have completed modifying your document for now, so you can save it.

9. Click the Save button 💾 on the Standard toolbar

FIGURE F-10: View tab in Options dialog box

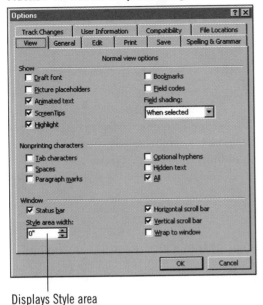

Displays Style area
in specified width

FIGURE F-11: Style area in document

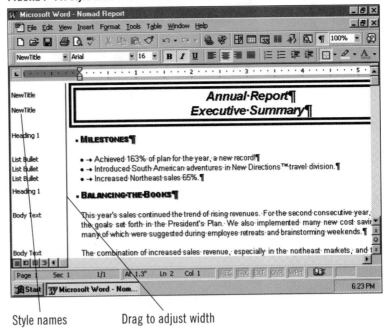

Style names   Drag to adjust width

FIGURE F-12: Completed document

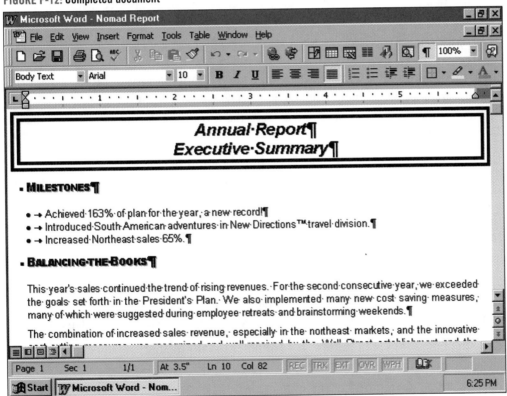

Printing styles

You can get a hard copy document that contains a description of the formatting used in each of the styles in a document. When you print a document using the Print command, click the Print What arrow in the Print dialog box, then choose Styles from the list. This feature prints a list of styles and a description of each one. Use this feature when you want to keep track of the styles in your document.

Moving Around with Styles

Styles can also play a valuable role as you move around in a longer document, because you can use styles to move to different parts of a document. For example, you can scroll through a document by "paging" through its headings. You can also use the Document Map to display headings on the left half of the window and the document text on the right half. By clicking a heading on the left, you can move the insertion point to the heading on the right. ✐ Angela wants to review each of the headings in the document, so will take advantage of the styles in the document to move to the locations she wants.

Steps 1 2 3 4

1. **Press [Ctrl] [Home] to place the insertion point at the beginning of the document**

2. **Click the Select Browse Object button ⊙ at the bottom of the vertical scroll bar**
   This button displays a menu of items you can use to scroll through a document, as shown in Figure F-13. You want to scroll through the headings.

3. **Click the Browse by Heading button ☰**
   The insertion point moves to the first heading in the document. Notice that the Previous and Next Page buttons in the scroll bar change color. The color indicates that clicking these buttons will move the insertion point from item to item, not from page to page as they normally do.

4. **Click the Next Heading button ⬇ and Previous Heading button ⬆ to move from heading to heading in the document, and back to the start of the document**
   To view all the headings at once and still see the text of the document, you can use the Document Map feature.

5. **Click the Document Map button 🔍 on the Standard toolbar**
   The window splits into two parts. On the left side you see the headings in the document. On the right side is the document text, as shown in Figure F-14.

6. **On the left side of the window, click the last heading in the document, Corporate Mission Statement**
   The insertion point moves to that heading on the right side of the window. You can now edit the text in this heading.

7. **Select the text Mission Statement and type Vision**
   Notice that the heading on the left is also updated. Turn off the Document Map feature.

8. **Click the Document Map button 🔍 on the Standard toolbar**
   Compare your document to Figure F-15.

9. **Click the Save button 💾 on the Standard toolbar**

FIGURE F-13: Search Items box

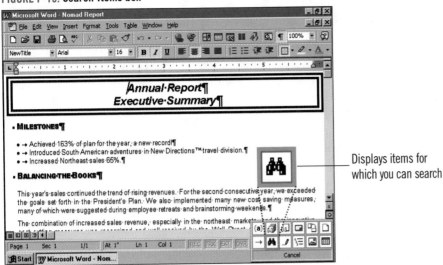

Displays items for which you can search

FIGURE F-14: Document Map

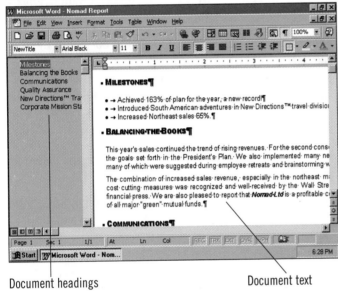

Document headings

Document text

FIGURE F-15: Completed document

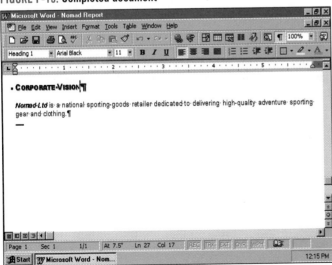

Replacing Styles

The same way you search for and replace text and formatting in a document, you can use the Replace command to locate and replace each instance of a style. For example, suppose you decide to change all instances of the Heading 3 style with the Heading 2 style. With the Replace command you can instruct Word to search for text formatted in the Heading 3 style and format it in the Heading 2 style instead. ◤━━ Angela wants to align the body text in her document with the text (after the bullets) in the bulleted list at the start of the document. Because there is a Body Text Indent style available, she will use the Replace command to substitute this style for the current Body Text style throughout the document.

Steps 1234

1. Press **[Ctrl][Home]** to place the insertion point at the start of the document

2. Click **Edit** on the menu bar, click **Replace**, then click **More** to extend the dialog box if all the options are not displayed

The Find and Replace dialog box opens. You can specify the formatting you want to replace by clicking the Format button.

3. With the insertion point in the Find What box, click **Format** near the bottom of the dialog box, then click **Style** from the list

The Find Style dialog box opens, as shown in Figure F-16. From this dialog box you can select the style for which you want to search. Select the current style applied to the body text in your document.

4. Click **Body Text**, then click **OK**

The Format area below the Find What box indicates that you are searching for the Body Text style. Next, you can specify the style you want to use instead.

5. With the insertion point in the Replace With box, click **Format**, then click **Style** from the list

You can select a new body text style.

6. Click **Body Text Indent**, then click **OK**

The Format area below the Replace With box indicates that the text should be formatted in the Body Text Indent style, as shown in Figure F-17. You are now ready to replace the styles.

7. Click **Replace All**

A message indicates the number of changes made.

8. Click **OK** to return to the dialog box, then click **Close**

Compare your document to Figure F-18. Then save your changes and close the document.

9. Click the **Save button** 💾 on the Standard toolbar, then close the document

FIGURE F-16: Find Style dialog box

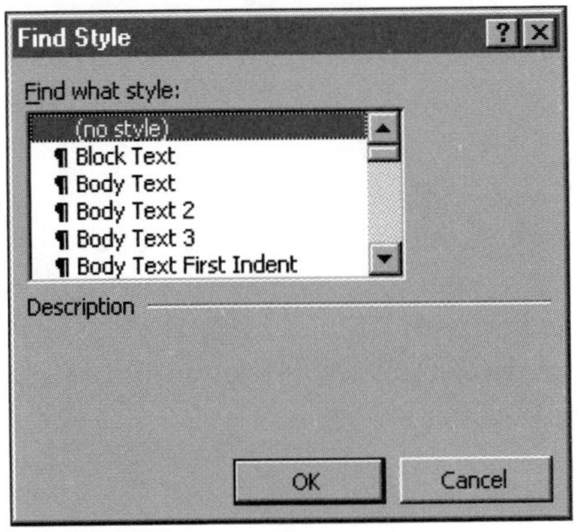

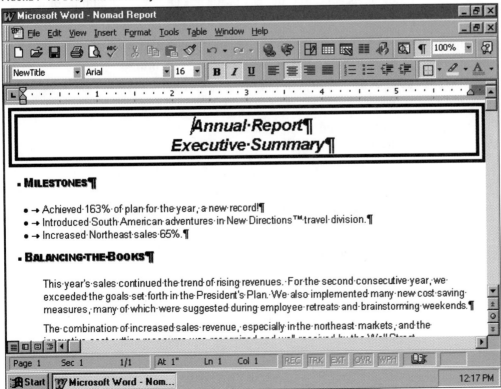

FIGURE F-17: Find and Replace dialog box

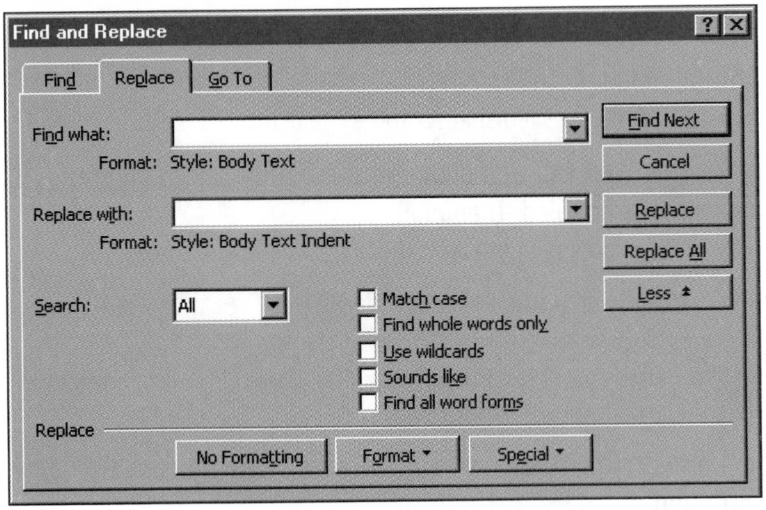

FIGURE F-18: Body Text Indent style in document

Formatting as You Type

Formatting a new document in Word can be as easy as typing. When you type certain combinations of text and formatting, Word formats the text as you type. For example, when you type a hyphen and then press the [Tab] key, Word formats the line with a bullet. ✒ The next document Angela would like to create is a draft document describing a new promotion. As she types the document, Word applies the appropriate formatting.

Steps 1234

1. Click the **New button** 🗋 on the Standard toolbar

2. Click **Tools** on the menu bar, click **AutoCorrect**
   In this case, verify the options for the AutoFormat As You Type feature.

3. Click the **AutoFormat As You Type tab** and compare the dialog box to Figure F-19, clicking any options not already enabled, then click **OK**
   The dialog box closes, and you are now ready to type the text of your document.

4. Type **Announcing new discount pricing for our "favorite" retailers** and press **[Enter]** twice
   When you press [Enter] twice after entering a line of text (that does not end in a punctuation mark), Word formats the line in the Heading 1 style.

5. Type **o** (a lowercase "o"), press **[Tab]**, then type **Sell at least 1/2 of your quota in the 1st week of each month** and press **[Enter]**
   Notice that as you type, the fraction "1/2" changes to a fraction symbol "½," the text "1st" changes to "1ˢᵗ" and bullets appear at the start of the line and at the beginning of the new line. Continue typing the document.

6. Type the following two lines, pressing **[Enter]** at the end of each line:
   Sell at least 3/4 of your quota in the 2nd week of each month
   Sell at least 100% of your quota in the 3rd week of each month
   Next, add a blank line.

7. Press **[Enter]** again at the end of the last line
   Pressing [Enter] twice stops the AutoFormatting in a bulleted list.

8. Type **Your store needs to meet only two of the above milestones to qualify**
   Compare your document to Figure F-20. You have completed typing and formatting your document for now, so print and save your work and close the document.

Time To
✔ Save

9. Print the document, click **File** on the menu bar, click **Close**, then click **Yes** and save the file with the name **Promotion**, then exit Word

FIGURE F-19: AutoFormat As You Type tab

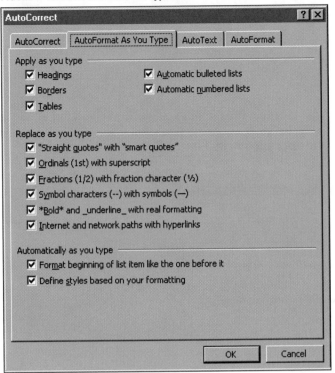

FIGURE F-20: Document formatted as you type

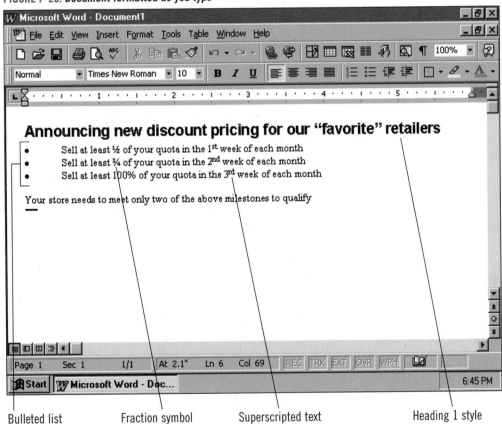

Practice

► Concepts Review

Label and describe each of the parts of the document shown in Figure F-21.

FIGURE F-21

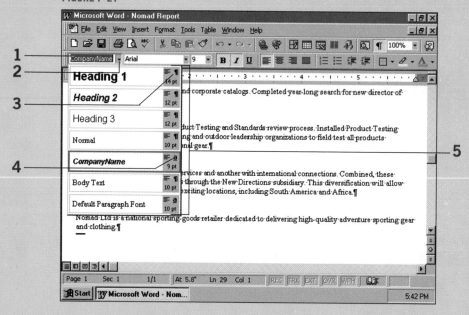

Match each of the following descriptions with the term that it describes best.

6. AutoFormat
7. Paragraph style
8. Templates
9. Style Gallery
10. Character style

a. A named set of paragraph format settings
b. Displays document in another set of styles
c. A named set of character format settings
d. Special documents containing styles and other options specific to different kinds of documents
e. Improves a document's appearance by applying styles and inserting symbols

Select the best answer from the list of choices.

11. Which of the following is true about replacing formatting in the Replace dialog box?
    a. You can click Replace All to review each occurrence of replaced formatting.
    b. To remove formatting from the search or replacement text, you click the Clear button.
    c. You can use buttons on the Formatting toolbar to select formatting options.
    d. You cannot use the Font or Paragraph dialog boxes to select formatting options.

12. To create a character style, you
    a. Type a name in the Style box on the Formatting toolbar and press [Enter].
    b. Click Format on the menu bar, then click Style.
    c. Click Format on the menu bar, then click Style Gallery.
    d. Select a style from the Style list on the Formatting toolbar.

13. **Which of the following is not a benefit of using styles?**
    a. Checks your document for proper grammar and word usage so it is appropriate for the kind of document you are creating
    b. Quickly applies format settings in one step
    c. Modifies style characteristics and reapply to all occurrences
    d. Previews a document in styles from other templates

14. **Which statement is not true about character styles?**
    a. You can create a character style using the Style dialog box.
    b. You can create a character style by using selected text as an example.
    c. Character styles affect the entire current paragraph.
    d. You can redefine a character style based on a selected example.

15. **Which statement best describes when to use styles in a document?**
    a. When text or paragraphs scattered throughout a document require similar and consistent formatting
    b. When text or paragraphs on the same page require the same format settings
    c. When text or paragraph formatting is not likely to change
    d. When text or paragraphs do not require many different format settings

16. **Which statement best describes the AutoFormat feature?**
    a. The AutoFormat command allows you to review changes before accepting them.
    b. AutoFormat corrects grammatical and spelling errors in a document.
    c. AutoFormat sorts items in a list for you.
    d. The AutoFormat command allows you to apply and reject formatting changes to improve the appearance of your document in one step.

17. **Which of the following changes is not made by AutoFormat?**
    a. Applies paragraph styles to all paragraphs in the document
    b. Adjusts spacing and inserts appropriate indentation
    c. Applies character styles to appropriate text
    d. Inserts appropriate symbols and characters

18. **Which of the following statements is NOT true about modifying styles?**
    a. You can modify a style based on the formatting in the current selection.
    b. You must open the Style dialog box and click the Modify button, and then open the dialog boxes for the type of formatting you want to use in the style.
    c. The Reapply Style dialog box gives you the option to redefine the style or apply original formatting.
    d. Redefining the style based on the current selection is the default option in the Reapply Style dialog box.

▶ Skills Review

1. **Format text with AutoFormat.**
    a. Start Word and open the document named WD F-2. Save the document as "Healthy Home".
    b. Click Format on the menu bar, then click AutoFormat to apply standard styles and formatting to your document.
    c. Click OK.
    d. Scroll through the document and review the changes.

2. **Use the Style Gallery.**
    a. Click Format on the menu bar, then click Style Gallery.
    b. Select different templates and examine your document as it would appear with these templates.
    c. Click Elegant Memo in the list of templates.
    d. Click OK.
    e. Save your changes.

3. Apply paragraph formatting and styles.

 a. With the insertion point in the first paragraph in the body of the document, click Paragraph on the Format menu. In the Line spacing list, select 1.5 Lines, then click OK.

 b. Select the Body Text style from the Style list box on the Formatting toolbar.

 c. Make sure the first option for updating the style is selected in the Modify Style dialog box, then click OK.

 d. In the first list in the document (near the top of page 3, depending on your monitor), select the first line (yoga).

 e. Click Paragraph on the Format menu. Change the Spacing After to 3 pt. Click OK to close the dialog box.

 f. With the same line still selected, click Bullets and Numbering on the Format menu. On the Bulleted tab, change the bullet style to a diamond. Click OK to return to the document.

4. Create and apply new styles.

 a. Select the text "EnviroTech" near the beginning of the second page. Change the formatting of the text by choosing Arial from the Font box and 9 pt from the Font Size box then click the Bold button.

 b. Click Format on the menu bar, then click Style. Click New. In the Name box, type "EnviroTech" and from the Style Type list choose Character. Then click OK and in the Style dialog box, click Apply.

 c. Apply the EnviroTech character style to each occurrence of the company name "EnviroTech".

 d. Select the heading "Introduction" and apply the Document Label style.

 e. With the heading still selected, click Format on the menu bar, click Paragraph, then apply 18 pts of spacing after.

 f. Click the Lines and Page Breaks tab, then click the Keep with next checkbox. Click OK.

 g. Reapply the Document Label style and update the style to reflect these changes in formatting.

 h. Deselect the heading.

5. Replace styles in a document.

 a. Click Edit on the menu bar, then click Replace. Click Format and then click Style.

 b. Choose Heading 1 from the list of styles, click OK.

 c. Click in the Replace with box, then click the Format button and then click Style.

 d. Choose Document Label from the list of styles, click OK.

 e. Click Replace All. There were two replacements made.

 f. Close the dialog box and save the document.

6. Display style names in the document.

 a. Click Tools on the menu bar, click Options, then click the View tab.

 b. Click the up arrow in the Style area width box until you see 1", then click OK.

 c. Position the pointer over the vertical line that separates the Style area from the rest of the document and, when the pointer changes shape, drag the line so that the Style area is no wider than the longest style name.

 d. Scroll (if necessary) to a paragraph formatted in the List Bullet style and double-click the style name.

 e. Click Modify, click Format, then click Paragraph from the list.

 f. On the Indents and Spacing tab, type "6" in the Spacing After box, to change the spacing to 6 pt, then click OK until you return to the Style dialog box.

 g. Click Apply.

 h. Position the pointer over the vertical line that separates the Style area from the rest of the document and, when the pointer changes shape, drag to the left until the Style area disappears.

 i. Preview then print your document.

 j. Save your changes.

7. Format text as you type.

 a. Click the New button on the Standard toolbar.

 b. Click Format on the menu bar, click AutoFormat, then click the Options button.

 c. Click the AutoFormat As You Type tab, clicking any options not already enabled, then click OK twice.

 d. Type "Customer Satisfaction Survey Results" and press [Enter] twice.

 e. Type at least six hyphens in a row and press [Enter] (this creates a line border).

f. Type o (an "o"), press [Tab], then type "More than 1/2 of catalog customers received their orders within the 1st week of placing their order" and press [Enter].

g. Type the following two lines, pressing [Enter] at the end of each line:
Just under 3/4 of retail customers returned to make 2nd and 3rd purchases
Over 1/2 of the customers surveyed expressed positive comments regarding their 1st purchase experience

h. Press [Enter] again at the end of the last line.

i. Type "These survey results mean that while generally positive, we must continue to pursue even higher customer satisfaction results. Let's all strive to ship orders within the 1st week for 1/2 of our customers, and increase positive purchase experiences to at least 3/4 of the customers."

j. Save your document as "Sales Promotion" and print it.

k. Close both documents, saving any changes.

l. Exit Word.

► Independent Challenges

1. As a member of the acquisitions team for an investment research company called Expansion Inc., you have been asked to improve the formatting of a summary analysis prepared by a colleague. Open the document named "WD F-3" and save it as "New Growth". Using Figure F-22 as a guide, apply the following formatting.

To complete this independent challenge:

1. Use the AutoFormat command to apply styles.
2. Use the Style Gallery to apply styles from the Professional Memo template.
3. Apply Heading 2 style to the six sub-headings "The Benefits of Growth", "Future Expansion", "Initial Expansion", etc.
4. Use the Replace command to format all occurrences of the name "World Travel Airlines" in bold italics.
5. Change the formatting for the Heading 1 style so that it appears with a bottom border and in 18 pts. Reapply and update the style.
6. Apply the Heading 2 style to the text "Cruise Lines Offer Opportunity for Growth" and the next two headings.
7. Preview, save, and print the document before closing it.

FIGURE F-22A

NewHorizons

Hurricane Hugo did more than damage property when it blew through the Caribbean and up the coast of the United States in 1989; it virtually devastated Caribbean tourism. Although more than 49 million tourists visited the region during the past several years, it has only been during the past year that regional services and accommodations have been restored to levels that will entice large numbers of tourists to return to the Caribbean. *World Travel Airlines*™ believes our company is uniquely positioned to capitalize on this expanding service area.

Benefits of Growth
World Travel Airlines for over 50 years has been a leader in the charter vacation travel industry. Our dedicated award-winning staff has achieved this leadership role. But they could not achieve this excellence if it wasn't for the management's commitment to embrace the future by staying abreast of vacation travel trends. Excellence is not achieved without a commitment to improve.

Expanding into the Caribbean

Capitalizing on the resurgence of the Caribbean as a vacation destination, *World Travel Airlines* can increase market share and offer our customers quality destinations at affordable prices. Key to our goal's success are the Keys, and to a lesser degree, Miami. By extending our routes from Key West and Miami, *World Travel Airlines* can venture into the Caribbean and near Atlantic easily.

Future Expansion
Expanded routes into Jamaica, the Cayman Islands, and the Bahamas could begin two years after the initial phase begins. Full service into these five island locations could be complete by 2002, pending board approval.

Initial Expansion
The initial expansion includes two new routes: San Juan, Puerto Rico, and St. Thomas in the Virgin Islands. By keeping the initial expansion to these two United States territories, *World Travel Airlines* avoids placing customers through customs.

Market Research

Our market research has shown that vacationers prefer to visit places they perceive as exotic while at the same time they choose destinations that ensure certain cultural "comfort zones." What makes these five locations particularly attractive for our potential customers, who will be predominately from the United States, is that English is widely spoken. In addition, the historical European influence on the cultures of these particular Caribbean locations makes them a comfortable choice for travelers, while the island location satisfies their desire for a "foreign" experience, romance, excitement, and sun.

World Travel Airlines market research also indicates that the "niche" vacation market is growing at exponential rates. The Caribbean is an area of wide ecological diversity and beauty. Form lush rain forests to mountains that will challenge any trekker, the markets we seek to develop offer enormous opportunity for travelers seeking educational or offbeat vacations. *World Travel Airlines* is working with government-sponsored agencies, such as the Institute of Puerto Rican Culture and with major area universities, to explore the promise of this peripheral vacation market.

FIGURE F-22B

Logistics

Cruise Lines Offer Opportunity for Growth
Arrangements are pending from major cruise lines to use *World Travel Airlines* as their official carrier to bring passengers to eastern and southern Caribbean ports for cruises that stop along South America and Trinidad and Tobago. Our commitment to expand coverage into the Caribbean could bring stand-alone passengers as well as residual passengers from agreements with cruise lines. *World Travel Airlines* is considering offering joint cruise package deals with Queen Cruises. Many of Queen's customers live in Chicago and the Midwest. Chicago is one of *World Travel Airlines'* regional hubs. An agreement with Queen is expected soon.

Aircraft
Existing aircraft could make most of these ports of call within two hours. Shorter flights, such as to New Providence in the Bahamas, could use Boeing 727 or 737 aircraft, which require fewer staff and less fuel.

Launching from Miami/Key West
Projections show our passengers could double to the Key West and Miami markets, with those cities being our launchpad into the Caribbean. The Miami Board of Tourism and the Keys Regional Commerce and Growth Association will waive certain fees and taxes for a two-year period.

Strategic Alliances

Tourism is the largest source of revenue for most countries and territories in the Caribbean region. It is the third largest source of revenue for Puerto Rico and dominates the economy of the U.S. Virgin Islands. Jamaica, the Cayman Islands, and the Bahamas all rely on tourist dollars to drive their economies. As a result, these governments are willing to work with us in partnership as we seek ways to expand the region's tourism market. Moreover, they are eager to provide a business environment that is favorable for all parties involved.

Currently, peak travel to the Caribbean occurs during the winter, from December to March. In an effort to expand the tourist season, various cultural institutions in these five target locations are working in collaboration with *World Travel Airlines* marketing representatives to heighten awareness of the region's rich cultural heritage. For instance, the world-famous Casals Festival held every June in Puerto Rico is being used as a model to develop other cultural celebrations that will attract visitors.

Conclusions

Surveying the Caribbean, its cobalt-blue waters and breathtaking scenery encapsulate a fantastic vacation destination. *World Travel Airlines* hopes to capitalize on this ever-growing hot spot so close to the United States by offering flights directly to some of the best areas within the Caribbean.

Our commitment to this expanding vacation area is based on *World Travel Airlines'* well-researched projections of travel trends and airline capacity in the near Atlantic, and our close collaboration with various governments and tourism officials in each of the five island locations.

2. As an executive member of an organization dedicated to the improvement of media services called "Communication for the Future", you are in charge of planning the upcoming 1998 convention. While in town, many of your members will want the opportunity to explore the Boston area. You have contracted with a travel agency to prepare a visitor's guide. The travel agency has prepared a draft, and you have decided to make the document more attractive. Open document named WD F-4 and save it as "Tourist Info".

To complete this independent challenge:

1. Use the AutoFormat command to apply styles.
2. Change the formatting for the Heading 1 style so that the text is 18 pt and italics. Reapply and update the style.
3. Change the formatting for the Heading 2 style so that the text is 14 pt and 4 pts of spacing after. Reapply and update the style.
4. Change the List Bullet style so that it is formatted with the left indent of 0.50 inches, a hanging indent of 0.50 inches, and 2 pt spacing before and after. Reapply and update the style.
5. Create a character style called Highlight that is 9 pt, bold, Arial. When you create this style, assign a keyboard shortcut to the Highlight style, [Alt] + [Shift] + [H]. Apply this style (using the keyboard shortcut) to the first few words or phrase in each paragraph formatted in the List Bullet style. Be sure to save the shortcut in the document and not in the template.
6. Preview, save, and print the document before closing it.

3. As volunteer at your local health food co-op, you have signed up for producing a flyer that describes the co-op's features to new members. Using text already located on the co-op's Web site on the Internet, apply attractive formatting to improve the appearance of the document.

To complete this independent challenge:

1. Log on to the Internet and use your browser to find a Web page of a co-op in your area or of special interest to you. If you can't find one, go to http://www.course.com. From there, click Student Online Companions, click the link for this textbook, then click the Word link for Unit F. Click on one of the links provided, then copy all the text in the document that appears. Paste the contents of the clipboard into a new blank document. Save the document with the name Co-op Flyer.
2. First improve the appearance of the document using AutoFormat (in the AutoFormat dialog box, choose Letter as the document type), then apply the styles in the Contemporary Memo template in the Style Gallery.
3. Edit the list of items in the store's inventory so that each group of items appears on a separate line. Apply the List 2 style to the first list. Then change the Spacing after to 6 pts, click the Increase Indent button three times, apply bullets, then redefine the List 2 style. If your document does not have a list of products, format the second, third, and fourth paragraphs. Create a List Number style that is similar to the List 2 style, but formatted with numbers.
4. Apply the List Number style to another list in the document. Or apply it to the first list if your document has only one.
5. Apply text flow formatting so that the lines of the store's address are never separated by a page break. Then create a new paragraph style called StoreAddress based on this formatting. Apply the StoreAddress style to the list of the hours at the end of the document.
6. Delete any extra paragraph marks that were used for spacing between paragraphs, and spell check the document.
7. Preview, save, and print the document before closing it.

4. As the marketing director for a small adventure travel agency, Majica Tours, you would like to announce a new tour offering. Using the AutoFormat As You Type in Word, create an attractive document that describes the tour features. Use Figure F-23 as a guide to complete this independent challenge:

1. Create a new blank document and save it as Majica Sea Tours. On the AutoFormat As You Type tab in the AutoCorrect dialog box, verify that all check boxes are checked.
2. Type "Announcing Seabreeze Sailing Adventures" and then press [Enter] twice to create a heading formatted in the Heading 1 style.
3. Change the Heading 1 style so that the font size is 18pts, and the paragraph formatting is 10 pts before and 18 points after, and centered.

4. Type ">" followed by a tab and then type the text shown in Figure F-23. Press [Enter] after each line.
5. Press [Enter] twice to stop bulleted formatting.
6. Under the heading, type 5 hyphens and then press [Enter] to create a solid line.
7. Change the formatting of the text in the bulleted list, so that it is formatted in Arial, 14 pts and 1.5 Line Spacing. Create a new paragraph style based on this formatting, name it Arrow List, and apply it to the bulleted list.
8. At the end of the document, type another set of hyphens and then press [Enter].
9. Type "Majica SeaTours Offices:" and apply the modified Heading 1 style to this text. Press [Enter] to create a new line.
10. Type the names of three cities (each on a separate line) and apply the Arrow List style to the list.
11. Preview, save, and print the document before closing it.

FIGURE F-23

Announcing Seabreeze Sailing Adventures

➢ Small groups, 8-10 guests

➢ Low cost, only $599 complete

➢ Gourmet meals, crew includes a gourmet chef

➢ Expert crew, 5 members with over 50 years of guiding and

sailing experience

Majica SeaTours Offices:

➢ Lake of the Woods

➢ Big Mountain

➢ Lake Pacifica

▶ Visual Workshop

As conference coordinator for Creative Consultants, Inc.'s 1998 Creativity Conference, you are in charge of developing an attractive document that describes the conference seminars to interested participants. A draft document contains the text you want to include. Open the document WD F-5 and save it as "Conference Overview". Figure F-24 serves as a guide for what your completed document should look like. Begin by using AutoFormat to apply consistent styles to the document. Then use the Style Gallery to apply the styles contained in the Contemporary Memo template. Create and apply a character style named "Planners" to the text "Artistic Planners." Continue formatting the document using the features you have learned in previous units, such as borders and shading, modifying bullets, and paragraph alignment. Remember to modify and reapply styles to quickly and consistently make changes throughout the document.

FIGURE F-24

Artistic Planners'
Creativity Conference
1998

Welcome to *Artistic Planners'* 1998 Creativity Conference™! This year's conference combines traditional creativity enhancing techniques with new methods tested in a variety of human endeavors. Learn how to become a more creative individual no matter what your field or interests. Today's sessions will help you:

❖ Learn to use guided imagery to focus your creative energies.

❖ Apply creativity enhancing techniques in everyday problem solving.

❖ Learn how to find your creative "zone" and stay in the zone through to the completion of a project.

❖ Discover how massage and relaxation techniques can enhance creativity.

Guided Imagination
Learn new techniques for finding the images that guide you towards your goals. Not all images work in every situation, so in this session you learn how to clarify your objectives to select the appropriate images. *Artistic Planners'* presenters will provide structures for interweaving images are also identified for gaining heightened integration.

Creativity Every Day
Creativity is not just for the traditional "artists" or traditional "artistic" endeavors. Employing creative thinking and creative problem-solving can help us achieve success in everyday activities at work, at home, and even at play. In this session, learn how to think "outside of the lines" no matter what you do.

The "Zone"
Sometimes our creativity comes unbidden, and if we are fortunate enough to take the time and energy to act on it, we are satisfied. But what to do when you "have" to be creative and your muse has abandoned you? In this session, we explore writer's block (and similar disabilities) in an effort to understand and triumph over them. Learn how to call up hidden stores of creativity, even when you feel dull and uninspired.

Enlightened Massage
View demonstrations of deep breathing, massage, and creative visualization exercises. Learn how various relaxation techniques can enhance your creative abilities. An informal dinner and discussion (with *Artistic Planners'* panel of experts) is scheduled after this final session.

Merging
Word Documents

Objectives

► **Create a main document**
► **Create a data source**
► **Enter records in a data source**
► **Insert merge fields**
► **Work with merged documents**
► **Create a label main document**
► **Merge selected records**
► **Format labels**

Mail merge is widely used by companies who need to send similar documents to many individuals at once. The recipient's name and other personal information are often added to a document to create a more personal impression. The Word Mail Merge Helper guides you step-by-step through the **mail merge process**, which combines a standard document with customized information. ✐ Angela wants to respond to several customers' requests for information about upcoming alpine adventure tours. She'll use the Mail Merge Helper to create a form letter, enter names in a mailing list, and generate a mailing label for each envelope.

Creating a Main Document

In the mail merge process, the **main document** contains **boilerplate text**, basic text that is common to all the versions of the merged document. The Mail Merge command on the Tools menu makes it easy to create and edit each of the merge elements. Table G-1 defines the basic elements of the mail merge process. Be sure to view the CourseHelp "Understanding Mail Merge" before completing this lesson. ✎ Instead of retyping each letter to each customer, Angela will use the Mail Merge Helper to modify a standard cover letter and merge it with a mailing list of customers, creating a personalized letter for each customer. First, she'll open the document that contains the boilerplate text for the letter.

Steps 1234

CourseHelp

To view the CourseHelp for this lesson, click the Start button, point to Programs, point to CourseHelp, then click Microsoft Word 97 Illustrated. Choose the Understanding Mail Merge CourseHelp.

1. Start Word, open the student file **WD G-1**, then save it as **Response Letter Main**
This document contains the boilerplate text for the main document. First you will insert today's date.

2. With the insertion point at the beginning of the document, click **Insert** on the menu bar, then click **Date and Time**
The Date and Time dialog box opens.

3. Verify that the Update Automatically check box is cleared, click the fourth option in Available Formats list box, and then click **OK**
The current date appears in the format you specified. Clearing the Update Automatically check box ensures that the date will not be updated each time you save or print the document. Now you are ready to start the Mail Merge Helper.

4. Click **Tools** on the menu bar, then click **Mail Merge**
The Mail Merge Helper dialog box opens. Helpful instructions regarding the next step in the merge process appear at the top of the dialog box.

5. In the Main Document section, click **Create**, then click **Form Letters**
You will create a form letter using Letter Main as the main document, which is already open and is the active window.

6. Click **Active Window**
The merge type and main document name appear in the Main Document section of the Mail Merge Helper dialog box, as shown in Figure G-1.

TABLE G-1: Definition of mail merge elements

term	definition
Main document	The document containing the standard information that is the same for each merged document. It also contains the field names that represent the variable information to be inserted during the merge
Data source	The document containing the personalized information that varies for each merged document, such as name and address, payment due amount, appointment date and time, etc.
Data field	An attribute that describes an item or individual. A group of data fields that relate to a specific item is called a record
Merge field	The merge fields you insert in a mail merge main document instruct Word where to insert unique information from the selected data source. These fields appear with chevrons («») around the name
Record	The entire collection of fields related to an item or individual, contained in the data source
Header row	The field names, which appear in the first row of the data source
Boilerplate text	The text in the main document that is the same for each version of a merged document

FIGURE G-1: Mail Merge Helper dialog box

Watch this area for instructions

Click to create a main document

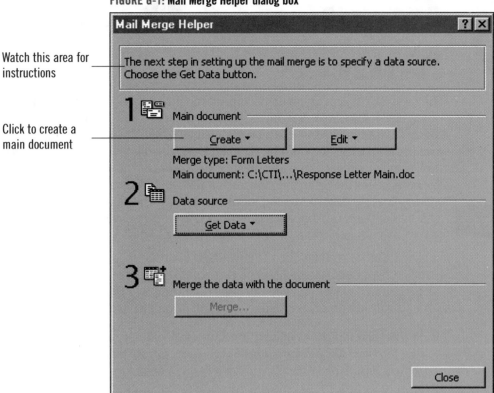

Viewing CourseHelp

The camera icon on the opposite page indicates there is a CourseHelp available for this lesson. CourseHelps are on-screen "movies" that bring difficult concepts to life, to help you understand the material in this book. Your instructor received a CourseHelp disk and should have installed it on the machine you are using. To start CourseHelp, click the Start button, point to Programs, point to CourseHelp, then click Microsoft Word 97 Illustrated. In the main CourseHelp window, click the topic that corresponds to this lesson. Because CourseHelp runs in a separate window, you can start and view a movie even if you're in the middle of completing a lesson. Once the movie is finished, you can click the Word program button on the taskbar and continue with the lesson, right where you left off.

Creating a Data Source

Once you have specified a main document, you are ready to create the **data source**, which will contain the information that differs in each version of the merged document. The **data source** consists of fields related to an item or individual. A **field** is a specific item of data (such as a first name or a zip code) for a product or individual. A group of data fields that relate to a specific item is called a **record**. You can create a new data source, or specify an existing source that already contains the fields and information you would like in your form letter. ▰▰▰▰ Angela will create a new data source and specify the fields it will contain—in this case, the names and addresses of the Nomad customers to whom she wants to send the letter.

Steps 1234

1. **Click Get Data, then click Create Data Source**
   The Create Data Source dialog box opens, as shown in Figure G-2. Several commonly used field names appear, and you can also create your own field names. First, you must remove any fields you don't need to use in the letter from the data source.

2. **In the Field names in header row box, click JobTitle, then click Remove Field Name**
   The JobTitle field is removed from the header row list and will not be included in the data source. Next, remove the other fields you don't need.

3. **Repeat Step 2 to remove the following field names: Company, Address2, Country, HomePhone, and WorkPhone**
   These fields are removed from the header row list. After removing or adding fields to the data source, you can close the Create Data Source dialog box.

4. **Click OK**
   The Save As dialog box opens. When you save your data source (which is a Word document) and give it a name, the data source becomes attached to the main document. Next, enter a name for the data source so that it is attached to the main document.

5. **Type Response Letter Data in the File name box, then click Save**
   Be sure to save the document in the same drive and folder as your other practice documents. After you click Save, the dialog box shown in Figure G-3 appears, indicating that there are currently no records in the data source. In the next lesson, you will add individual customer records to the data source.

Trouble?

If you accidentally remove a field name from the data source in the Create Data Source dialog box while the field name still appears in the Field name box, just click the Add Field Name button. If the Field name box shows a different name, type the name of the field you accidentally removed in the Field Name box, and then click the Add Field Name button.

Helpful information
and instructions

Type new field
name here

Click to add field
name specified in
Field name box

Click to remove a
selected field name

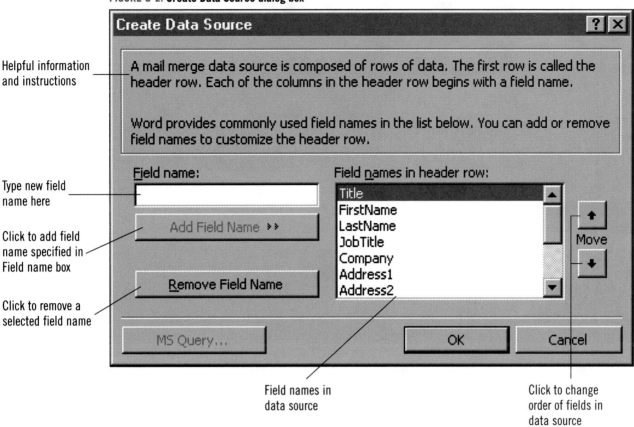

Field names in
data source

Click to change
order of fields in
data source

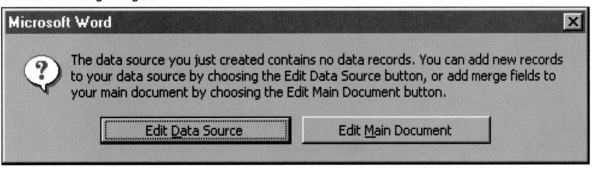

Entering Records in a Data Source

Once you have created the fields for your data source, you are ready to add records. **Records** contain the information related to each individual to whom you want to send a letter. The Data Form dialog box makes it easy to quickly add records to a data source. This dialog box shows a form that includes text boxes corresponding to the field names in the data source. You can also edit a data source directly from the main document. ⬦⬦⬦⬦ Angela needs to enter records that contain the names and addresses of the Nomad customers who have requested alpine expedition information.

Steps

1. Click **Edit Data Source** to add the new records
   The Data Form dialog box opens, as shown in Figure G-4.

2. Place the insertion point in the Title field if it's not already there, type **Ms.**, then press **[Tab]** or **[Enter]**
   The text "Ms." appears in the Title field and the insertion point moves to the FirstName field. Pressing [Tab] or [Enter] moves the insertion point to the next field. Pressing [Shift][Tab] returns the insertion point to the previous field. You are now ready to enter more records.

3. Enter the following for the fields in the first record:

Title	FirstName	LastName	Address1	City	State	PostalCode
Ms.	**Lilly**	**Thomas**	**346 Lake St.**	**Cooper**	**MN**	**55321**

   Remember to press [Tab] or [Enter] to move to the next field.

4. Click **OK**
   Clicking OK closes the Data Form dialog box. You can always return to this dialog box.

5. Click **Tools** on the menu bar, click **Mail Merge**, then click **Edit** in the Data Source area

6. Choose **Response Letter Data**
   When you click Edit then Response Letter Data in the Data Source area, the Data Form dialog box opens.

⬦ **Trouble?**

Take care not to press [Esc] or you will lose the record you are currently entering.

7. Click **Add New** to show the blank data form, then enter the following data records:

Title	FirstName	LastName	Address1	City	State	PostalCode
Mr.	**Joe**	**Blondel**	**843 2nd St.**	**Midtown**	**TX**	**75150**
Ms.	**Leslie**	**Rauh**	**56311 S. Main Rd.**	**Canton**	**IL**	**60072**
Mr.	**Max**	**Bruni**	**358 Park Lane**	**Northport**	**WA**	**98023**

   Remember to click Add New after completing the data forms for the second and third records. Pressing [Enter] at the end of each record will also show a blank data form.

8. Click **OK** after completing the data form for the last record, then click Save 🖫 on the Standard toolbar
   All records and changes to the data source are saved, and the dialog box closes. You return to the main document. Note that the Mail Merge toolbar appears in the document window, as shown in Figure G-5. This toolbar offers easy access to the commands you need when merging documents.

FIGURE G-4: **Data Form dialog box**

Fields in data source

Number of current record

Go to previous record

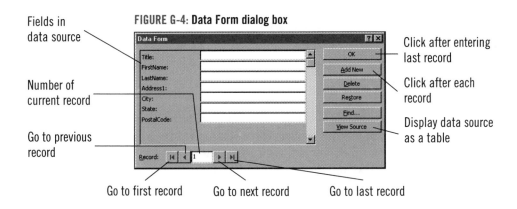

Click after entering last record

Click after each record

Display data source as a table

Go to first record   Go to next record   Go to last record

FIGURE G-5: **Mail Merge Toolbar**

Click to choose a field from attached data source

Choose fields to insert Word information

Click to return to Mail Merge Helper

FIGURE G-6: **Data records displayed in table format**

Click to return to main document

Edit Data Source button

Fields in header row

Data records

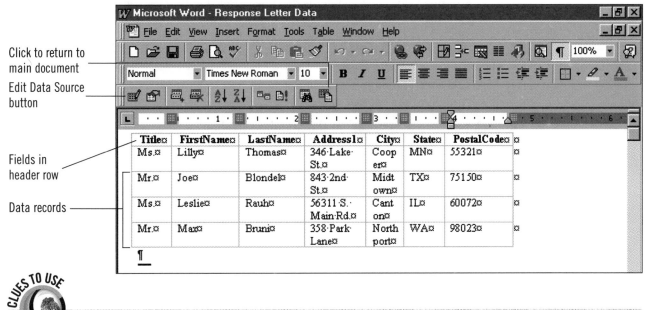

CLUES TO USE

Editing the data source

It is easy to make changes to your data source. The Edit Data Source button ✎ on the Mail Merge toolbar opens the Data Form dialog box, as shown in Figure G-4. Here you can click the View Source button to show the data records in table format, as shown in Figure G-6. Each field in the Data Form

dialog box corresponds to a cell in the header row of the table. You can click the Manage Fields button in this view to add new fields or delete those you no longer need. Click the Mail Merge Main Document button when you are ready to return to the main document.

Inserting Merge Fields

After specifying a data source, entering records, and returning to the main document, you see the Mail Merge toolbar. You can use this toolbar when you are ready to insert the field names from the data source into the main document. When you finish inserting fields, the main document will contain boilerplate text and the fields that indicate where variable information will be inserted during the merge. This is the last step before performing the actual merge. 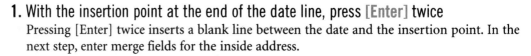 To merge her main document and the data source, Angela will insert the merge fields that make up the inside address and greeting of the letter to Nomad's customers.

1. **With the insertion point at the end of the date line, press [Enter] twice**
Pressing [Enter] twice inserts a blank line between the date and the insertion point. In the next step, enter merge fields for the inside address.

2. **Click Insert Merge Field on the Mail Merge toolbar, click Title in the list of fields, then press [Spacebar]**
The Title field is inserted in the document, surrounded by chevrons (« »). The chevrons distinguish merge fields from the rest of the text in the main document. The space separates the Title field from the next field you enter.

3. **Click Insert Merge Field, click FirstName, then press [Spacebar]**
The FirstName field is inserted in the document, followed by a space.

4. **Click Insert Merge Field, click LastName, then press [Enter]**
The LastName field is inserted in the document. Pressing [Enter] places the insertion point in a new blank line.

5. **Insert the remaining merge fields for the inside address and greeting, as shown in Figure G-7**
Be sure to insert proper punctuation, spacing, and blank paragraphs to format the inside address and greeting correctly.

6. **Click the Save button 🖫 on the Standard toolbar**

Go to previous record
Current record
Check main document for errors
Click to merge documents to another document
Click to merge documents to the printer
Merge options

FIGURE G-7: Main document with merge fields

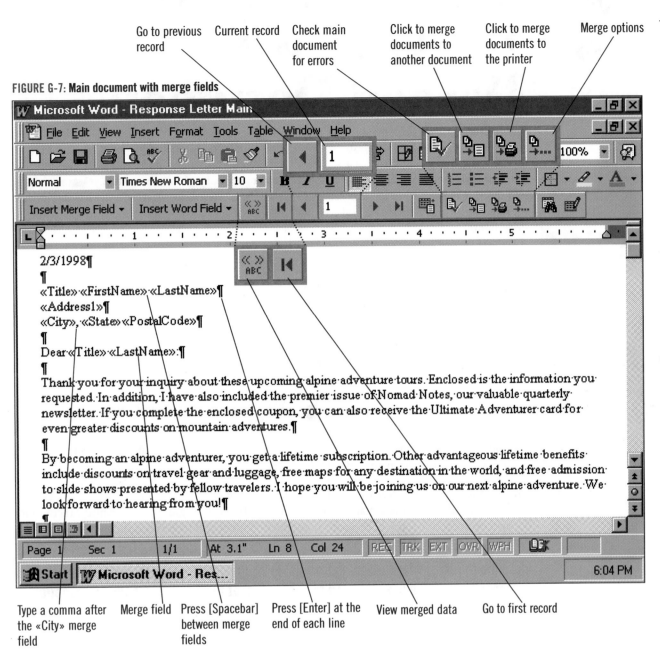

Type a comma after the «City» merge field
Merge field
Press [Spacebar] between merge fields
Press [Enter] at the end of each line
View merged data
Go to first record

Word 97

Working with Merged Documents

Performing the actual merge operation is as simple as clicking a button. You can merge all of your documents to a separate file or to a printer, or you can specify only certain records to merge. Even though merging to a separate file requires more disk space, you gain the ability to edit and review before printing. See Table G-2 for a summary of merge options. ✐ Angela will merge the Nomad letter to a separate file so she can view the merged documents in print preview, verify the page layout, and complete any necessary customization for individual merged documents.

1. Click the Merge To New Document button 🗐 on the Mail Merge toolbar
The main document and data source are merged to a new document called "Form Letters1". Each merged letter is separated with a section break, which you can see by scrolling through the document.

2. Click the Print Preview button 🔍 on the Standard toolbar
The document appears in print preview.

3. Click the Multiple Pages button 🖿 on the Print Preview toolbar, then drag to select four pages
You see all of the merged letters. In the Print Preview window, you can make last minute adjustments to customize a specific form letter.

4. Double-click in the body text in the second page
The second merged letter appears close-up, as shown in Figure G-8. Because Mr. Blondel will be attending a travel exposition at which Nomad will have a booth, customize the last sentence of the letter to this customer.

5. Click the Magnifier button 🔍 on the Print Preview toolbar, then edit the last sentence to read: We look forward to seeing you at the Adventures Plus Convention in Dallas!

6. Click File on the menu bar, then click Save
The Save As dialog box opens.

7. In the File name box, type Response Letter Merge, then click Save
The document containing all the merged letters (and the changes) is saved with the name Response Letter Merge. You can now print the letters.

8. Click the Print button 🖨 on the Print Preview toolbar, then click Close on the Print Preview toolbar after printing the documents
All the merged letters print on the printer connected to your computer. You can close all open documents.

9. Hold down [Shift] while you click File on the menu bar, then click Close All
Click Yes in response to any messages asking you to save your changes.

Text insert from
data source

FIGURE G-8: **Close-up of merged letter in print preview**

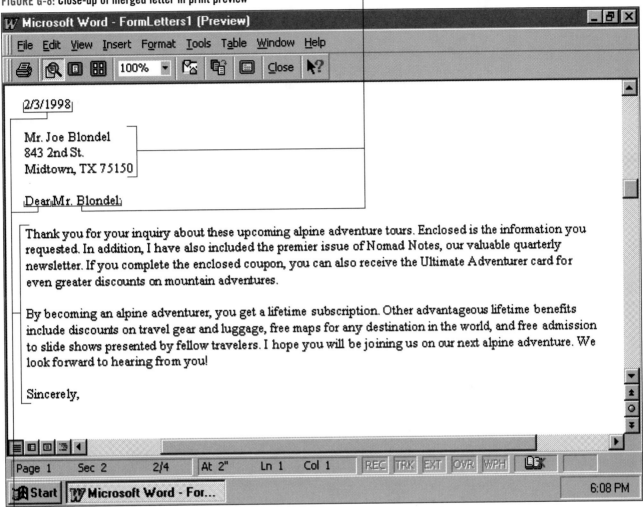

Boilerplate text

TABLE G-2: **Merge options**

click this button	or press	to
(button)	[Alt][Shift][N]	Merge the main document and all records of the data source to a new file
(button)	[Alt][Shift][M]	Send the merged main document and data source to the printer; does not create a new file
(button)		Specify a range of records to include in the merge; also shows the Query options dialog box

Creating a Label Main Document

Using the data source you created earlier in this unit, you can easily print envelopes or labels for mailing the letters. Simply specify a new main document, attach the existing data source, and select a setup format. You will learn about many standard formats that correspond to name brand business labels and envelopes, including index cards, postcards, name tags, and disk labels. You can also customize labels and envelope sizes. ◀━━ Angela will use a data source that her assistant has already created.

Steps 1 2 3 4

1. **Click the New button ▢ on the Standard toolbar to create a new document**

2. **Click Tools on the menu bar, then click Mail Merge**
   The Mail Merge Helper dialog box opens. Now create a new main document for the mailing labels.

3. **Click Create, click Mailing Labels, then click New Main Document**
   A temporary name for the main document appears in the Mail Merge Helper dialog box.

4. **Click Get Data, then click Open Data Source**
   The Open Data Source dialog box opens. You will use a data source that has already been created.

5. **Click WD G-2, then click Open**
   A message box appears, prompting you to finish setting up your main document.

6. **Click Set Up Main Document**
   The Label Options dialog box appears. In this dialog box, you need to select the appropriate type of label. The default brand name Avery standard appears in the Label Products box. You need to select the product number for the label.

7. **In the Product number box, scroll to and click 5161 - Address, then click OK**
   The Create Labels dialog box opens. Here, you can enter the field names for the labels.

8. **Click Insert Merge Field, click Title, press [Spacebar], then continue entering the remaining merge fields and appropriate punctuation, as shown in Figure G-9**
   Note that nonprinting characters (spaces and paragraph marks) are not visible in the Sample Label box.

9. **Click OK to return to the Mail Merge Helper dialog box, as shown in Figure G-10**
   In the next lesson, you will specify only selected records for the labels merge.

Read this area for instructions

Click to choose a field you want to insert

Insert a space after the merge field

Type a comma and space after the «City» merge field

Press [Enter] at the end of each line

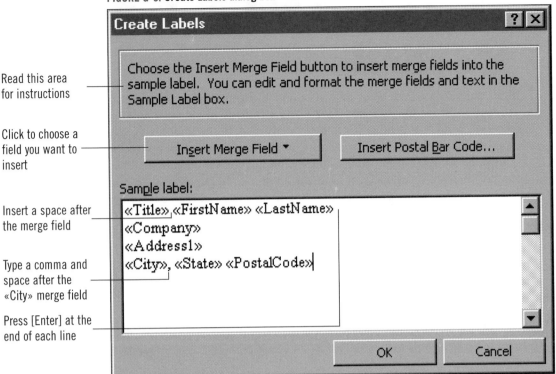

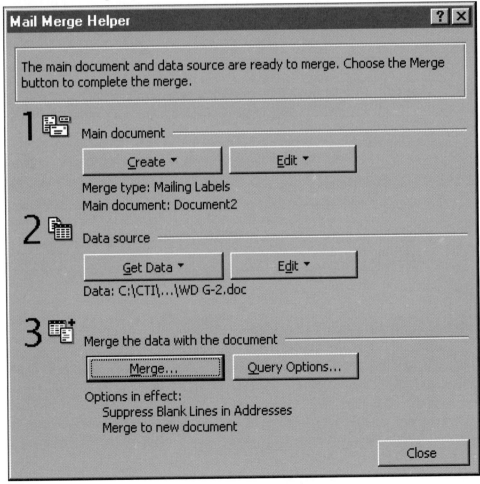

Word 97

Merging Selected Records

Sometimes you do not want to send a document to all the individuals in a data source. For example, you might want one group of individuals to receive one kind of document, and another group of individuals to receive another. With the Mail Merge Query Options feature, you can specify the criteria for choosing which records in a data source should be merged with a main document. When you use Query Options, you can identify the fields and their contents that each record must match to be included in the merge.  Angela is sending letters to Nomad customers in Massachusetts. She will only need labels for customers living in this state. In the Query Options dialog box, Angela puts MA in the state field to be included in this merge.

Steps

1. In the Mail Merge Helper click Merge

The Merge dialog box opens. In this dialog box, indicate that you want to use Query Options to select records to merge.

2. Click Query Options

The Query Options dialog box opens. In this dialog box, describe the criteria to use when selecting records to merge.

3. In the Field column, click the fields list arrow and scroll down to select State

This is the field you want to include when selecting records. Next, verify how the field should be evaluated.

4. In the Comparison column, be sure Equal to appears in the first box

This selection specifies that the contents of the State field in a record must exactly match the contents you will specify.

5. In the Compare to column, type MA

Your selection criterion appears in the column. Compare your dialog box to Figure G-11. You can specify additional selection criteria in the subsequent rows of the dialog box. You have completed specifying your selection criteria, so continue with the merge process.

6. Click OK

You return to the Merge dialog box, as shown in Figure G-12 so you can merge the records.

7. Click Merge

The selected records are merged to a new document. The labels are arranged in a Word table. Each label appears in separate cells that are divided by grey (non-printing) gridlines. Notice that only those customers with an address in Massachusetts are merged on the labels. You have finished merging documents for now. Compare the merged label document to Figure G-13. With the labels in a Word table, you can quickly format the labels so they are easier to read.

CLUES TO USE

Using multiple selection criteria

When you specify selection criteria for the data records to include in a merge, you are not limited to specifying a single field's contents. In fact, you can specify up to six criteria in the Query Options dialog box. After entering criteria in the first line of the dialog box, you click the operator arrow at the start of the next line. When you click the arrow, you can choose the And operator or the Or operator. Choose the And operator to identify additional required criteria that a record must match so that it is included in the merge. Choose the Or operator to identify additional optional criteria that a record can contain so that it is included in the merge.

FIGURE G-11: **Query Options dialog box**

Specify contents or value

Specify fields

Specify conditions

Specify comparison

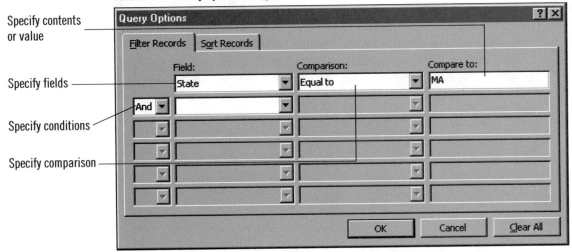

FIGURE G-12: **Merge dialog box**

FIGURE G-13: **Merged label document**

Merged records in label format

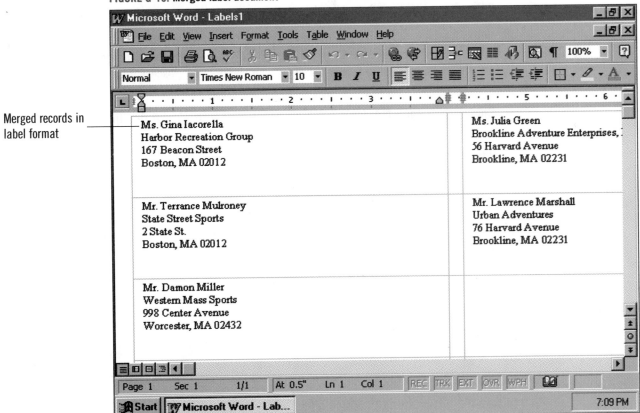

Formatting Labels

If you have merged your main document and data source to a new file (rather than to a printer), you can format the merged documents to make them more attractive before printing them. To make her labels easier to read, Angela will format the label. After editing the merged label document, she will print the labels using ordinary paper in her printer.

Steps 1 2 3 4

1. **Click Edit on the menu bar, then click Select All**
   This command selects all the text in the merged label document.

2. **Click the Font Size arrow on the Formatting toolbar, then click 14, and click the Bold button B on the Formatting toolbar**
   Increasing the font size makes the labels clearer and easier to read. To get an overall view of the page, preview the document before printing it.

3. **Deselect the text, then click the Print Preview button 🔍 on the Standard toolbar**

4. **Click on the document**
   Compare your document to Figure G-14.

5. **Click the Print button 🖨 on the Preview toolbar**
   Remember you can print from print preview. Next, close all open documents. To choose this command, press and hold down [Shift] (otherwise, the Close command will appear on the File menu instead of Close All).

6. **Hold down [Shift] while you click File, then click Close All**
   When you choose the Close All command, you are prompted to save changes to any open documents and to name any unnamed documents before you close each file. Be sure to carefully watch for the message box that indicates which document is currently being closed and saved.

7. **Click Yes in each message box that prompts you to save a document, save the files with the file names listed below, click No if you are asked to save any changes in the data source WD G-2, then Exit Word**

Save this file	With this content	With this filename
Labels merged document	the final merge product, labels with customer information	**MA Only Labels Merge**
Labels main document	the document with the merge fields	**Labels Main**

   The changes to each document are saved and all open documents are closed.

FIGURE G-14: Merged label document in print preview

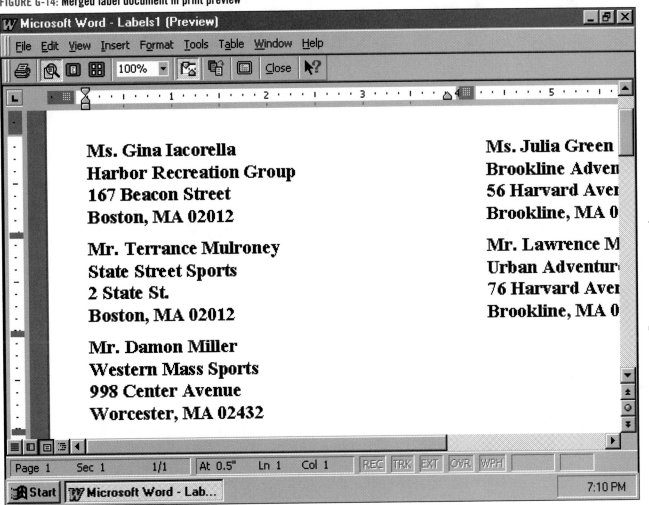

Practice

▶ Concepts Review

Label each part of Figure G-15

FIGURE G-15

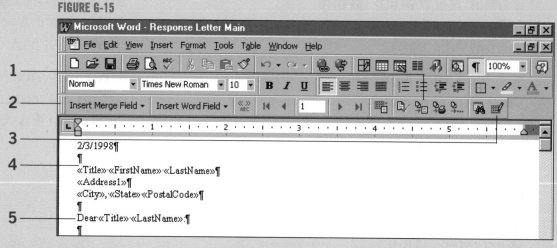

Match each of the following terms with the statement that best describes its function. Write the letter of the statement next to the appropriate term.

6. Data source
7. Data record
8. Boilerplate text
9. Main document
10. Field
11. View Source
12. Merge Field button
13. Mail Merge Helper
14. Data records

a. A piece of information specific to an item or individual
b. The entire collection of fields related to an item or individual
c. Contains the customized information that differs in each merged document
d. The text that is the same for each version of a merged document
e. Contains the common text for all versions of the merged document
f. Shows data records in table format
g. Are added to the data source in the Data Form dialog box
h. The Mail Merge command on the Tools menu shows this dialog box
i. Shows the list of fields to be entered in the main document

Select the best answer from the list of choices.

15. Which of the following is NOT a benefit of merging to a new file, rather than to a printer?
  a. You can format the merged documents to enhance their appearance.
  b. You can view the layout of merged documents in print preview.
  c. You save space on your hard disk.
  d. You can edit individual documents.

16. Which of the following statements best describes what you can accomplish when you show data records in table format?
  a. Add merge fields to the main document
  b. View one data record at a time
  c. Edit the merged document
  d. Add or delete fields from the data source

17. Which of the following tasks cannot be accomplished in the Query Options dialog box?

   a. Sort records by fields in ascending or descending order

   b. Save query specifications for future merge operations

   c. Select fields to be included in the data source

   d. Select records to be included in the merge operation

▶ Skills Review

1. Create a main document.

   a. Start Word, open the document named WD G-3, then save it as "Ideas Main".

   b. Select the text "[your name]" and replace it with your own name, then select the text "[Click here and type subject]" and replace it with "Ideas Wanted".

   c. Open the Mail Merge Helper dialog box using Tools, then Mail Merge, and choose the Form Letters option to create a form letter main document based on the memo document in the active window.

2. Create a data source.

   a. Click Get Data then click Create Data Source.

   b. In the Field Names in Header Row box, remove all the fields except FirstName, LastName, and JobTitle.

   c. In the Field Name box, type "Mailstation", click Add Field Name, then click OK.

   d. Type "Ideas Data" in the File name box, then click Save.

3. Enter records in a data source.

   a. Click Edit Data Source to add new records.

   b. Enter the following information in the appropriate fields to complete the data form for each of the recipients of this memo.

	FirstName	LastName	JobTitle	Mailstation
Record 1	Jules	Martinez	Marketing Manager	34
Record 2	Carl	Ortez	Customer Service Manager	18
Record 3	Sandy	Woodward	Vice President of Sales	48
Record 4	Elizabeth	Lewis	Charter Sales Division	45

   c. Click OK after completing the data form for the last record.

   d. Click the Save button on the Standard toolbar.

4. Insert merge fields.

   a. Place the insertion point after the tab character that follows the heading TO:.

   b. Click Insert Merge Field on the Mail Merge toolbar and click FirstName, then press [Spacebar].

   c. Click Insert Merge Field and click LastName. Then type a comma and press [Spacebar].

   d. Click Insert Merge Field and click JobTitle.

   e. Place the insertion point after the tab character that follows the Mailstation: heading.

   f. Click Insert Merge Field and click Mailstation.

   g. Click the Save button on the Standard toolbar.

5. Preview and edit merged documents.

   a. Click the Merge To New Document button on the Mail Merge toolbar.

   b. Click the Print Preview button on the Standard toolbar.

   c. Click the Multiple Pages button on the Print Preview toolbar, and select four pages.

   d. Click the magnifier pointer anywhere in the first page.

    e. Click the Magnifier button on the Print Preview toolbar.

    f. Select the last sentence of the letter and type "Please begin design for tour brochures". Close print preview, then print the first page.

    g. Click File on the menu bar, click Close then click Yes.

    h. In the File name box, type "Ideas Merge" and save the file.

    i. Press and hold [Shift], click File on the menu bar, click Close All, then click Yes to save all versions.

6. Create a label main document.

    a. Click the New button on the Standard toolbar, creating a new blank document.

    b. Click Tools on the menu bar, then click Mail Merge.

    c. Click Create, click Mailing Labels, then click Active Document Window.

    d. Click Get Data, then click Open Data Source.

    e. Click Ideas Data, then click Open.

    f. Click Set Up Main Document.

    g. In the Product Number box, click 5161-Address, then click OK.

    h. Click Insert Merge Field, click FirstName, press [Spacebar], insert the LastName field, then press [Enter].

    i. Click Insert Merge Field and click JobTitle. Press [Enter].

    j. Click Insert Merge Field and click Mailstation.

    k. Click OK to return to the Mail Merge Helper dialog box, then click Close.

    l. Save the document as "Ideas Labels Main".

7. Merge and format labels.

    a. Click the Merge to New Document button on the Mail Merge toolbar.

    b. Click Edit on the menu bar, then click Select All.

    c. Click the Font Size list arrow on the Formatting toolbar, then click 14.

    d. Click the Bold button on the Formatting toolbar.

    e. Preview the labels.

    f. Close Print Preview.

8. Merge selected records.

    a. Click Window on the menu bar, then click the Ideas Labels Main document.

    b. On the Mail Merge toolbar, click the Mail Merge Helper button to show the Mail Merge Helper dialog box.

    c. Click Query Options.

    d. In the Field column, click the arrow and scroll down to choose Mailstation.

    e. In the Comparison column, be sure "Equal to" appears in the first box, then in the Compare to column, type "45".

    f. In the next line, click the operator arrow and choose Or.

    g. In the Field column, click the fields list arrow and scroll down to choose Mailstation.

    h. In the Comparison column, be sure "Equal to" appears in the first box, then in the Compare to column, type "34", then click OK.

    i. Click Merge twice (be sure New Document is selected).

    j. Click Edit on the menu bar, then click Select All.

    k. Click the Font Size list arrow on the Formatting toolbar, then click 14. Click the Bold button on the Formatting toolbar.

    l. Hold down [Shift] while you click File, then click Close All.

   m. Click Yes and save your merged query label document with the name "Ideas Label Merge". You do not need to save the first merged document.

n. Click Yes to save changes to Ideas Label Main.

o. Click File on the menu bar, then click Exit.

► Independent Challenges

1. As an account representative for Lease For Less, a company that rents office equipment such as fax machines and large copiers, you previously drafted a letter describing the corporate discount program to a current customer. Open the document named WD G-4 and save it as "Discount Main" and save WD G-5 as "Discount Data", then close "Discount Data". Complete the following steps to edit a main document, attach an existing data source, and create and edit a merged document.

To complete this independent challenge:

1. Open the Mail Merge Helper and specify Discount Main as the form letter main document.

2. Attach the existing data source Discount Data to the main document.

3. Insert today's date at the top of the main document, adding a blank line after the date. Edit the signature block to show your name.

4. In the main document, replace the placeholder text enclosed in brackets with the merge fields in the data source.

5. Merge the documents to a new file named "Discount Merge".

6. Preview the documents. Add the following sentence to the end of the last letter, "P.S. I hope the above information has answered your questions about Lease For Less services. If you have any further questions, please contact me at 666-2345".

7. Print the merged documents. Compare the later letter to Figure G-16. Save any changes to all open files before closing them.

FIGURE G-16

March 15, 1998

Ms. Brittany Brinig
Independent School Dist. 667
200 Gervais Pkwy.
Plains, NY 54012

Dear Ms. Brinig:

Thank you for your inquiry about a corporate discount for our copier rentals. Enclosed is the information you requested. In addition, I have also included the premier issue of WorkADay, our exclusive management newsletter.

To be eligible for a corporate discount, you must contact to rent 2 or more of our fax or copier machines for at least six months. Of course all of our machines come with unlimited service by our highly trained technicians. As a corporate customer, you will receive a 20% discount on general office rentals and a 30% discount for our industrial copiers including color copy machines. As your account representative, I would be pleased to discuss your office requirements with you. I will call you to arrange a time when we can meet.

Sincerely,

[your name]
Lease for Less
Account Representative

P.S. I hope the above information has answered your questions about Lease for Less services. If you have any further questions, please contact me at 666-2345.

2. As an executive assistant, you are responsible for the distribution of your company's newsletter to consultants at various other companies. Your company has just purchased a new printer that can print address labels. Using the printer for labels will save time when distributing the newsletter. Newsletter recipients in New York City will receive their documents via a hand-delivered courier (who has already provided the required labels), while the remaining companies will receive their documents via U.S. Mail and will require printed labels. Use the Mail Merge Helper to create a label main document named "Newsletter Main". You can also choose to create envelopes instead of labels if your printer has this option.

To complete this independent challenge:

1. Open the document WD G-6 and save it with the name "Newsletter Data" and close the document.
2. Use the Mail Merge Helper to attach the existing data source Newsletter Data to the label document.
3. If you are using labels, use the Avery label 5161-Address. If you are merging to envelopes, use the default envelope style. Insert the merge fields in the main document and save it as "Newsletter Main".
4. Enter your own address in the Return Address area (if you are creating envelopes, not labels).
5. Add an additional record to the data source using any name and address you wish.
6. Use the Query Options feature to specify a selection criterion. Use the "Not Equal To" comparison operator in your selection criterion to select records that do not contain "New York City" in the City field.
7. Merge the label (or envelope) and data source to another document named "Newsletter Merge".
8. Print your labels(or envelopes), then save any changes to all open files before closing them.

3. You are the fundraising coordinator for Companies for Kids, a non-profit organization that collects money and materials for children housed in local shelters. In response to requests for information from potential corporate sponsors, you previously drafted a short letter describing the benefits of being a sponsor. Open the letter named WD G-7 and save it as "Children Main". Complete the following steps to edit a main document, and create a data source and a merged document.

To complete this independent challenge:

1. Open the Mail Merge Helper and specify "Children Main" as the form letter main document.
2. Insert today's date at the top of the main document, adding a blank line after the date. Edit the signature block to show your name.
3. Create a new data source with the following merge fields: Title, FirstName, LastName, Company, Address1, City, State, PostalCode. Save the data source with the name "Children Data".
4. Add at least three records to the Data Form dialog box using any contact names, company names, and addresses you wish.
5. In the main document, replace the placeholder text (enclosed in brackets) with the merge fields created in Children Data.
6. Merge the documents to a new file named "Children Merge".
7. Preview and print the merged documents.
8. Create and print labels (or envelopes) to send with the letters, you do not need to save the labels. Use any label type you wish. Save any changes to all open files before closing them.

4. As a recent college graduate, you have just begun your search for a position requiring a background in business administration. Complete the following steps to edit a main document, create a new data source, and create a merged document.

To complete this independent challenge:

1. Create a new document that is a generic letter of inquiry. Leave blanks (or some other indicator) for where variable information (such as names, addresses, company names, and area of companies' specialization) belongs. Use Figure G-17 as a guide for inserting variable information that will be provided by your data source. Save the letter as "Inquiry Main".
2. Open the Mail Merge Helper and specify "Inquiry Main" as the form letter main document.

3. Use your Web browser to search for financial or investment companies and note their names and mailing addresses. Create a data source using the names and addresses of at least five companies for whom you would like to work. Be sure to include a field for an area of specialization to which you would refer in your letter.

4. For an example of a good web source for locating companies, log on to the Internet and use your browser to go to http://www.course.com. From there, click Student Online Companions, click the link for this textbook, then click Word for unit G. Follow the link to the Business BigBook.

5. Save the new data source as "Inquiry Data".

6. Attach the data source to the main document.

7. In the main document, replace the placeholder text with the merge fields in the data source.

8. Merge the documents to a new file named "Inquiry Merge".

9. Perform a second merge, this time generate letters for only those companies in your home state (or some other state in which you might wish to live). Use the Query feature to specify the criteria. Save this second merged document as "Home State Inquiry Merge".

10. Print the merged documents. Save any changes to all files before closing them.

FIGURE G-17

Address fields

Name fields

Company name fields

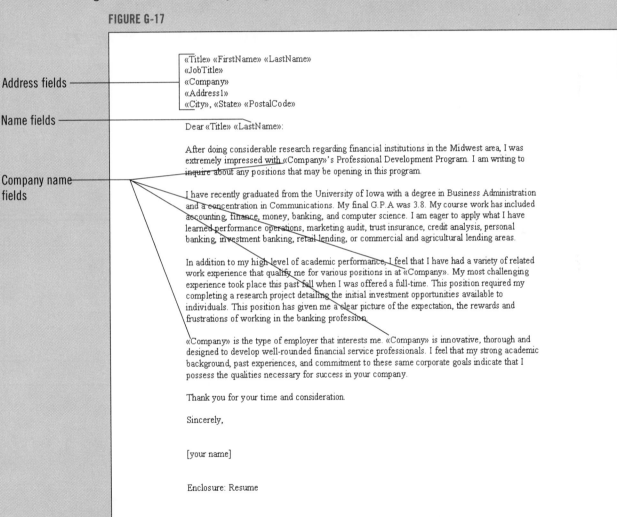

«Title» «FirstName» «LastName»
«JobTitle»
«Company»
«Address1»
«City», «State» «PostalCode»

Dear «Title» «LastName»:

After doing considerable research regarding financial institutions in the Midwest area, I was extremely impressed with «Company»'s Professional Development Program. I am writing to inquire about any positions that may be opening in this program.

I have recently graduated from the University of Iowa with a degree in Business Administration and a concentration in Communications. My final G.P.A was 3.8. My course work has included accounting, finance, money, banking, and computer science. I am eager to apply what I have learned performance operations, marketing audit, trust insurance, credit analysis, personal banking, investment banking, retail lending, or commercial and agricultural lending areas.

In addition to my high level of academic performance, I feel that I have had a variety of related work experience that qualify me for various positions in at «Company». My most challenging experience took place this past fall when I was offered a full-time. This position required my completing a research project detailing the initial investment opportunities available to individuals. This position has given me a clear picture of the expectation, the rewards and frustrations of working in the banking profession.

«Company» is the type of employer that interests me. «Company» is innovative, thorough and designed to develop well-rounded financial service professionals. I feel that my strong academic background, past experiences, and commitment to these same corporate goals indicate that I possess the qualities necessary for success in your company.

Thank you for your time and consideration.

Sincerely,

[your name]

Enclosure: Resume

▶ Visual Workshop

As the conference coordinator for the annual Texas Educators Convention, you are in charge of creating nametags for conference attendees. Using the Mail Merge feature in Word, create a mailing labels main document named "Conference Main". Then create a data source with the following merge fields: FirstName, LastName, Grade/Subject, and District. Save the data source with the name "Conference Data". Add at least four records in the Data Form dialog box. Using Figure G-18 as your guide, set up the main document by selecting the product 5095-Name Badge in the Label Options dialog box and inserting the merge fields in the Create Labels dialog box. Merge the labels to a new document named "Conference Labels". Use formatting to enhance the appearance of your nametags. Preview and print the labels on plain paper. Save any changes to all files, then exit Word.

FIGURE G-18

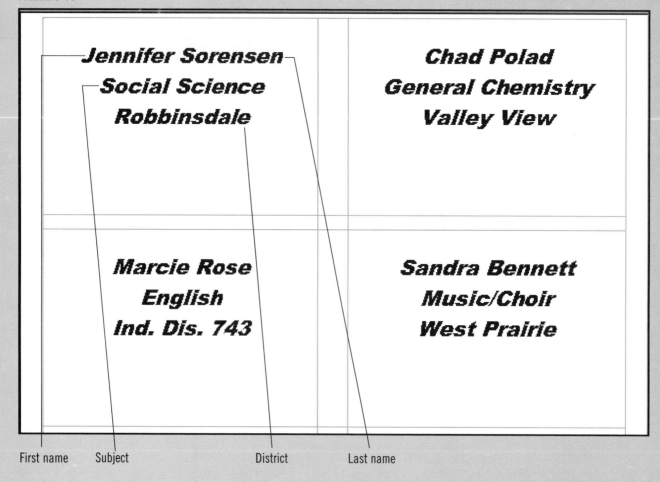

Working

with Graphics

Objectives

- ► Insert clip art graphics
- ► Modify clip art graphics
- ► Create custom graphics
- ► Modify custom graphics
- ► Apply special effects to graphics
- ► Position graphics and AutoShapes
- ► Insert a graphic from another program
- ► Create a callout

By adding and positioning graphics in a document, you can achieve dramatic effects. Graphics break up the monotony of large blocks of text and reinforce ideas presented in the text. Word provides many built-in graphics files (called **clip art**) covering a wide variety of topics, as well as decorative elements such as borders, bullets, and backgrounds. If the clip art collection provided with Word does not meet your needs, you can use the Drawing feature in Word to create your own graphics. Also, with the aid of the Drawing feature, you can create callouts, which draw your reader's attention to specific parts of a document. 🖌 Angela has produced a simple report summarizing the year's highlights. Now she would like to spice up the text by inserting graphics and borders to create a flyer for Nomad Ltd senior management called *NomadNotes*.

Word 97

Inserting Clip Art Graphics

In Word you can insert pictures (in the form of graphics files, many of which are provided with the Word program) to better illustrate ideas and enhance your document. With Microsoft Clip Gallery 3.0, you can view available clip art graphics side-by-side. In addition, the Clip Gallery gives you easy access to recorded sound and video clips that you can insert in a document. After you insert a graphic, you can size and position it to fit where you want on the page. In the NomadNotes flyer, Angela wants to insert a graphic in the article about the new travel division. She would also like to insert a border under the name of the flyer.

27.9.99

1. Start Word

2. Open the document named WD H-1 and save it as Flyer Graphics
   The document opens in page layout view.

Trouble?

If you do not see the Clip Art command, click the From File command. Double-click the Popular folder.

3. Scroll to the top of the document and place the insertion point in front of the title NomadNotes, click Insert on the menu bar, click Picture, then click Clip Art
   The Microsoft Clip Gallery dialog box opens, as shown in Figure H-1. The pictures you see in this dialog box are the figures available in the currently selected category. If you see different pictures, it could be because another category is already selected on the left side of the dialog box. You can choose a category to view a collection of related pictures.

4. From the Categories list, click Signs, select a graphic that looks like a sign post with arrows pointing in several directions, and then click Insert
   The selected graphic appears in the document at the insertion point. After inserting a graphic, you often need to resize it to fit in the document. You can size a graphic object by dragging its sizing handles, which appear on all four sides and corners of a graphic.

Trouble?

If the Picture toolbar doesn't appear when the graphic is selected, click View on the menu bar, click Toolbars, then click Picture. If you accidentally moved the graphic, click Undo and be sure to drag the sizing handles, not the figure.

5. Select the graphic (if necessary), position the pointer over the lower-right sizing handle, when the pointer changes shape ↖ then drag up and to the left until the graphic is about 1" wide and 1.5" tall
   The Picture toolbar appears when a picture is selected. Compare your document to Figure H-2. In addition to the pictures shown in Clip Gallery, you can also insert lines, backgrounds, and bullets. To better separate the title from the rest of the document, insert a decorative border.

6. Place the insertion point in front of the heading Corporate Vision, click Insert on the menu bar, click Picture, and then click From File
   The clip art folders include various folders with graphics and other decorative elements. Next locate the Lines folder.

7. Click the Up One Level button 🗁 if necessary, then double-click the Lines folder

8. Select Green and Black Stripe, then click Insert
   Compare your document to Figure H-3. For now, don't be concerned about the position of your graphics in the document. You will learn how to position graphics later in this unit. For now save your changes to the document.

Trouble?

If you do not see the file in the Lines folder, it means that the correct graphics filters were not installed on your computer. You can continue working in this unit but your document will not contain the line shown in the figures.

9. Click the Save button 💾 on the Standard toolbar

FIGURE H-1: Clip Gallery dialog box

FIGURE H-2: Sized graphic

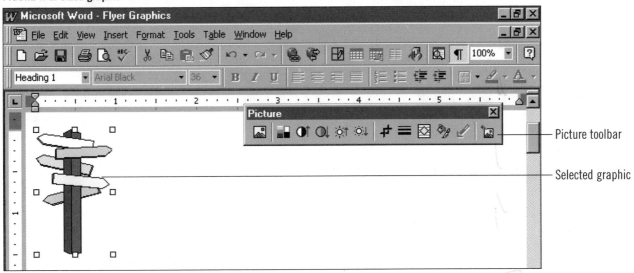

Picture toolbar

Selected graphic

FIGURE H-3: Border graphic inserted

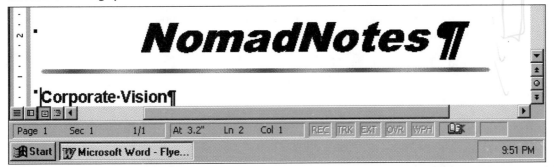

Modifying Clip Art Graphics

In Word you can modify clip art graphics to meet your needs. You might decide to change the color of the graphic or add a border around the picture. The Picture toolbar, as shown in Figure H-4, contains the buttons that provide easy access to the commands you need to modify clip art graphics. For example, with the Format Picture command on the Picture toolbar, you can specify color, line, position, and text wrapping options. ✎ Angela would like to modify the arrows sign graphic. Along with changing the color and adding a border, she would also like to modify the picture so that the text will wrap around the graphic instead of displacing the text.

Steps 123 4   27. 0. '09

1. **Select the arrows sign graphic you inserted in the previous lesson**
   The Picture toolbar appears in the document window. Because the document might not be printed on a color printer, change the image color.

2. **Click the Image Control button 🖼 on the Picture toolbar, then click Grayscale**
   The color in the graphic changes to shades of gray. This option can be helpful if your printer does not print in color.

3. **Click the Text Wrapping button ⬦ on the Picture toolbar, then click Square**
   The text wrapping feature allows you to specify how you would like the text to be arranged around the picture. Some text wrapping options include text being placed only above or below the picture, text going through or behind the picture, and text arranged tight against all sides of the graphic. With square text wrapping, the text will flow around all sides of the graphic evenly. You can add a border around a graphic to enhance its appearance.

4. **Click the Line Style button ≡ on the Picture toolbar, then select the 3 pt double line**
   A double line border appears around the graphic. You can also change the color of a graphic.

5. **Click the Format Picture button 🖌 on the Picture toolbar**
   The Format Picture dialog box opens. In this dialog box you can specify a variety of colors, patterns, and other characteristics for your picture. Next, you will change the background color of the graphic.

6. **Click the Colors and Lines tab**
   On the Colors and Lines tab, you can specify fill color, line style, and arrow styles as shown in Figure H-5.

7. **In the Fill area, click the Color list arrow**
   A color palette appears, allowing you to choose from a variety of colors. At the bottom of the palette, you see the More Colors and Fill Effects options. These options allow you to choose from a larger variety of colors or create your own hue and apply texture to your fill.

8. **Choose the last color in the fourth row, then click OK**
   The graphic now has a gray background. You have finished modifying this graphic for now. Compare your graphic to Figure H-6.

9. **Click the Save button 💾 on the Standard toolbar**

FIGURE H-4: Picture toolbar

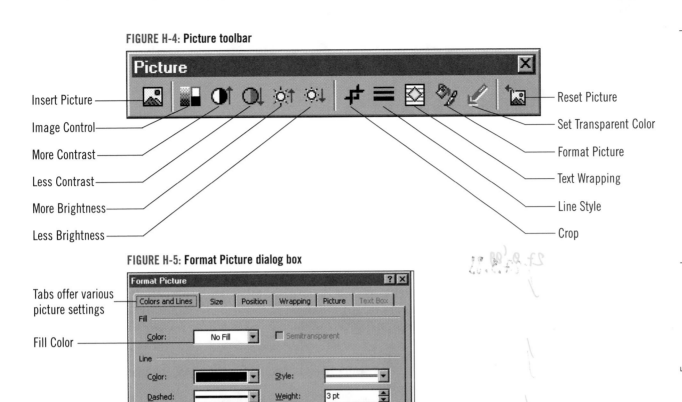

Insert Picture

Image Control

More Contrast

Less Contrast

More Brightness

Less Brightness

Reset Picture

Set Transparent Color

Format Picture

Text Wrapping

Line Style

Crop

FIGURE H-5: Format Picture dialog box

Tabs offer various
picture settings

Fill Color

FIGURE H-6: Modified graphic

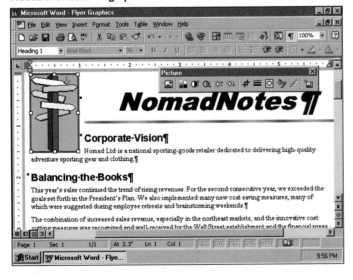

Using the cropping tool to modify a graphic

Occasionally you will want to use only a small part of a graphic offered by Word. In this case you can use the cropping tool on the Picture toolbar to crop or cut away the undesired parts. To crop a picture, first select the graphic, then click the Crop button ⊹ on the Picture toolbar. After clicking the Crop button the pointer will change to ↖. Click this pointer on any of the sizing handles and drag over the areas you wish to crop.

Creating Custom Graphics

When you want to insert graphics in your document, you are not limited to the clip art files provided by Word. In Word, you have the ability to create your own custom graphics using simple (but powerful) drawing tools on the Drawing toolbar. You can create lines and shapes, and apply colors to them. With the AutoShapes button on the Drawing toolbar you can create simple shapes quickly without having to draw them from scratch. AutoShapes include squares, triangles, lightning bolts, block arrows, and stars and banners. Angela would like to use a graphic to accompany the article about environmental relations in her newsletter. Because Word does not provide a graphic that she feels is relevant, she creates her own.

27.3.33

1. Click the **Drawing button** 🗗 on the Standard toolbar
   The Drawing toolbar appears at the bottom of the Word document window, as shown in Figure H-7. You use the buttons on this toolbar to create your own graphics in your Word documents.

2. Click **AutoShapes** on the Drawing toolbar, click **Basic Shapes**, then click the **Isosceles Triangle** in the second row
   When you click an AutoShape feature, the pointer changes shape to $+$. With this pointer, you can drag and draw the selected shape to a desired size. The AutoShape option on the Drawing toolbar offers a variety of presets you can draw.

3. Scroll to the end of the document, click the pointer in a blank area (below the text) at the bottom of the page, then drag the pointer down and to the right until you have a triangle with a **1" base** and **1" tall** (you do not need to be very exact).
   Compare your shape to Figure H-8. Just as you can copy and paste text, you can also copy and paste selected graphics and AutoShapes.

4. Select the triangle shape, if it is not already selected, click the **Copy button** 🖺 on the Standard toolbar, then click the **Paste button** 🖺 on the Standard toolbar
   Another triangle shape appears near the original shape.

5. With the second shape selected, drag the bottom right sizing handle up and to the left so the new shape is just slightly smaller than the first shape
   With the shape selected you can drag it to a new position.

6. With the second shape still selected, position the pointer near the shape until the pointer changes to ✥, then drag the second shape so that it overlaps the first shape, as shown in Figure H-9
   The overlapping triangles will represent the mountains in the graphic.

7. Click the **Oval button** ⬭ on the Drawing toolbar
   You can use this tool to draw circles, as well as ovals.

8. Press and hold down **[Shift]** and, near the top of the triangle shapes, drag a circle that is about one-half inch across
   Holding down the [Shift] key as you drag with the Ellipse tool creates a perfect circle. Compare your document to Figure H-10.

9. Click the **Save button** 🖫 on the Standard toolbar

Trouble?

If you don't see the second shape, it is because Word pasted it exactly on top of the first shape. Click the shape and then drag it to the right, so you can work with the new one.

FIGURE H-7: **Drawing toolbar**

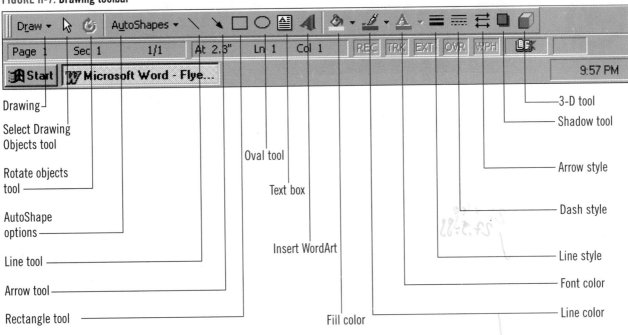

Drawing

Select Drawing
Objects tool

Rotate objects
tool

AutoShape
options

Line tool

Arrow tool

Rectangle tool

Oval tool

Text box

Insert WordArt

Fill color

3-D tool

Shadow tool

Arrow style

Dash style

Line style

Font color

Line color

FIGURE H-8: **AutoShape**

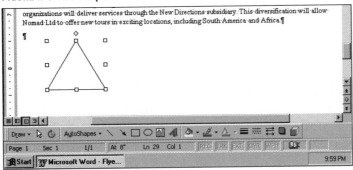

FIGURE H-9: **Overlapping shapes**

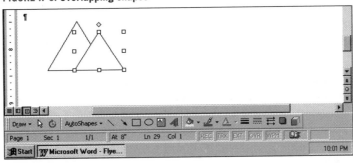

FIGURE H-10: **Completed custom graphic**

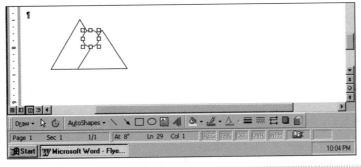

Modifying Custom Graphics

You are not limited to only drawing lines and shapes in your custom graphics. You can also fill your shapes with colors and rearrange shapes (as well as make many other modifications) to make your creations look the way you want. ◢◣ Angela's drawing needs color to make it look more realistic. Angela adds color to her shapes and makes other changes to her graphic to achieve the effect she wants. First, she adds color to the circle shape.

Steps 1234   27.8 '99

1. Select the circle in the drawing, then click the Fill Color list arrow 🎨▾ on the Drawing toolbar

   Clicking the Fill Color button shows a palette of colors from which you can choose to fill the selected shape, as shown in Figure H-11.

2. Click the Yellow color on the Palette

   The circle is filled with the yellow color, as shown in Figure H-12. Only the circle will be filled with yellow because this is the selected shape.

3. Select the larger triangle and click the Fill Color list arrow 🎨▾ on the Drawing toolbar, then click a Dark Blue color on the Palette

   The triangle is filled with dark blue. Now, fill the other triangle with another color.

4. Repeat step 3 for the other triangle, this time choosing the Dark Green color

   The second triangle is filled with dark green. Objects you draw appear in layers, one on top of another. The sequence in which you draw a shape determines the order in which the shapes are layered. For example, because the circle is the last object you drew, the circle appears on top of the other shapes. The Drawing button on the Drawing toolbar offers options for placing shapes in relation to each other and to text.

5. Click the circle shape, click Draw on the Drawing toolbar, click Order, then click Send to Back

   The circle appears behind the triangle, giving the appearance of a sun setting between two mountains.

6. Adjust the position of each of the shapes (as necessary) by clicking and dragging them so that your picture approximates the illustration in Figure H-13

   Do not be concerned if the colors for your two mountains are reversed. What is important is that your mountains are different colors from the sun shape and from each other. After you have finished modifying the various shapes in a custom graphic, you can group the shapes together, so that you can work a group of objects as a single shape.

7. Click the Select Objects button 🔖 on the Drawing toolbar, then drag a rectangle to surround all the objects

   With all the shapes selected, you see the sizing handles for each of the objects. So that you can work with the objects as a single item, you group the objects together.

8. Click Draw on the Drawing toolbar, then click Group

   With the objects grouped, you see only one set of sizing handles as shown in Figure H-14. Grouping the shapes makes a single drawing object, so you can now select the entire arrangement by clicking only one shape. Having the shapes grouped together will make it easier to move the graphic in the document.

9. Click the Save button 💾 on the Standard toolbar

FIGURE H-11: Fill Color palette

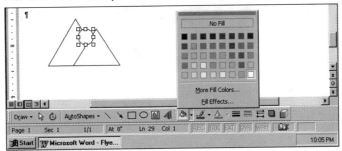

FIGURE H-12: Filled circle

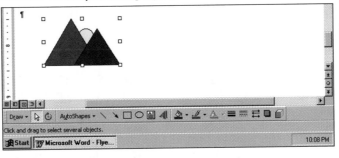

FIGURE H-13: Circle object sent to back

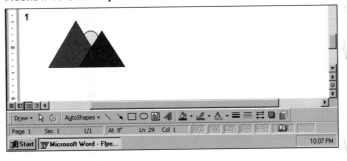

FIGURE H-14: Grouped drawing objects

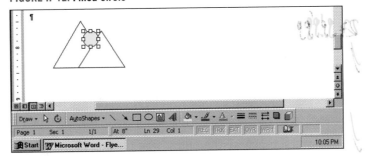

Sizing shapes with precision

As you size shapes, you might have noticed that the lines in the shapes appear to "jump" as your pointer moves. This is because the shapes are automatically aligned to an invisible grid. The Snap to Grid, which is turned on by default, aligns shapes along a very tightly spaced grid. This feature makes it easier to align shapes with one another. If you want more flexibility to create and drag shapes exactly where you wish, you can turn off the Snap to Grid feature. Click the Draw button on the Drawing toolbar and then click Grid. Clear the Snap to Grid check box and click OK.

Applying Special Effects to Graphics

The Drawing toolbar contains many features you can use to enhance the shapes you insert in a document. For example, you can give a shape a unique appearance by adding special fill patterns, such as gradient. You can display a shape in three-dimensions. You can even rotate the shape to an exact angle you choose. ✐ Angela would like to add a block arrow to emphasize the section on Balancing the Books. She would also like to experiment with some of the more dramatic fill effects found in the Fill Effects Dialog box.

Steps 1 2 3 4

27. 8. 99

1. Click **AutoShapes** on the Drawing toolbar, click **Block Arrows**, then select the **Down Arrow**

   After selecting an AutoShape, the pointer will change to ✚. With this pointer, you can click and drag the selected shape to any size and anywhere in the document.

2. In the white space at the end of the document, click and drag down 1" and to the right .5"

   Just as you modify custom graphics, you can modify AutoShapes using the Drawing toolbar.

3. Click the **Fill Color list arrow** on the Drawing toolbar, then click **Fill Effects**

   The Fill Effects dialog box opens as shown in Figure H-15.

4. Select the **Gradient tab** if it is not already selected, then click the **Preset option button** in the Color area

   Notice the Variants and Shading styles at the bottom of the dialog box. You can also preview the fill effects in the sample box in the lower right corner. You can choose from a list of preset color options.

5. Click the **Preset colors list arrow**, select **Desert**, then click **OK**

   The arrow is filled with the Desert fill effect.

6. Click the **Line Color list arrow** on the Drawing toolbar, choose **Red**

   You can use the Line Style arrow to choose new colors and patterns for the lines outlining your AutoShapes. The 3-D feature can add an even greater dramatic effect to AutoShapes.

7. Click the **3-D button** on the Drawing toolbar, then select **3-D Style 1**

   The arrow appears with a 3-D effect. With the Free Rotate feature, you can rotate your figure to point in any direction that you choose.

QuickTip

Drag when the green dot appears in the center of the pointer.

8. Click the **Free Rotate button** on the Drawing toolbar, click any **rotate handle**, drag the arrow around until it points up, then click the **Free Rotate button** again to turn it off

   You can also change the size of the pointed part of the arrow. For example, you can squeeze down the top part of the arrow. (You need to turn off the Free Rotate feature to see the yellow sizing diamond you use in the next step.)

Time To

✔ Save

9. Position the pointer over the **yellow diamond** under the pointed part of the arrow and drag up a short distance

   Compare your document to Figure H-16.

FIGURE H-15: Fill Effects dialog box

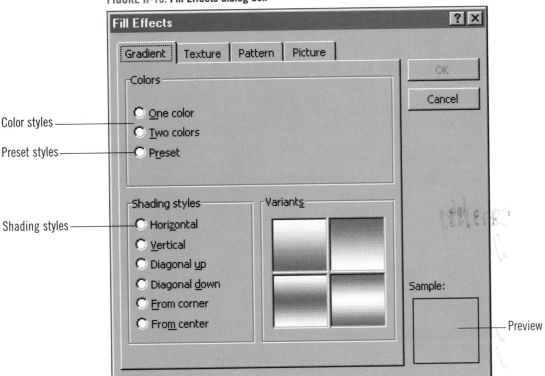

Color styles ——————
Preset styles ——————

Shading styles ——————

Preview

FIGURE H-16: Modified AutoShape

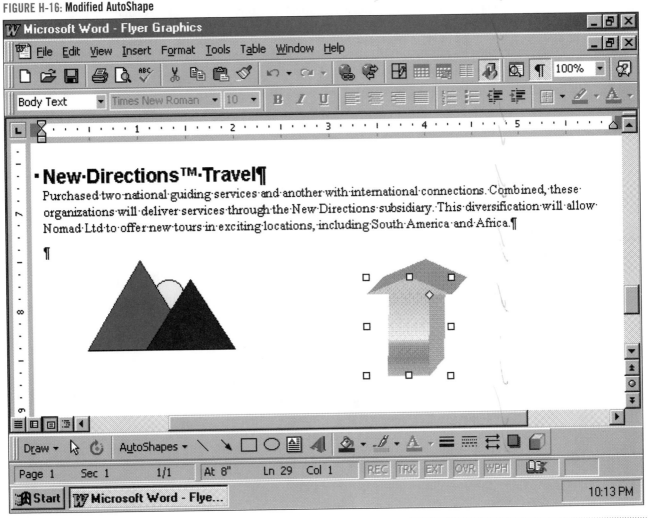

- New·Directions™·Travel¶
Purchased·two·national·guiding·services·and·another·with·international·connections.·Combined,·these·
organizations·will·deliver·services·through·the·New·Directions·subsidiary.·This·diversification·will·allow·
Nomad·Ltd·to·offer·new·tours·in·exciting·locations,·including·South·America·and·Africa.¶

Positioning Graphics and AutoShapes

Word offers various options when positioning graphics. To move a graphic, you simply select the graphic and drag it to the desired location. When positioning a graphic near text, you can specify how you would like the text to wrap around the graphic. The Format AutoShapes and Format Object dialog boxes contain options for positioning, text wrapping, and other types of formatting for graphics. You can open these dialog boxes by double-clicking the graphic. Angela has finished modifying her graphics and would like to position them throughout the document. She will specify how she would like the text to wrap before moving the graphics.

 27.9.99

1. **Select the border graphic and drag it so it appears under the paragraph below the heading Corporate Vision**

   You will need to position the border about .25" below the paragraph. Placing graphics can often require several attempts before you get the results you want. Keep positioning it by releasing the mouse and re-selecting the graphic until it appears in the proper location. If text is misplaced, simply reselect and position the graphic again.

2. **Double-click the Up Arrow graphic, then click the Wrapping tab (if it is not already in front)**

   Double-clicking an AutoShape opens the Format AutoShape dialog box, as shown in Figure H-17. The Format AutoShape dialog box offers various formatting options such as positioning, text wrapping, and size.

3. **Select Tight in the Wrapping Style area and Right in the Wrap to area, then click OK**

   After you have specified the text wrapping style, you can move the graphic to the desired position.

4. **Click inside the Up Arrow graphic, drag the graphic and place it under the heading Balancing the Books**

   Make sure the heading is above the graphic with the paragraph text to the side of the graphic, as shown in Figure H-18. Notice the text wraps to the shape of the AutoShape.

5. **Double-click the custom mountain graphic**

   Double-clicking a custom graphic opens the Format Object dialog box. The Format Object dialog box offers the same options as the Format AutoShape dialog box.

6. **Select Tight in the Text Wrapping area, select Left in the Wrap To area, then click OK**

   With the wrapping options specified, you can position the custom graphic.

7. **Drag the graphic to the right of the paragraph below the Environmental Relations heading**

   The text flows to the left of the mountain graphic. To enhance the effect, format the paragraph so that both left and right edges of the paragraph are even.

8. **Click anywhere in the paragraph below the Environmental Relations heading, then click the Justify button on the Formatting toolbar**

   Compare your document to the illustration shown in Figure H-19.

9. **Scroll to the top of the page, then select and drag the arrow signs graphic so that it is to the left of the heading New Directions Travel**

   Compare your document to Figure H-20.

QuickTip

You do not need to be concerned if your text does not wrap exactly the same as shown in the figure. You can adjust the size of the arrow, if you wish.

Time To

✔ Save

FIGURE H-17: Format AutoShape dialog box

Text wrapping options

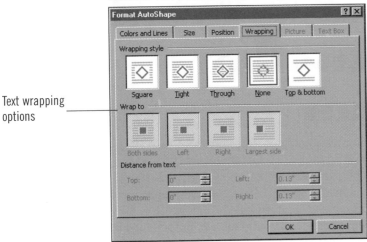

FIGURE H-18: Positioned graphic

Text wraps tight and to the right

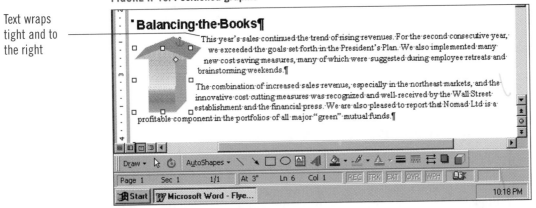

FIGURE H-19: Custom graphic positioned

Justified paragraph

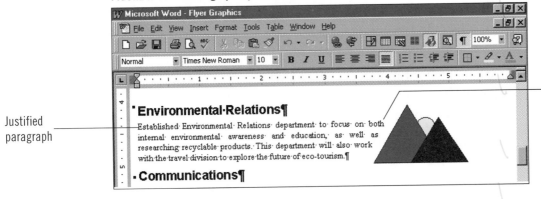

Text wraps tight and to the left

FIGURE H-20: Clip art positioned in document

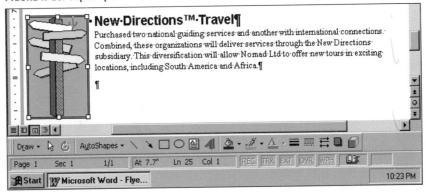

Inserting a Graphic from Another Program

You are not limited to working with graphics either provided in Word's clip art collection or those you create with the Drawing toolbar. There are many drawing programs on the market with which you can create sophisticated graphics, and you can insert graphics created in these programs into your Word documents. The advertising department at Nomad has been busy creating a new logo in a graphics program called Paint, which is provided with Microsoft Windows 95. Michael Belmont has created a new graphic to use as a logo for Nomad Ltd, which Angela would like to insert in the newsletter.

Steps 1234

1. Place the insertion point at the end of the title NomadNotes

2. Click Insert on the menu bar, then click Object
   The Object dialog box opens. You can click the Create from File tab to help locate a file. The Nomad logo file is located on your Student Disk.

3. Click the Create from File tab
   The Create from File tab is now foremost in the dialog box, as shown in Figure H-21. On this tab you can locate the Paint file.

4. Click Browse, then locate and double-click the drive that contains your student files
   With the appropriate drive selected, you can select the file you want to insert.

5. Click the Preview button (if it's not already selected), scroll to and select the file WD Logo, click OK in the Browse dialog box
   The logo filename appears in the File Name dialog box.

6. Click OK in the Object dialog box
   The picture appears in the document.

7. Select the Paint object, click the Text Wrapping button on the Picture toolbar, then click Square
   The Picture toolbar appears when you select an object, as it does when you select a picture.

8. Drag the object to the right of the title NomadNotes
   Compare your document to Figure H-22.

9. Click the Save button on the Standard toolbar

Modifying a Paint object

When you insert an object that was created in another program, you can edit the object in the original program (provided that the program is installed on your computer). For example, if you insert a Paint file as an object, you can modify the graphic using Paint without actually leaving Word. To edit an object, you simply double-click the object to display the object's original program environment. You will still be able to see the Word document in the original program window. To move back to the Word program simply click outside the object.

► WD H-14   **WORKING WITH GRAPHICS**

FIGURE H-21: **Create from File tab in Object dialog box**

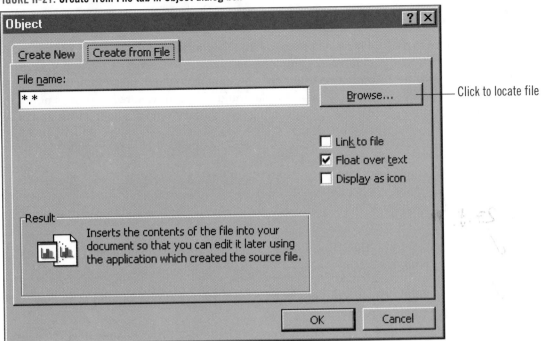

Click to locate file

FIGURE H-22: **New picture in document**

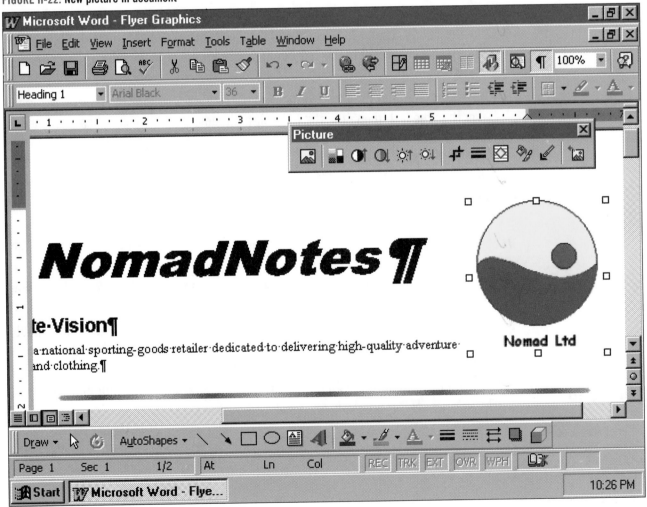

Word 97

Creating a Callout

When you want to draw your reader's attention to a specific item in a document, you can create a callout to that item. A **callout** is a graphic object containing text and a line pointing to a location in a document. You can enter any text you want in a callout. In addition, you can position it exactly where you wish. Angela would like to make sure her readers notice the new tour destinations available in the upcoming year, so she creates a callout to this part of the document.

Steps 1234

27.8. 88

1 Click **AutoShapes** on the Drawing toolbar, click **Callouts**, then select **Line Callout 2**
With the Callout tool selected, you can drag your callout anywhere in the document.

2 Click the pointer near the end of the **New Directions** paragraph, and drag down and to the right about one-half inch
A callout appears next to the text, as shown in Figure H-23. Immediately after you insert a callout, you can enter text.

3 Type **New for 1998!**
You can use the yellow sizing handles to adjust the callout position.

4 Click the **callout frame** to select it and display its sizing handles, then drag the yellow sizing handle connected to the text box and pull down and to the left
Notice that the first yellow sizing handle stays anchored.

5 Click the callout and drag the bottom sizing handle up so that the callout box is not larger than the text, then drag the right sizing handle until the text appears on one line
With the callout still selected you can use the buttons on the Drawing toolbar to modify the text box itself.

6 Click the **Dash Style button** ▦ on the Drawing toolbar, and select the **Round Dot line**
The callout appears with dashed lines.

7 Select the text in the callout, then click the **Bold button** B on the Formatting toolbar, then click the **Font list arrow** on the Formatting toolbar and click **Arial**
To display the callout more clearly without the paragraph marks, you can hide the non-printing characters.

8 Click the **Show/Hide button** ¶ on the Standard toolbar, then deselect the callout
Compare your document to Figure H-24. You have finished working with graphics in your document, so you can hide the Drawing toolbar and save your changes.

9 Click the **Drawing button** 🎨 on the Standard toolbar and save your changes
The Drawing toolbar is hidden.

Time To
✔ Save
✔ Print the document
✔ Close
✔ Exit Word

FIGURE H-23: Creating a callout

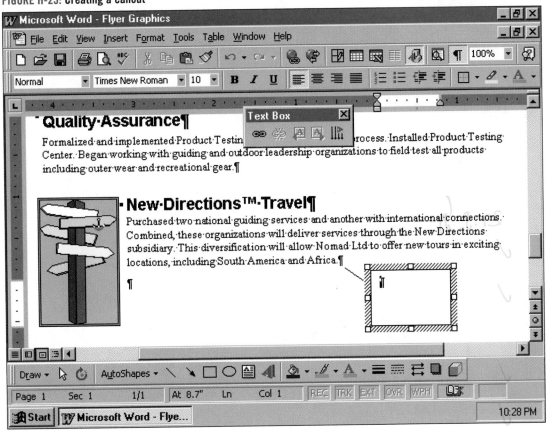

FIGURE H-24: Completed callout

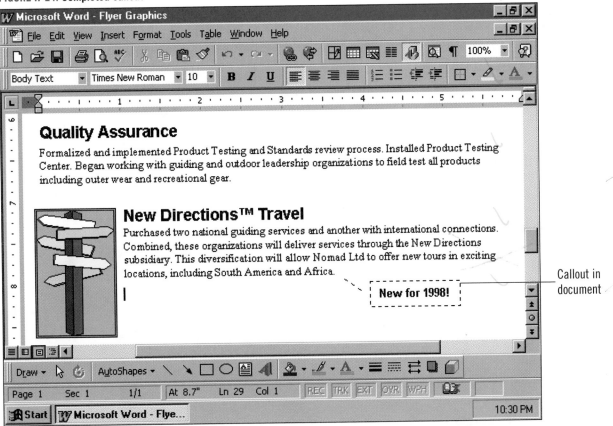

Callout in document

Practice

► Concepts Review

Label each of the elements in Figure H-25.

FIGURE H-25

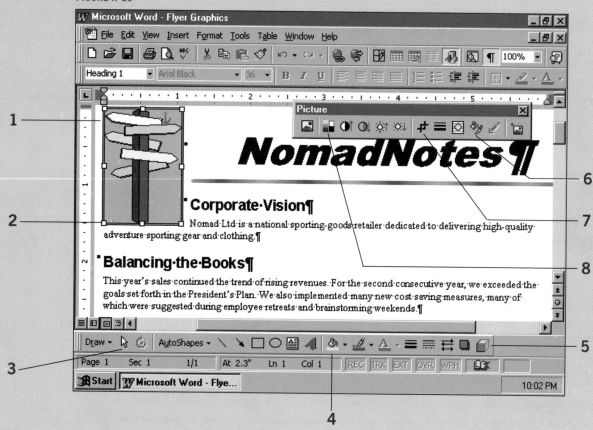

Match each of the following features with the correct descriptions.

9. Callout
10. Oval button
11. Select Objects button
12. Sizing handle
13. Drawing toolbar

a. Allows you to draw a circle or oval shape
b. Allows you to group custom shapes or AutoShapes into one graphic
c. Contains buttons you can use to create custom graphics
d. Framed text pointing to an area in a document
e. Allows you to size an object

Select the best answer from the list of choices.

14. To insert a graphic provided by Word, you
   a. Click Insert, then click Picture.
   b. Click the Drawing button on the Standard toolbar.
   c. Click the Picture button on the Drawing toolbar.
   d. Click View, then click Picture.

15. To draw your own custom graphic, you must first
   a. Click Insert, then click Picture and select the picture you want.
   b. Click the Drawing button on the Standard toolbar.
   c. Click the Picture button on the Drawing toolbar.
   d. Click View, then click Picture.

16. Which of the following is NOT true about using graphics in Word?
   a. You can create your own graphics in another program and insert them in Word.
   b. You can select graphics from Word's collection of clip art.
   c. You cannot modify graphics you insert in Word.
   d. You can edit graphics created in another program.

17. To modify a graphic, you need to
   a. Click Edit, then click Graphic.
   b. Exit Word and start the program that was used to create the graphic.
   c. Select the graphic and use the Picture toolbar.
   d. Triple-click the graphic.

18. To change the color of a shape, you
   a. Select the Fill Color button on the Drawing toolbar.
   b. Select the shape then click the Fill Color button.
   c. Delete the shape, click the Fill Color button and redraw the shape.
   d. Select the shape, click the Fill Color button, then select a new color.

19. To draw a perfect circle, you
   a. Click the Circle button and drag a circle.
   b. Click the Oval button and press [Ctrl] as you drag a circle.
   c. Click the Freeform button and carefully draw a circle.
   d. Click the Oval button and press [Shift] as you drag a circle.

20. To insert an AutoShape, you
   a. Click Insert, then click AutoShapes.
   b. Click AutoShapes on the Drawing toolbar.
   c. Click Tools, then click AutoShapes.
   d. Choose AutoShapes in the Picture dialog box.

▶ Skills Review

1. Insert a graphic.
   a. Start Word.
   b. Open the document named WD H-2 and save it as "Theatre Graphics".
   c. Place the insertion point at the beginning of the document.
   d. Click Insert, click Picture, then click Clip Art.
   e. In the Screen Bean category, select the graphic that looks like someone scratching his head, then click Insert.

2. Modify a graphic.
   a. Select the graphic and drag individual sizing handles until it is .75" wide and 1.25" tall.
   b. Click the Line Style button on the Picture toolbar, then select a 1 ½ pt line.
   c. Click the Format Picture button on the Picture toolbar.
   d. Click the Wrapping tab, click the Tight option, then Wrap to the Right option.
   e. In the Distance form text area, click the down arrow until 0" is shown in the Right box.
   f. Click the Color and Lines tab, click the Fill Color list arrow, select Lavender.
   g. Click OK.
   h. Position the graphic to the left of the bulleted list under the heading Still Can't Decide?

3. Create a custom graphic using AutoShapes.
   a. Click the Drawing button to display the drawing toolbar, if necessary, click Rectangle tool, and on the blank area of the document (if needed, create a blank page), draw a square by holding down [Shift] as you draw. The square should be about two inches on each side.
   b. Click the Fill Color list arrow and select a dark blue color.
   c. Click the Oval tool, and below the square, draw a circle by holding down [Shift] as you draw. The circle should be about two inches in diameter.
   d. Click the Fill Color list arrow and select a bright pink color.
   e. With the circle selected, drag it to place it over the square.
   f. Click AutoShapes on the Drawing toolbar, click Basic Shapes, then select the Diamond.
   g. Holding down [Shift] drag a diamond 2" by 2".
   h. Click the Fill Color list arrow and select a dark green color.
   i. Position the diamond over the circle.
   j. Click the Select Objects button and drag a rectangle around all three objects (if you cannot drag a rectangle around all of the objects, hold down [Shift] as you click each shape).
   k. Click Draw on the Drawing toolbar, then click Group.
   l. Hold down [Shift] and drag a corner sizing handle so that the graphic is about 1.5" on all sides.
   m. Double-click the graphic, click the Wrapping tab, click Tight, then click OK.
   n. Position the graphic to the left of the title.

4. Insert a Paint object.
   a. Place the insertion point near the middle of the page and click Insert on the menu bar, then click Object.
   b. Click the Create from File tab.
   c. Click the Browse button.
   d. Locate the student file called WD LOGO2, then click OK until you return to the document.
   e. Position the graphic to the left of the paragraph that is under the heading Othello, then size it attractively.
   f. Click the Text Wrapping button on the Picture toolbar, then click Tight.

5. Create a callout.

   a. Click the AutoShapes button on the Drawing toolbar, then click Callouts.

   b. Select Line Callout 3 (No Border), the third callout in the fourth row.

   c. Drag the callout down and to the right just under the shaded paragraph at the end of the document.

   d. Enter the text "Experience the classics in a modern setting!"

   e. Drag the sizing handles on the callout to fit just the text.

   f. Preview, save, and print the document, then close it.

▶ Independent Challenges

1. As the communications coordinator for the annual Students for Peace Conference, you are responsible for designing attractive note paper for the staff. Begin by creating a new document and save it as "Peace Paper". Use Figure H-26 as a guide for how the completed note paper should look.

To complete this independent challenge:

1. Draw a rounded-rectangle 1.5" high and about 7" wide. (Hint: Use the Rounded Rectangle AutoShape found under Basic Shapes.) Position the rectangle just below the top of the page. Fill the rectangle with the sky blue color.

2. Insert the Dove graphic in the Animals category.

3. Size the graphic and position it so that it fits in the left side of the rectangle.

4. Using the Lines Autoshape, draw a long line down the left edge of the page. Format the line so it is 6 pts thick. Apply the sky blue color to the line.

5. Draw two horizontal lines near the bottom of the vertical line. Apply the color yellow to both these lines. Format them so that they are 6 pts thick. Send the upper yellow line behind the other lines.

6. Select all three lines and group them. Copy the grouped shapes and paste the graphic near the right edge of the page.

7. Select the second group of lines, click the Rotate or Flip command on the Draw button, then click Flip Horizontal. Position the lines so that the vertical line is aligned with right edge of the rectangle.

8. Preview, save, and print the document, then close it.

FIGURE H-26

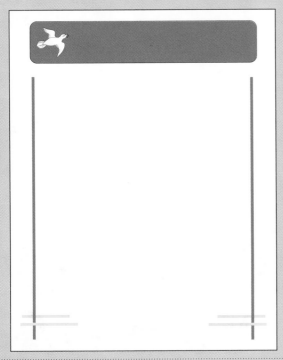

2. As marketing communications specialist for The Magic Shop, a chain of stores selling magic supplies and costumes, you have decided to create your business card. Begin by creating a new document and saving it as "Magic Card". Use Figure H-27 as a guide for how the completed card should look.

To complete this independent challenge:

1. Type the company name, your name, an address, and a phone number, each on a separate line.
2. Format the text in the font you wish. Size the name of the shop at 14 pt. Right-align all the text.
3. Insert the graphic that looks like a magic hat in the Entertainment category.
4. Size the graphic to be about 1" by 1".
5. Apply tight and wrap to the right text wrapping. (Hint: Use the Format Picture dialog box, not the toolbar.)
6. Position the graphic to the right of the text so that the magic wand extends over the store name slightly.
7. Create a border around the graphic and text using the Rectangle tool. Modify the Rectangle so that it has no fill and 3 pt double-lines.
8. Preview, save, and print the document, then close it.

FIGURE H-27

3. As the marketing communications specialist at Sunset Travel, an international travel agency, you have been asked to design a new company logo that will adorn all company documents. You can begin your design using the Drawing toolbar. Create a new document and save it as "Sunset Logo". Use Figure H-28 as a guide for how the completed logo should look.

To complete this independent challenge:

1. Draw a rectangle 2" wide and 1" high.
2. Copy the rectangle and position it directly under the first shape.
3. Fill the bottom rectangle with the dark blue color.
4. Size the bottom rectangle so that it is only ¾" high. The top edge of the bottom rectangle should still be touching the bottom edge of the top rectangle.
5. Fill the top rectangle with the preset Late Sunset fill Effect. (Hint: Use the Gradient tab in the Fill Effects dialog box.)
6. Draw an oval about .5" across and fill it with the gold color.
7. Position the oval over the two rectangles.
8. Select the bottom rectangle and choose the Bring to Front option.
9. Group the three objects together.
10. Preview, save, and print the document, then close it.

FIGURE H-28

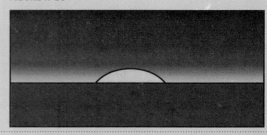

4. As communications director of the City of Boston's tourism department, you have recently written the text for a flyer for city visitors. Now you would like to add graphics to make the document look more attractive. Open the document called WD H-3 and save it as "Boston Graphics".

To complete this independent challenge:

1. Insert the graphic line Neighborhood. Size the graphic so that it is the width of the text on the page, not including margins, and position it above the title.
2. Insert the champagne bottle graphic, size it so that it is about 1" by 1".
3. Adjust the text wrapping around this graphic to be tight and to the right.
4. Position the graphic next to the heading Night Life.
5. Log on to the Internet and use your browser to search for information about Boston. Search for museums in the Boston area and add at least one name to the bulleted list in your document. If you can't locate a Boston museum, use your browser to go to http://www.course.com. From there, click Student Online Companions, click the link for this textbook, then click the Word link for Unit H. Insert another graphic of your choice (preferably a graphic that reflects the name of a museum you've identified). Size the graphic so that it is about one inch on each side and position it near the bulleted list.
6. Preview, save, and print the document, then close it.

▶ Visual Workshop

Your work at the local state tourism office has taught you a great deal about what your state has to offer in the area of tourism and outdoor recreation. Every quarter you print a newsletter to promote exploration of your state. It's time to publish the Spring/Summer Issue. Use the draft document WD H-4 and save it as "Tourism Graphics". Figure H-29 serves as a guide for how your completed document should look. Use AutoShapes to create the triangle and sun graphics. You'll also insert the sailboat graphic from the transportation category.

FIGURE H-29

Glossary

Alignment The horizontal position of text within the width of a line or between tab stops; for example, left, center, or right.

AutoCorrect A feature that automatically corrects a misspelled word. Word provides several entries for commonly misspelled words, but you can add your own.

AutoFormat A feature that improves the appearance of a document by applying consistent formatting and styles based on a default document template or a document template you specify. The AutoFormat feature also adds bullets to lists and symbols for trademarks and copyrights where necessary.

AutoText entry A stored text or graphic you want to use again.

Border A straight vertical or horizontal line between columns in a section, next to or around paragraphs and graphics, or in a table. You can assign a variety of widths to a border.

Bullet A small graphic, usually a round or square dot, often used to identify items in a list.

Callout A graphic element used to label or point to an item in a document. It consists of text and a line pointing to the item.

Character style A stored set of text format settings.

Clipboard A temporary storage area for cut or copied text or graphics. You can paste the contents of the Clipboard into any Microsoft program file. The Clipboard holds the information until you cut or copy another piece of text or a graphic.

Cut To remove selected text or a graphic from a document so you can paste it to another place in the document or to another document. The cut information is placed in a temporary storage area called the Clipboard. *See also* Clipboard.

Data source The document containing the variable information to be used with the mail merge feature.

Field Variable information in a document that is supplied by a file or by Word. In a mail merge operation, individual items (such as a name or state) are stored in fields in the data source. A merge field inserted in the main document (such as a form letter) instructs Word to provide that field's contents from the data source. A Word field is variable information provided by Word. For example, if you insert the Filename field in a footer, the document's filename appears in the footer.

Font A collection of characters (letters, numerals, symbols, and punctuation marks) with a specific design. Arial and Times New Roman are examples of font names.

Font effects Refers to enhanced formatting you can apply to text, such as Shadow, Engraved, all caps, and hidden, among others.

Font size Refers to the physical size of text, measured in points (pts). The bigger the number of points, the larger the font size.

Font style Refers to whether text appears as bold, italicized, or underlined, or any combination of these formats.

Footer The text that appears at the bottom of each printed page of a document.

Format The way text appears on a page. In Word, a format comes from direct formatting and the application of styles. The four types of formats are character, paragraph, section, and document.

Formatting toolbar A bar that contains buttons and options for the most frequently used formatting commands.

global template In Word, a template with the filename NORMAL.DOT that contains default menus, AutoCorrect entries, styles, and page setup settings. Documents use the global template unless you specify a custom template. *See also* template.

Graphic A picture, chart, or drawing in a document.

Graphic object An element in a document that can be moved, sized, and modified without leaving Word.

Hanging indent A paragraph format in which the first line of a paragraph starts farther left than the subsequent lines.

Header The text that appears at the top of each printed page of a document.

Indent The distance between text boundaries and page margins. Positive indents make the text area narrower than the space between margins. Negative indents allow text to extend into the margins. A paragraph can have left, right, and first-line indents.

Landscape A term used to refer to horizontal page orientation; it is the opposite of "portrait," or vertical, orientation.

Line break A mark inserted where you want to end one line and start another without starting a new paragraph.

Line spacing The height of a line of text, including extra spacing. Line spacing is often measured in lines or points.

Mail merge The process of creating personalized form letters or labels by combining boilerplate text with variable information.

Main document In the mail merge process, the main document is the document containing the boilerplate text; the text that is the same in each version of the merged document.

Margin The distance between the edge of the text in the document and the top, bottom, or side edges of the page.

Normal view The view you see when you start Word. Normal view is used for most editing and formatting tasks.

Page break The point at which one page ends and another begins. A break you insert (created by pressing [Ctrl] + [Enter]) is called a "hard break"; a break determined by the page layout is called a "soft break". A hard break appears as a dotted line and is labeled Page Break. A soft break appears as a dotted line without a label.

Page Layout view A view of a document as it will appear when you print it. Items such as headers, footnotes, and framed objects appear in their actual positions and can be dragged to new positions. You can edit and format text in page layout view.

Paragraph style A stored set of paragraph format settings.

Paste To insert cut or copied text into a document from the temporary storage area called the Clipboard.

Point size A measurement used for the size of text characters. There are 72 points per inch.

Portrait A term used to refer to vertical page orientation; it is the opposite of "landscape", or horizontal, orientation.

Record The entire collection of fields related to an item or individual contained in the data source.

Redo The ability to repeat reversed actions or changes, usually editing or formatting actions. Only reversed changes can be repeated with the redo feature.

Repetitive text Text that you use often in documents.

Resize The ability to change the size of an object (such as framed text or a graphic) by dragging sizing handles located on the sides and corners of the selected object.

Resolution Refers to the size of your monitor's screen display. Resolution is measured in pixels; a typical resolution is 640 x 480. The illustrations in this book were taken on a computer with these resolutions. Because a higher resolution results in more space visible on the screen and smaller text, your screen might not exactly match the illustrations in this book. You can change the resolution of the monitor using the Control Panel on the Start menu.

Sans serif font   A font whose characters do not include serifs (the small strokes at the ends of the characters). Arial is a sans serif font.

ScreenTip   When you place the pointer over a button, the name of the button is displayed and a brief description of its function appears in the status bar.

Section   A part of a document separated from the rest of the document with a section break. By separating a document into sections, you can use different page and column formatting in different parts of the same document.

Selection bar   An unmarked column at the left edge of a document window used to select text with the mouse. In a table, each cell has its own selection bar at the left edge of the cell.

Serif font   A font that has small strokes at the ends of the characters. Times New Roman and Palatino are serif fonts.

Shading   The background color or pattern behind text or graphics.

Soft return   A line break created by pressing [Shift] + [Enter]. This creates a new line without creating a new paragraph.

Style   A group of formatting instructions that you name and store and can modify. When you apply a style to selected characters and paragraphs, all the formatting instructions of that style are applied at once.

Style Gallery   A feature that allows you to examine the overall formatting and styles used in a document template. With the Style Gallery, you can also preview your document formatted in the styles from a selected template.

Template   A special kind of document that provides basic tools and text for creating a document. Templates can contain the following elements: styles, AutoText items, macros, customized menu and key assignments, and text or graphics that are the same in different types of documents.

Text flow   Refers to paragraph formatting that controls the flow of text across page breaks. Controlling text flow prevents awkward breaks within paragraphs or ensures that related paragraphs appear together on the same page.

Vertical ruler   A graphical bar displayed at the left edge of the document window in the page layout and print preview views. You can use this ruler to adjust the top and bottom page margins as well as to change row height in a table.

Word 97

Index

Index

Index